Sex, Death and Witchcraft

Other titles from Bloomsbury

Ritual: Key Concepts in Religion, Pamela J. Stewart and Andrew J. Strathern
PB: 978-1-44118-569-3
HB: 978-1-44113-729-6

Death, Ritual, and Belief, Douglas J. Davies
PB: 978-0-30433-822-1

Myth: Key Concepts in Religion, Robert Ellwood
PB: 978-1-84706-235-2
HB: 978-1-84706-234-5

Sex, Death and Witchcraft

A Contemporary Pagan Festival

DOUGLAS EZZY

BLOOMSBURY

LONDON • NEW DELHI • NEW YORK • SYDNEY

Bloomsbury Academic

An imprint of Bloomsbury Publishing Plc

50 Bedford Square	1385 Broadway
London	New York
WC1B 3DP	NY 10018
UK	USA

www.bloomsbury.com

Bloomsbury is a registered trade mark of Bloomsbury Publishing Plc

First published 2014
Reprinted 2014

© Douglas Ezzy, 2014

British Library Cataloguing-in-Publication Data
A catalogue record for this book is available from the British Library.

ISBN: HB: 978-1-47252-246-7
PB: 978-1-47252-758-5
ePub: 978-1-47253-363-0
ePDF: 978-1-47252-201-6

Library of Congress Cataloging-in-Publication Data
A catalog record for this book is available from the Library of Congress.

Typeset by Newgen Knowledge Works (P) Ltd., Chennai, India
Printed and bound in Great Britain

CONTENTS

LIST OF FIGURES

ACKNOWLEDGEMENTS

To the participants of Faunalia. This is for you. Thank you for your generosity and courage. In particular, thanks to those who shared their stories with me in a formal interview.

To Kira, without whom this would not be.

To Hawthorn and Seline. Respect and gratitude.

To Emily, Tim and Jill. You help me find a life with soul.

To Ruth Sansom, who was one of the first to guide me in understanding mystical experience. I honour you as an ancestor.

Thanks to my academic colleagues who helped me see there was something important to say, and helped me find the courage to say it. They shared their homes with me, invited me to speak at their universities and contributed in various other ways: Graham Harvey, Adrian Harris, Jone Salomonsen, Grant Potts, Chas Clifton, Jenny Blain, Robert Wallis, Susan Greenwood, Sara Pike, Marianne Lien, Ute Huesken, Robert Puckett, Nikki Bado, Shawn Arthur, Lynne Hume, Andrew Francis, Kathleen McPhillips, Carole Cusack, Gary Bouma, Rowan Ireland, Garry Deverell, James Collins, Helen Collins, Anna Halafoff, Julia Verdouw, Morgan Leigh, Katie Wright and Kesherie Gurung. Thanks to Sam Peek, Sean Scullion and the crew of PA Tas for being an inspiration to me. Thanks to Edan Mumford, Philippe Duquesnoy, B. Dalton, Seline, Michelle Maddern, Gavin Andrew, Hawthorn, Sean Scullion, Vinde, Pan, Danny and Tania LeNoir, for permission to use the photos in the book. Thanks to my academic mentors: Allan Kellehear and Gary Easthope. Thanks to those who, for various reasons, I cannot name.

Thanks also to the University of Tasmania, which granted me two periods of study leave during which the vast bulk of the work was conducted for this book.

An earlier version of Chapter 3 was published in 2011 as: 'An Underworld Rite: A Pagan Re-enactment of Persephone's Descent into the Underworld'. *Journal of Contemporary Religion*, 26, 2: 245–259; www.tandfonline. com. Some paragraphs distributed throughout the book were previously published in 2010 in a chapter titled 'The Ontology of Good and Evil: Spirit Possession in Contemporary Witchcraft and Paganism'. In Andrew Dawson (ed.), *Summoning the Spirits: Possession and Invocation in Contemporary Religion*. London: I. B. Taurus, pp. 179–198. Thanks to the publishers for permission to reprint these.

Introduction

A Witches' Sabbat

Harrison: We built this monster bonfire, 20 feet high. The ritualists are up the top of the hill. The whole hill is covered in fog. We light the fire and it just blazes. That is the signal for everyone to come up. Hatty is leading [the procession of the participants coming up the hill]. We can hear the drums start, and then we hear them get louder and louder. We hear the excitement and the chanting. We are really hyped up because we can hear boom, boom, boom, boom, boom, boom. Ooohhh, hhhooo, the sabbat is coming.

Phoebe: The beats of the drum were like my heart. I was almost able to feel everyone's excitement, the anticipation of it all. I was no longer I. I was something so great that I do not have words. Did it blow my mind? It blew my mind. Did it blow every inch of me? It totally did. The craziness, the chaos and the confusion. The sitting and appreciating people being very sensual with each other. I sit and I watch and observe. The energy is spiralling, and spiralling, and spiralling. It was very animalistic. It was very primal. It was a world between worlds. Looking in the trees and you can see faces looking back at you, energies that are not of this world. I do not have the words. The feelings, the excitement, I can see it. I am looking at you but I can see it. Oh [sighs].[1]

Beating drums accompany the participants as they approach the hill. In the dark of night their path is lit by a full moon. The air is still. Through the fog they can see their destination: a massive bonfire. A black-robed priestess stands silhouetted against the flames. Emerging from the forest the 70 participants form a circle in the clearing around the bonfire. A priest stands beside the priestess. The ritual begins with invocations, collective chants, drumming, laughter and shouting. It feels like riding a tidal wave of energy. Participants growl, snarl and chant 'Baphomet!'[2] Eventually Baphomet appears. Baphomet is unforgettable: the black wings, the goat mask, the torch burning between the goat's horns. Baphomet does not speak. Baphomet communes directly with people's hearts with a sigh, a held hand, a caress. Ritual wine is shared as the rite transforms from a scripted performance into an ecstatic communal dance lasting into the small hours of the morning. People sit by the fire, rotating to keep warm against the freezing cold night air. As dawn approaches they gradually drift off to bed in bunkhouse accommodation down the hill.

Baphomet is a window into a hidden world. This world is not only hidden on remote hilltops or in Pagan rituals, but deep in people's hearts. It is hidden because it is both feared and desired. People are afraid of what might happen if it is allowed into the open. Fearful echoes of otherworldly demons unsettle those who approach Baphomet. Desire draws participants towards Baphomet, struggling against restraint and guilt. The ritual provides a passage into this hidden world, into the presence of Baphomet, and then safely returns participants to everyday life and normality. The ritual forges courage and trust. Participants dance naked. Fire and passion keep them warm. Respect and love keep them safe. The otherworld seeps into their souls. The Baphomet rite is a mystic encounter with the 'disturbing familiarity . . . of the Other' (de Certeau 1992: 10). The mystery is revealed, but refuses to be grasped. The fears are only empty mirages. After the ritual, the elusive Baphomet is hidden again. The balance of everyday life is restored. Yet, the participants feel different. Their lives are changed. Something from this hidden world stays with them. They hold in their hearts a memory of passionate, all-embracing joy.

Baphomet is a hybrid animal/human, male/female, goat-headed deity who developed from the medieval depictions of the Witches' sabbat. At Faunalia, Baphomet is reinvented as a contemporary Pagan deity who represents the animalistic and sexual side of being human. As they dance with Baphomet participants become more accepting of their sexual and erotic selves. This does not necessarily mean that they indulge their sexual desires, although some do. Rather, it means that naked bodies and erotic desire are celebrated as normal and healthy aspects of being human. This stands in stark contrast to the fear, guilt and loathing that is often associated with bodies and sexuality. These oppressive self-understandings have been the source of considerable pain and suffering for many participants.

Faunalia is a Pagan festival that opens people's hearts and blows their minds. The Baphomet rite is at the heart of Faunalia. It is performed on the third night of this five day festival. Sexual desire, death and self-transformation are central themes of the rituals at Faunalia. In theatrically elaborate immersive experiences that last through the night participants dance naked around a huge bonfire in the Baphomet rite and role-play their

IMAGE I.1 *Sitting around at Faunalia: Gavin, Danny, Doug and two other participants.*[3]
Photo by B. Dalton.

own death in the Underworld rite. These rituals transform participants' understandings of sexual desire and the inevitability of death. Participants become more comfortable with sexual desire, less afraid of death and more confident in themselves. This book describes the festival and explains how the rituals have such powerful effects.

Phoebe and Harrison created and lead Faunalia. The quotes that open this Introduction describe their experiences of the Baphomet rite at the first Faunalia in 2000. Phoebe is 41-years-old and has been a Witch for nine years. Harrison is 47-years-old and has been a Witch for 25 years. Phoebe and Harrison are similar to most people who attend Faunalia. Participants tend to work in middle-class or service-sector occupations and are often married or in long-term relationships. Many are well-educated, although some have limited education. These people are attracted to Faunalia because it provides an intense and transformative emotional experience, a powerful moment of ritual engagement with the hidden core of their lives.

In the quotation above, Phoebe describes how her self-awareness expands well beyond the everyday sense of self. This experience of transcendence is produced by the ritual process. Carefully crafted theatrical props and costumes contribute to the power of the ritual. While the ritual is partially scripted, there is also considerable scope for improvization. As the night progresses the ritual becomes increasingly free-form in structure. It is a deeply spiritual experience. The altered states of consciousness and the intensity of the emotions generated during the Baphomet rite are central to the power of the ritual to transform deeply embedded self-understandings, fears and habits. The Baphomet rite is described in detail in Chapter Five.

> **Harrison:** I wanted to create a rite that would challenge people's prejudices. There was a certain element of shit stirring and iconoclasm. At first it was going to be a mere Pagan revel with just a few elements drawn from the [medieval Witches'] sabbat. It would be evocative and Pagan and ecstatic. A lot of modern Paganism in my opinion is way too sanitized and inoffensive and not challenging to the status quo. I wanted to have an experience that was an emotional experience, that was moving and wonderful and magical. I got some ideas from the legend [of the Witches' sabbat. I said to myself] I will use that bit, but not that bit.

Harrison identifies two motivations for creating the Baphomet rite. First, it is challenging, very challenging. The ritual deliberately draws on symbols and myths that are confronting and stir up strong reactions. The goat-headed deity Baphomet, with all the associations with the Christian devil, is at the heart of the confronting nature of the ritual. Second, the ritual creates a moving and powerful experience of deep emotional intimacy, trust and joy. Participants enter into trance and altered states of consciousness while they dance and taste the *mysterium tremendum*. As Harrison puts it: 'They raise erotic energy, sensual energy and . . . they experience magic. People's hearts do open up from the experience. You can see that year after year.'

The Baphomet rite was first performed at The Pagan Mardi Gras in 1999. Faunalia was created in the following year. The Pagan Mardi Gras is an Australian Pagan festival located in a different state to Faunalia and has a similar structure to other mainstream Pagan festivals such as those described by Pike (2001) and Hume (1997). Pagan festivals are discussed in more detail below. In the months prior to The Pagan Mardi Gras, Heath approached Harrison about performing a ritual at the festival. Harrison had been thinking about creating a ritual based on the medieval Witches' sabbat and said to Heath: 'I have got just the thing'. They formed a group who began work on creating the ritual.

> **Harrison:** Then we started writing the Baphomet rite [to perform at The Pagan Mardi Gras]. There were a few minor things that needed to be sorted out. Heath, Daisy, and then Phoebe and I got together and wrote a few more lines for it and just knocked it into shape so that it was a doable ritual. Then we organized a ritual team.

Phoebe joined the group rehearsing to perform the Baphomet rite. Phoebe and Harrison knew each other through participation in an earlier Pagan group of which Phoebe had been a leader and that had subsequently disbanded. At first Phoebe was a bit cautious about going to the festival because it was about a ten-hour drive, they would be away for several days and it would be 'the first time I had gone away on my own without my family'. Phoebe is married and has three children. She describes doing the rehearsals for the Baphomet ritual:

> **Phoebe:** So we started working on the ritual. Harrison already had ideas for Baphomet. The rehearsal times were so in your face. The energy [of the other ritualists] was a bit overwhelming when I first met them. We started doing rehearsals for Baphomet. But before the rehearsal stage, Harrison asked us who wanted to take on the role of Baphomet. It was too confronting for me the first time, it was too associated to Catholicism and Satan, the Devil. [I said] 'No, I am happy to do one of the elements.' Baphomet is the god form, or Baphomet/Dionysus is the god form, that the Catholics chose to represent [as] Satan in the Bible and in their teachings.

Most Witchcraft rituals include invocations of the four elements of Earth, Air, Fire and Water. In the Southern Hemisphere these are typically 'called in' at the four directions of South, East, North and West respectively. While important, calling in an element is a less demanding ritual role in comparison to performing the character of Baphomet. Very few Witchcraft rituals involve the deity Baphomet.

Having completed the rehearsals, the group of ritualists travelled to The Pagan Mardi Gras. It was held over a long weekend at a large campground facility with bunkhouse accommodation. On the first evening they participated in some enjoyable rituals arranged by other people. The Baphomet ritual was scheduled for the second night.

> **Harrison:** [At the appointed time] we started doing the ritual. We were about an hour or so late. We had organized with some drummers to bring their instruments along and play music, and then promptly forgotten all about it. Just before the ritual, they said, 'Well, what do you want us to do?' [We said] 'when the priestess is not talking, play the drums. Go with the energy'. So they set their drums up, we set the circle up, we started the ritual. I think they had about two hundred people over the weekend but I'm not sure how many were there for the actual ritual, but there were a hell of a lot. I started sweeping the circle area. I started with the chant, 'Come cast the circle widdershins'. [People started saying] 'Did he say widdershins?' 'Widdershins! What's this about widdershins?' Something like that, but anyway. So I kept going. It took ages to get everyone in the circle. We started casting the circle. So I presume that the people that were upset with the fact we were working widdershins had either left or resigned themselves to doing it anyway. So I walked the whole circle, chanting, 'The line is

drawn, the circle is cast'. And that is all fine. I've done that. It was a big circle.

'Widdershins' is understood to mean 'against the direction of the sun'. In the Southern Hemisphere the sun rises in the East, travels through the North sky, and sets in the West. So, the sun appears to travel anti-clockwise through the sky.[4] Witches therefore cast their circles anti-clockwise as a way of indicating they are working with the forces of nature in a positive and constructive way. Casting a circle widdershins, or clockwise in the Southern Hemisphere, can be done for a variety of reasons. It is often associated with rituals for self-empowerment and self-discovery, or where the ritualists seek to break or transform something. Widdershins sometimes has a connotation of evil or maliciousness. People who have recently become Witches are often very uncomfortable casting a circle widdershins, although more experienced practitioners seem to feel comfortable with the practice. Harrison's use of a widdershins circle casting was clearly intended to indicate that the ritual broke with tradition and sought self-discovery and empowerment.

> **Harrison:** So the circle has been cast with the four elements, the drums have kicked in, we had done the invocations and invoked Baphomet, and Heath is there playing Baphomet, and we were getting ready to build up the energy and break into wild dancing. Then these people started chanting, 'We're off to see the wizard' and obviously trying to drown out the ritualist. So we just got louder and the drummers [became] a lot more enthusiastic. The ritual went well, the hecklers got drowned out.
>
> The ritual went off. We had so many people coming up and saying how great the ritual was. I was still awake at dawn. That was the first big ritual I had been to where we had a lot of drumming and energy like that and that ecstatic energy. People were hugging; people were standing in circle just hugging. I had not seen or felt that emotional reaction to a ritual. [There were] heaps of people skyclad [naked] by that time. They hadn't started skyclad. It was just incredible. The whole thing was really magical from start to finish.
>
> The next day we found out that the people had been deliberately trying to disrupt it because they thought the Baphomet energy was too dangerous to invoke. I think it is a rubbish argument in any context. I agree that there are risks in doing the Baphomet ritual, but I think there are risks in doing any real magic. To me a fundamental part of doing magic is that it is the art of change. It changes things. To do that is risky. Change is always risky. There is no two ways about that.

Some of those present at the ritual found it unsettling. However, for a large group of people the ritual worked really well. For example, Phoebe describes how her participation in the Baphomet ritual 'blew my mind':

Phoebe: Doing Baphomet at The Pagan Mardi Gras blew my mind [laughs]. It was an amazing experience. There was an issue with my husband before I left about going skyclad or not. At that stage I had not gone skyclad at all. In my head I thought, well, look, whatever happens, happens. But, Doug, when the revelry started, it was me that ran up to the central fire and I literally ripped my dress off and threw it into that fire. I wasn't ready to take my undies off, but that was enough, that was all I needed for that moment. I tore this cheesecloth dress off and threw it in [the fire]. It was almost like that just went 'whooph', and even more energy for me. I did not sleep for two days. I was awake for two days, walking around the woods, the forest. I saw fairies. I would go off with my cigarettes and I would sit on my own throughout the day many times. I couldn't settle.

There was a massive dispute over the Baphomet ritual the next day. We were hauled into a meeting. I don't recall the whole meeting. They just felt that we were working with forces and energies that we had no understanding about. Now, if I had [chosen] to open my mouth, I would have turned around and said something like, 'Harrison's been doing this for 18 years and there is no way he would be presenting something that he did not understand.' I trusted him in that respect, and still do.

Sauvage, a 41-year-old male, was at the first Baphomet rite at The Pagan Mardi Gras and captures the tension between the unsettling nature of the Baphomet rite and its emotionally and spiritually rewarding outcomes.

Sauvage: This group of people came up from another state and were going to put on a rite. It was meant to be the re-enactment of the sabbat. I was looking for options to be confronted a little about myself and as a way to grow. [The Baphomet rite] was a real celebration of being alive and being human. It was more than your usual circle dance [short laugh]. There was a lot more raw energy, a lot more erotic elements. There was a fierceness to it, and an unrestrained passion. I saw people enjoying themselves. I saw that same sense of awe and wonder that I had seen at some other Pagan rituals when people just lost themselves in the moment, and in being magical. Yeah. I enjoyed what they did.

I remember Harrison and Phoebe being particularly down after that event because there was this whole discussion around the camp of how irresponsible [the Baphomet rite] was. I [didn't think it was] irresponsible. I made the point of going up to each of them and saying, 'Look, I really enjoyed that, and thanks for putting it on'. I remember particularly having a conversation with Phoebe about it, saying: 'I think it was brave but it was important, and I think it is what we need, and it was great. Don't give up'. Yes, it was a bit 'dark', and there were foreboding energies. [But] I actually found it quite liberating.

Phoebe mentions a compliment she received at this time, that may have been Sauvage's: 'I was given a really, really, amazing compliment, which did blow me away. Until then I still doubted the fact that I [was] on the right track.'

> **Sauvage:** I remember a real genuineness about the people that organized that rite. I just felt good about it. I felt that there was a trust there. I felt better about putting myself in a space that minds like that would create. I felt quite safe. Strangely more [safe] than some other [more straightforward Pagan] ritual spaces that I had been in.

Sauvage felt safe and trusted the creators of the Baphomet rite. At the heart of Faunalia is a strong ethic of mutual respect that allows participants to engage with the confronting and challenging aspects of Baphomet. The ethic of mutual respect is to a large extent a product of the leadership style of Phoebe and Harrison. Trust at Faunalia is examined in more detail in Chapter Six on the ethical dimensions of the festival. Faunalia combines ritual practices that are extraordinarily confronting with a respectful relational ethics that allows participants to safely open their hearts to their deepest fears and desires. In these moments of extreme vulnerability they find new hope, courage, purpose and self-worth.

The Baphomet rite, and the annual Faunalia festival that followed, deliberately draw on symbols, practices and emotions that are unsettling and disturbing. For Phoebe and Harrison the unsettling nature of the Baphomet rite is partly what allows it to be such a rewarding experience. The ritual challenges and transforms them through intense emotional experiences.

> **Harrison:** In a sense, for a lot of people, Phoebe is the mother of Faunalia. She is the nurturing side of Faunalia. The one you can talk to and approach. Whereas I am the father figure. When it comes to stuff like talking about the thou shalt nots, I am the one who gets that job. But in another sense when Phoebe and I think about the genesis or the birth of Faunalia, Phoebe is the father and I am the mother [laughing]. It was her idea. She was like the impetus, the drive to get it happen, but I am the one who gave it shape. I mean, we both did.

IMAGE I.2 *Baphomet banner from Faunalia.*
Photo by B. Dalton.

Phoebe and Harrison, like most other participants at Faunalia, sought out Witchcraft as a way of finding meaning, rewarding friendships and a sense of confidence and purpose in life. They feel that Witchcraft, and Faunalia in particular, allowed them to discover a life with 'soul'. Phoebe's story is told in more detail in Chapter One, and in the vignette that precedes Chapter Seven. Harrison's story of his path into Witchcraft beautifully illustrates why the people who attend Faunalia seek out emotionally intense rituals such as the Baphomet rite. The rituals at Faunalia are a particular form of ecstatic and shamanistically oriented Witchcraft that contrasts with the more traditional and formalistic forms of Witchcraft.

Harrison's path into Witchcraft in the early 1980s followed one similar to other Witches at that time: reading books and magazines, and making contacts through occult bookstores and responding to advertisements (Luhrmann 1989). Starhawk's (1979) *The Spiral Dance* is an early important publication in the popularization of contemporary Witchcraft, alongside Janet and Stewart Farrar's (1981) *Witches Bible* and several other similar books. These books describe the rituals of 'the wheel of the year' that celebrate the changing of the seasons, and how to cast a circle.

These foundational practices of Witchcraft inform the Pagan practices at Faunalia, and are described in more detail below.

Early in his discovery of Paganism, Harrison had an experience that was pivotal in shaping his ritual practice, and, as a consequence, the Baphomet rite:

> **Harrison:** I was doing this Wiccan studies correspondence course. It was very expensive. It was more eclectic neo-Pagan nature stuff. I met one of their initiates through a contact advertisement in their paper, and it was one of the most demoralizing experiences in my life. It was terrible. I met this guy. [He wanted] to see if I was fair dinkum or not. I think once he established that I wasn't looking for a sex club, he said come along. So I went there and it was just terrible. They had their altar set up with the candles on it. They left the electric lights on through the whole ritual. They read everything. The circle casting, the whole lot, they read in a dull monotone. It was just woeful. There was no energy, no feeling. Then they said, 'Ok, that's the end of it'. They did the cakes and wine, then they pulled their cigarettes out from under the altar and we all lit up and had a smoke. I was devastated. I'd had all these imaginings of how magical experiences would be, and this was totally crap.
>
> So I went back [to some other people that I knew] and we ended up doing a ritual with the four of us the next night. [It was] really awesome. We had a big bonfire going, and we called in the quarters, and I called in fire. As I called in fire, this wind blew up behind me and blew the flames from the fire all around me. So for a second I was just totally engulfed in flames. Then it blew away. It was just brilliant. That was a turning point, because I lost faith in the idea of an initiatory succession, or at least the necessity of it, and developed a much greater trust in experiences. Magic is something experienced, not something you have conferred by someone else.

Harrison's experience led him to the conclusion that the critical issue was not who trained or initiated you, but the quality of the ritual and the experiences it generated. Some groups within contemporary Witchcraft are very concerned about whether people have been properly initiated and trained (Hutton 1999). Harrison had a number of experiences of emotionally powerful rituals that reinforced his sense that what mattered was not training or initiatory lineage, but rather the quality of the ritual experience. In the following account Harrison describes a ritual experience that some people might find unsettling. Many people, including some Pagans, avoid emotionally intense experiences such as these. In contrast, Harrison came to value and seek out emotionally powerful and unsettling ritual experiences.

Harrison: [A few years later] Hatty took a group of twenty or so [Pagans] off into a clearing in the forest. We did a shamanic vision journey, guided visualization. We all sat around in this big circle, and one at a time we would get up and dance, and I jumped up and did my [turn]. At first I thought it was just a bit of play-acting, and then this rush of energy hit me, it swept me off my feet. It spun me round and smacked me into the ground, and I thought I was going to die, I had never felt anything like it. This animal just took over. I [shouted] 'rroaaarrraaaaggghh!' It was so intense and so physical. It blew me away. That is when I started to realize that magic is about that energy, the transformation of consciousness, rather than just saying the words.

'Energy' is a term commonly used in contemporary Pagan and New Age discourse to refer to those aspects of self and relationships that are difficult to put into words. The term 'energies' is also used to refer to spiritual beings and experiences. While Harrison links his experience of energy to the transformation of consciousness, it is the somatic, emotional and performed aspects of the experience that are primary. Energy is 'worked with' through ritual, dance, Reiki, touch, music and symbols. The accounts of the energy experienced at Faunalia point towards the sorts of experiences described in feminist psychoanalytic theory as 'communion' (Benjamin 1988) and 'the caress' (Irigaray 2001). These are discussed in more detail in Chapter Six.

'Energy' is central to rituals that are experientially demanding and ecstatic. These rituals transform participants' emotions and self-understandings in powerful ways. While formal and traditional rituals can also be transformative, this is often not the case. In the mid-1990s Harrison saw a video of a ritual that drew on Vodou, and another that included a Chinese dragon. Both seemed to provide the sort of profound and emotionally intense experience that he had come to value. This led him to begin searching for something similar in the Pagan tradition. Many contemporary Pagan rituals are inspired by Irish, English and Norse mythologies and the literature of classical Greece, Rome and Egypt. The Greek myth of Persephone's descent into the underworld, for example, is often acted out as a role-play during a ritual and inspired the Underworld rite described in Chapter Three. Harrison looked for a mythological inspiration to provide an emotionally powerful, unsettling and transformative ritual:

Harrison: I started thinking about the Witches' sabbat. I am much more drawn to the archetypal energy of Witchcraft as something socially challenging, and something magical, weird and mythical. I get a bit impatient with Pagans when they don't let go of their Christian baggage. Pagans are scared of the devil. But it is not my job to change or judge others, so I just found people like Phoebe who I resonated with.

This is where Harrison and Phoebe, and as a consequence Faunalia, begin to place themselves on the margins of mainstream Witchcraft and Paganism. It is also why the Baphomet rite was only performed once at The Pagan Mardi Gras. Many contemporary Witches, although not all, would be uncomfortable with participating in a ritual inspired by the medieval Witches' sabbat because of the centrality of the Christian Devil, or Satan, to this mythology (Lewis 2001). Pagans and Witches work very hard to make it clear that they are not evil, or worshipping Satan, but are instead invoking Pagan Gods. Many Christians remain suspicious of Witches and Pagans because of a mistaken association between Pagan Gods and Satan. Harrison and Phoebe's choice to use the medieval Witches' sabbat as an inspiration for creating a Pagan ritual places Faunalia at the controversial edge of contemporary Paganism and Witchcraft.

In the Baphomet rite participants dance with Baphomet. They learn new ways of relating to sexual desire. Desire is honoured, but desires are not always acted upon. Desire is sometimes moderated and sometimes fulfilled, when it is bound up with respect, trust and love. This complex and ambivalent understanding is very different to conservative Christianity's black and white moral ontology. The Devil symbolizes Christianity's understanding of sexual desire, nudity, pleasure and dancing as inherently evil. At Faunalia sexual desire, nudity, pleasure and dancing are catalysts, doorways into a life with soul. The symbolic resonances of Baphomet with the Devil are part of what makes the ritual so powerful.

While the choice of mythology is controversial, the striking thing about the participants at Faunalia is how ordinary they are. Participants attend Faunalia and then return to mundane jobs and established relationships with the same level of commitment as anyone else in the community. They are typically in their thirties or forties with careers and relatively stable family lives, or at least their relationships reflect the patterns of relationships in contemporary Australia. Their occupations include: a disability worker, a bus driver, a policy analyst, computer programmers, systems analysts, a fitness instructor, administrative workers, a real estate salesperson and a massage therapist. They mostly think of themselves as part of contemporary Paganism, and do not think of themselves as worshipping the devil. At Faunalia Baphomet is reinvented as a contemporary Pagan deity.

Harrison saw something in the mythology of the Witches' sabbat that he thought could be used to create a good ritual. Carlo Ginsburg (1992) argues that the myth of the medieval Witches' sabbat is a Christian overlay on Pagan indigenous folk religion of medieval Europe. The sabbat myth could therefore be understood to embody something of the shamanic and ecstatic ritual tradition that Harrison, and those he did ritual with, had come to value. It is this Pagan heritage that Phoebe and Harrison seek to reclaim in the Baphomet rite.

In the quotation above, Harrison explains his choice to use the Witches' sabbat as myth around which to build a ritual. He emphasizes his desire

IMAGE I.3 *Ritualists at Faunalia.*
Photo copyright Edan Mumford. Reproduced with permission.

to 'challenge people's prejudices'. The desire to create a moving emotional experience through ritual is bound up with the choice to challenge the status quo. The numbing and emotionally barren character of contemporary life is one of the central themes of social theory (Ruti 2006). Intense emotional experiences of any kind are often considered threatening and dangerous. This theme is taken up in Chapter One. Some forms of Paganism and Witchcraft are more formalistic and traditional. Other forms of Paganism and Witchcraft, such as Faunalia, are more ecstatic and improvized.

Paganism, Witchcraft and Faunalia

'Paganism' is an umbrella term that refers to a group of religious movements broadly oriented towards honouring nature. Contemporary Paganisms include Wicca, Witchcraft, Druidry, Goddess Spirituality, Heathenry and a variety of other smaller traditions (Harvey 1997). Contemporary Wicca, or Witchcraft, is the most influential tradition that shapes the rituals at Faunalia. Witchcraft is the largest of the Pagan traditions and began in the 1940s in England and spread out from there around the world, splintering into a variety of subgroups (Hutton 1999). While the terms Wicca and

Witchcraft are used by some people to refer to specific traditions of practice (Hutton 1999), the terms are used interchangeably here, as is common among many Australian Pagans.

Witches share the practice of creating sacred space by casting a circle. This typically involves symbolically drawing a circle around participants, who stand in a circle. The circle is often drawn with a ritual knife (athame), or wand, and is followed by carrying symbols of the four primary elements around the circle (Air, Fire, Water and Earth) and then calling in the 'quarters': Air in the east, Fire in the north, Water in the west and Earth in the south. The directions of Fire and Earth are often reversed in the northern hemisphere, although the directionality of the elements is becoming increasingly idiosyncratic. Once the sacred space has been created, a variety of rituals may be performed. A prayer may be said to a deity. Tarot readings may be conducted. Participants may engage in a spiral dance, accompanied by drumming and chanting. Wine and cakes are often blessed and shared among participants. A ritual drama relevant to the time of year may be performed, celebrating, for example, the new growth of spring, or the harvest. Most contemporary Witchcraft groups perform their rituals wearing robes or other celebratory clothing. Nude (skyclad) rituals are rare, although they are practiced in some covens. Two of the main seasonal rituals are Beltane, which is a fertility rite that celebrates the coming of summer, and Samhain, that celebrates the coming of winter, reflecting on death and loss. These are two key festivals in the 'wheel of the year' that is a cycle of eight rituals celebrating the changing seasons of the year. Most covens are small, rarely numbering more than 20 people, and typically perform rituals on full moons, dark moons and the wheel of the year festivals. This form of Witchcraft is now well-documented in academic studies (Bado-Fralick 2005, Greenwood 2000, Hutton 1999, Hume 1997).

Paganism has an organizational structure quite different to other forms of contemporary religion, such as world-rejecting new religious movements, Christian churches and other religious congregations. The organizational structure of Paganism and Witchcraft in Australia is loose, ephemeral and voluntary in nature, similar to many New Age movements (York 1995). A chart of the structure would look like a web, with multiple links and nodes. There are a small number of groups that are more tightly organized, such as some covens, and some heathen groups, who might meet weekly, and have a more insular approach. However, these groups probably represent less than five per cent of Pagans in Australia. Most contemporary Pagans meet at various festivals, join covens or groups that last one to three years, then dissolve and reform reasonably freely. People drift in and out of these groups depending on other life commitments and inclination. The people who make money from Witchcraft do so mostly by selling books and Pagan paraphernalia. Some people make money from running workshops, but people rarely attempt to make money from running rituals or festivals. The cost of attending Faunalia, for example, only covers the accommodation, meals and other related expenses, such as firewood and ritual items. Paganism is structurally similar in organization to late modern 'subcultures' such as Goths (Hodkinson 2002), and other forms of 'neo-tribes' (Maffesoli 1996).

The larger Pagan organizations in Australia, such as the Pagan Awareness Network and the Pagan Alliance, function more like unions or educational associations (Hume 1997). These organizations do not prescribe beliefs or practices. They have elected officials and minimal membership costs. Their main functions are to provide newsletters and websites that facilitate networking among Pagans. They provide information about Paganisms to the media, police and other secular bodies. They sponsor some Pagan events, providing organizational expertise and insurance cover.

Pagan festivals are an important part of contemporary Paganism (Pike 2001). These are typically annual meetings, with participants numbering in the hundreds. Some people travel considerable distances to attend these events. They generate and sustain community on a broader scale, beyond the smaller covens and the virtual relationships of the internet. Festivals are usually held outside cities at campgrounds or recreational areas with tent and/or bunkhouse accommodation. Large bonfires are often part of the event where participants dance accompanied by drumming and chanting. Workshops facilitate information sharing and various forms of networking. The rituals at these events can be elaborate and transformative. Faunalia is one such event, albeit an unusual one.

'Faunalia' is a pseudonym for an Australian Pagan festival that has been a yearly event since it began in 2000 and ended in 2009. It takes place over a five-day extended long weekend in a secluded rural bush location approximately two hours' drive from a large Australian city. There is bunkhouse accommodation, a shared dining room, a gymnasium and a large open area with a central bonfire. About 80 people attended the 2005 festival. In 2005 I interviewed 11 male and 12 female attendees, of which six people were attending the festival for the first time. These proportions are similar to all those attending the festival. The interviewees ranged in age from 21 to 59 years old, and their average age was 37.

Information about Faunalia is disseminated in a variety of ways. Most people who attend know each other through participation in smaller covens or through other festivals. A small group, perhaps up to 20 people in 2005, only knew a few people at Faunalia. Reflecting the largely decentred and virtual nature of Pagan community in Australia, many people heard about Faunalia through online communities. For example, Ruth, a 25-year-old who had attended Faunalia three times reported that when she first became interested in Witchcraft she joined one of the online Witchcraft communities: 'There was an advertisement for Faunalia and I looked at it, and thought, hey, this sounds like fun. I didn't know anybody, but by the time I got there I knew a few people through email.'

The leaders of Faunalia explicitly resist any attempt to portray themselves as leaders of a movement. Faunalia is a peak experience, and the rituals are intense and profoundly transformative. However, it is ephemeral. While there are some continuing covens that Faunalia's participants could ask to join, this is not the main focus of Faunalia. Only a couple of people reported that they had been invited to join such groups, or that they had sought out such membership. Occasional events are organized between festivals, but participation is voluntary, and no one reported any social or emotional pressure placed on them to attend such events.

The rest of this book describes the rituals of the 2005 Faunalia, with the Baphomet rite at its heart. The book examines how the rituals allow participants to develop new forms of relationship with aspects of themselves and the world around them. The book follows the structure of the festival. The early chapters introduce the festival and the role of ritual. The later chapters describe the two main rituals of the Underworld rite and the Baphomet rite.

Chapter outline

Chapter One examines the concept of 'soul'. Drawing on sociological and psychoanalytic theory I develop a this-worldly understanding of soul. A life that is experienced as worthwhile, and performed with dignity and respect, is a life with soul. Participants recount how the rituals at Faunalia helped them find a life with soul. Soul is found in relationships. In soulful relationships people acknowledge and support each other, while recognizing and accepting difference. Soul is also found in ritual performances, in doing, acting and dancing.

The structure and organization of Faunalia are described in Chapter Two. The chapter develops Turner's concept of liminality, bringing it into dialogue with the relational, aesthetic and embodied aspects of the soulful experiences discussed in Chapter One. Liminality describes the experience of being briefly outside of the normal everyday world. Temporal factors and material objects play an important role in creating liminality at the festival. Liminality also creates communitas – a deep, if transitory, sense of community – and is bound up with a morality of authenticity. Liminal ritual events make space and time for transformations of soul. The chapter develops a relational theory of religion, arguing that religion at Faunalia is a set of ritual practices that engage symbolic resources to provide both an etiquette for relationships and an emotional and somatic sense of self-worth and purpose.

The Underworld rite is performed on the second night at Faunalia. Chapter Three describes the ritual, largely in the words of participants. In the Underworld rite participants come face to face with their mortality, and the suffering and loss inherent in many life transitions. For many participants, their sense of self is transformed in the ritual. It is confronting, painful and difficult to imagine one's own death. In the ritual, the pain is honoured, the fear is confronted and the awareness of a life lived 'towards death' becomes just a little more bearable. The Underworld rite illustrates how rituals help participants find a life with soul in the context of human suffering and mortality.

Participants understand rituals at Faunalia as 'shadow work'. This is examined in Chapter Four. The 'shadow' refers to those aspects of the self that are not completely consciously articulated, such as fears and anxieties. Shadow work engages with these aspects of the self primarily through the aesthetic and somatic aspects of ritual performance. The rituals transform participants' relationships to these shadow, hidden or repressed parts of their lives. For example, the Underworld rite does not seek to overcome or escape from fears and anxieties associated with death and suffering. Rather, participants reluctantly accept these as inevitable parts of life and discover a new strength to face suffering and the inevitability of their own mortality.

The Baphomet rite performed on the third night is described in Chapter Five. Drawing mainly on participants' own words, the chapter follows participants through the ritual briefings and preparation in the afternoon and early evening, into the procession and commencement of the ritual where they disrobe and enter a state of trance. The ritual involves chanting and dancing and an encounter with the hermaphroditic deity Baphomet, a goat-headed symbol of animalistic erotic desire. The chapter includes extensive participant accounts of both erotic encounters and spiritual experiences.

Ethics is discovered in the Baphomet rite through deliberately confronting participants' sexual and animalistic desires. Chapter Six reviews the ethical dimensions of Faunalia. Rather than seeking to overcome or deny sexual desire, participants develop a complex relationship with their desire, choosing when and how to contain it or to indulge it. This is understood as a form of shadow work. The ritual allows participants to 'dance' with their desires even though their desires are not fully articulated consciously. The Baphomet rite also confronts fears of the naked and erotic body. Drawing on Friedrich Nietzsche, Emmanuel Levinas and Jessica Benjamin the chapter considers how aesthetics and relational etiquette shape the development of a Pagan ethic of authenticity.

Chapter Seven examines the implications of the rituals at Faunalia for contemporary academic understandings of religious experience. Rituals that generate liminal experiences are transformative because of somatic and aesthetic dimensions that work alongside belief and cognitively articulated symbolic systems. Contemporary social theories that emphasize the inter-subjective and embodied aspects of being human are also discussed. The Dionysian elements of ritual and the experience of 'flow' draw participants into a religious etiquette of relating to both oneself and others that is associated with a somatic sense of self-worth and purpose.

The rituals at Faunalia transform participants' relationships to themselves and to the world around them. People learn to be less afraid, more confident, more self-accepting and respectful. These transformations are achieved through ritual performances that engage with emotional and somatic self-understandings. The participants at Faunalia are human: they make mistakes and are sometimes selfish and disrespectful. Beyond this, the rituals at Faunalia point to the power of ritual performance to transform self-understandings and the importance of bodies and emotions in shaping the way we live in the world.

CHAPTER ONE

Soul

Introduction

This chapter examines what it means to live 'soulfully'. People go to Faunalia because they choose to follow their heart, to live with passion and to be authentic. I use the phrase 'living with soul' to describe this sort of life. Living with soul is at the heart of what participants value about Faunalia. From a psychoanalytic perspective Mari Ruti (2006) describes a this-worldly, non-metaphysical understanding of 'soul'. A life with soul is one that is experienced as worthwhile and emotionally satisfying. A life with soul is something that participants find through rituals. A life with purpose and dignity can be found in many secular activities. However, religious ritual is attractive to many people because it provides practices that enable them to find a life with soul.

A life with soul has three main characteristics. First, it is found in relationships. In soulful relationships people acknowledge and support each other, while recognizing and accepting difference. To examine the relational aspects of soul, this chapter introduces Graham Harvey's (2013) conception of religion as an etiquette of relationships, and Jessica Benjamin's (1988) psychoanalytic discussion of mutual recognition in erotic relationships. Second, a life with soul is facilitated through ritual practices, in performances, in doing, acting and dancing. Here the chapter develops Benjamin's (1998) concept of 'acting' as half-conscious performances, and Carl Einstein's (Pan 2001) understanding of ritual as aesthetically mediated performances and relations. Third, a life with soul draws on symbolic resources such as myths and shared cultural understandings. The culture of contemporary Witchcraft and Paganism are the dominant symbolic resources utilized at Faunalia. Later chapters discuss Pagan culture in detail, along with other symbolic resources utilized by participants at Faunalia.

The term 'soul' is preferable to 'meaning' or 'purpose' because 'soul' points to the emotional, aesthetic and moral aspects of life, which are the focus of this book. 'Meaning' suggests cognition and belief, which are not central issues for the Pagan rituals discussed in the book. 'Purpose' suggests a teleological orientation towards the future, which, while important, is not central to the participants at Faunalia. Charles Taylor (1989: 33), following Ricoeur (1985) and MacIntyre (1981), argues that the self is more than either cognitively framed understandings or strategic abilities. A sense of self is linked to notions of 'the good'. I use 'soul' in a sociological and non-metaphysical way to indicate this moral dimension of self-understandings. It has some similarities to Grace Jantzen's (1998) concept of 'flourishing', although I am less concerned with the gendered nature of this experience, and to live a life with soul is also to know suffering. I do not discuss whether a soul is a thing that continues on after life, although many Pagans believe in an afterlife. Rather, in this book 'soul' describes a way of living this life.

Rituals play key roles in creating lives with soul. Think of funerals. Sometimes these rituals are powerful and we come away feeling transformed and with a sense that something important has happened. Yes, it is sad to farewell a loved one, and perhaps the tears flow freely, but it feels 'right'. The grief is honoured, the person remembered and life without them is just a little more bearable. The ritual performance changes something in us at an emotional level. It also changes the way we relate, both to the deceased person, and to other people who share our grief. If the ritual has 'worked' and been done well, it changes these things for the better. Rituals help us find a life with soul.

The reason people attend Faunalia is to find better ways of living soulfully. Yes, the rituals are confronting, but it is not the desire to confront death, or the thrill of dancing naked with 80 people around a bonfire that primarily motivates participation in the festival. This chapter explains how Phoebe, Sauvage and Lewis find soulful lives through their participation in Faunalia. The pursuit of soulful lives is central to Faunalia.

The rituals at Faunalia provide a window into contemporary society. They cast in sharp relief the features of our lives that cheat us of soul. Soulful lives are discovered in many places: loving relationships, all night dance parties, gardening and sometimes in religious communities in all their variety. This book examines just what it is that makes these activities important, and why we need them if we are to experience our lives as meaningful and worthwhile.

Soul: Phoebe

Phoebe is married to Matthew who is an agnostic. Early in her marriage to Matthew she attended a Spiritualist church for four months. Matthew was uncomfortable with this and following the birth of Phoebe's third child, she put religion 'on the backburner'. Her decision to become involved in Paganism came some time later, approximately nine years prior to our interview. It began with a phone call to the owner of a Pagan bookshop she found in the phone directory:

> **Phoebe:** For the first five years [after Matthew and I were married] I chose to take on the role as mother and housekeeper and all of that. I enjoyed it. It is a part of my nature that I enjoy very much. But I was dying spiritually. I would sit where you are now and Matthew would be there, and I would not know what I had just watched. I could be there with him for hours and just zone out. Nothing around me satisfied me or fed me internally anymore. Yes, my kids did. Yes, the moments with Matthew did. But that was on a very different level. The best way of putting it is my soul was dying. They are the words he actually used when he came in one evening and just looked at me, and I was just blank. There was no life. I became quite robotic. He just looked over at me and said: 'Your soul is dying. Go do what it is that you need to do'. And, Doug, I was out that door! [laughs.]

Phoebe talked to the Pagan bookshop owner for two hours on the phone. He gave her the phone number of a person who was running a Wiccan coven. Phoebe became heavily involved with the Wiccan group for nearly two years. Participation in the coven: 'gave me confidence, I found my voice. That to me is a very, very big positive.' She left that group prior to the creation of Faunalia. When I asked Phoebe to describe the overall influence of Faunalia, she replied:

> **Phoebe:** I think it has changed me. [When I speak,] I am heard because I am actually using my voice. I am not as intimidated with people, whereas I used to be. It has given me a lot more confidence to stand up. The amount of friends and heart connections that I have made with people has been enormous.

Phoebe felt that her soul was dying. The restoration of that soul through participation in contemporary Witchcraft has two main, and tightly interwoven, consequences: self-confidence and relationships. The rituals of contemporary Witchcraft, and Faunalia in particular, make both these possible. Contemporary Paganisms are primarily religions of practice, not overly concerned with theology (Hume 1997). Phoebe does not focus on trying to explain her religion philosophically. Rather, she focuses on the ritual experiences and relationship with deity. She feels that she is valued as a creative agent within the context of emotionally satisfying relationships.

Phoebe's observations about her soul dying point to something that many contemporary social commentators have described. As Mari Ruti (2006) puts it:

> One of the most persistently recurring themes of twentieth century theory . . . is the idea that there is something about the assaultive fragmenting and numbing quality of life in post-industrial Western societies that devastates human interiority in a manner that leaves us psychically crippled – that 'cheats us of soul'. (Ruti 2006: 73)

Ruti (2006: 20) is not using soul in a religious sense. Rather, soul refers to the person's attempt to find her or his 'place and purpose in the world' through reflexively and creatively working with symbolic resources from contemporary culture. Ruti's psychoanalytically informed definition of soul points to the importance of creative agency, but needs supplementing to embrace the religious ritual practices that are important to Phoebe.

'Religion' as practiced at Faunalia is primarily about rituals and relationships, not belief. Religion has often been defined as belief in God, or some variation on this that retains an emphasis on cognition and otherworldly transcendence. Perhaps it is because they are not overly concerned about such beliefs that many participants at Faunalia do not think of themselves as engaged in religion. Graham Harvey (2005, 2013) persuasively argues that such a conception of religion is misguided, drawing on the work of Vásquez (2011), Latour (2010) and Ingold (2011). For Harvey, religion is to be found 'elsewhere' in the practice of ritual and the etiquette of relationships to other-than-human persons. At the heart of religion as practiced at Faunalia is the development of an etiquette of relationships with other participants and with deities such as Baphomet. In this book I use a definition of religion that combines Harvey's emphasis on practice and relationships with Ruti's discussion of reflexivity and symbolic resources:

> Religion is a set of ritual practices that engage symbolic resources to provide an etiquette for relationships and an emotional and cognitive sense of self-worth and purpose.

I argue that religious ritual practices are foundational and make possible, or engage, particular types of meanings and values (Bell 1992). As Catherine Bell (1997: 82) notes: 'the study of ritual as practice has meant a basic shift from looking at activity as the expression of cultural patterns to looking at it as that which makes and harbors such patterns.' In other words, rituals and practices are not only expressions of beliefs and ideas. Rather, beliefs and ideas can also be outworkings of rituals and practices. This definition of religion is consistent with that given by those closely engaged with ritual studies. Grimes (2000: 70), for example, says: 'By spirituality I intend practiced attentiveness aimed at nurturing a sense of the interdependence of all beings sacred and all things ordinary . . . and by religion I mean spirituality sustained as a tradition or organized into an institution.' Similarly, Driver (1991: 97) notes the primacy of actions such as 'invoking, addressing, affecting, manipulating' in the interweaving of action and symbols in ritual: 'the ritual is not in the service of the symbols, but the other way round.'

This definition moves away from an emphasis on belief as the foundation of religion, an emphasis that probably derives from Protestant Christianity. In some senses, religious belief could be understood as a particular form of religious practice. This issue is discussed extensively and thoroughly by Harvey (2013): 'To understand believing as something done within Christianity we have to stop theorizing belief as connected to postulation, ideas, interiority, subjectivity. Rather, we have to think of believing as another kind of relational activity' (Harvey 2013: 124). Harvey here points to one of the key aspects of ritual practices that I focus on in this book: the relational etiquette facilitated by rituals.

The development of an etiquette of relationships is central to lives with soul. Mature and confident selves form by 'becoming more active and sovereign' *within* relationships (Benjamin 1988: 18). Jessica Benjamin's (1988, 1998) feminist psychoanalytic theory provides a sophisticated analysis of relational etiquette and ethics, mainly in the context of erotic relationships. She argues that ethics develop in the practice of relationships. Ethics is not something individuals discover on their own, by themselves. Ethics is discovered in relationships. Much contemporary thought suggests that maturation is a process of making ourselves independent and autonomous, incorrectly suggesting that we 'grow out of relationships'. Rather, Benjamin draws on psychoanalysis and sociological theory to emphasize the inter-subjective foundations of our lives. We mature as people through growing *into* relationships. A life with soul is found in relationships.

The relationships found in religious ritual practices reflect broader cultural forms and political structures (Arnal and McCutcheon 2013, Asad 1993, 2003). The rituals at Faunalia reflect participants' attempts to resist a broader culture that is afraid of suffering and sadness (Alexander 2012, Ahmed 2010, Horowitz and Wakefield 2007), and ambivalent about sexual desire (Irigaray 2001, Benjamin 1998). While religious practice at Faunalia is individualized, it also engages in a sophisticated attempt to resist and transform some central aspects of Western culture.

Ronald Grimes (2000: 3) argues that 'without rites that engage our imaginations, communities, and bodies, we lose touch with the rhythms of the human life course'. Grimes' point about life-course transitions such as weddings and funerals can be extended to other aspects of being human. Rituals bring humans into somatic and imagined relationship to the world in which we live. Rituals facilitate the transition from single to married, or from alive to deceased, and provide an important function in smoothing these transitions. Rituals also allow individuals to discover a sense of their place in the world, their ability to act in it and the etiquette of relational morality that links them to other humans and to the other-than-human world.

Mythology enables 'us to live more intensely' within the world, as Karen Armstrong (2005: 3) so beautifully puts it: 'In mythology we entertain a hypothesis, bring it to life by means of ritual, act upon it, contemplate its effect upon our lives, and discover that we have achieved new insight into the disturbing puzzle of our world' (Armstrong 2005: 10). While I disagree with Armstrong's apparent privileging of belief over ritual, she makes an excellent point. Those who dismiss religion as 'opting out' (Armstrong 2005: 3), or like Walter Benjamin consider religions to be 'archaic constructs that need to be replaced by rational critique' (Pan 2001: 9), miss the importance and complexity of the religious experience. Some religions may involve 'opting out' and others may be archaic and could benefit from a greater consideration of rational analysis, but to characterize all of religious experience in this way ignores the significance of religion as it is described by those who know it intimately.

Religion is attractive because it allows people to live in the world in healthy and soulful ways. This is a central argument of this book. This is one of the most common reasons people give for participating in religion. A life experienced as soulful appears to be an outcome of religious practices. This does not mean that a soulful life can only be found in religion. There are various secular ways of living that seem equally capable of producing lives with soul – Ruti's (2006) psychoanalytic practice is one of them. My point is simply that one of the main reasons people choose to live religious lives is that they find them rewarding, meaningful and emotionally satisfying.

Religion, and religious ritual, can also be oppressive and destructive. This is a product of the particular form of relational etiquette that is constructed in the ritual and religious culture. Jessica Benjamin argues that domination and oppression in erotic relationships are a product of: 'a breakdown in the necessary tension between self-assertion and mutual recognition that allows self and other to meet as sovereign equals' (Benjamin 1988: 12). Benjamin's central concept is that of *mutual recognition*, which she describes as 'the necessity of recognizing as well as being recognized by the other' (Benjamin 1988: 23). The concept of mutual recognition is discussed in greater detail throughout the book. A similar process operates in religion, where oppression and exploitation develop as a result of the breakdown of respect, and the failure to allow participants to engage in relationships as agents and equals. Rituals that entail mutual recognition involve both self-assertion, and the recognition of others in their own right. Oppression and domination are not related to the truth or falsity of religious beliefs, rather they are a product of the relational etiquette and practices of ritual participants.

Weddings are rituals that change the status of relationships. These ritually mediated relationships involve a process of mutual recognition. Participating in weddings helps make sense of a changed relationship; they help people find an etiquette for their new relationship status. Weddings mark the commitment of two people to share their lives in relationship. The marrying couple make their vows in which they commit to care for each other, and at the same time honour and respect their differences. They engage in mutual recognition. Weddings do not always create relationships of respect, self-confidence and resilience. There are patriarchal overtones still found in some weddings, for example, in the use of the word 'obey' in vows some women make to their husband. At this point I simply want to highlight that for many people marriage is a ritual that helps them live a life with soul because through participation in the ritual the couple reinforces an etiquette of relating that involves respect and mutual recognition.

Religious practices allow people to 'work' with the aspects of themselves that shape moral orientations, both towards themselves and others. The religious 'technology' of ritual is morally neutral, it can be used for good or evil, to create respect or domination. One of the primary consequences of participation in religious ritual is that it shapes people's moral orientations and self-understandings. This is a Durkheimian (1976) point, developed particularly in his later work (Shilling and Mellor 1998). The moral consequences of participation in the rituals at Faunalia are discussed in detail in Chapters Four and Six.

Contemporary religious ritual can be understood sociologically as a social technology for transforming people's self-understandings and their morality of relational etiquette. It is also more than this. In particular, for many religious practitioners, the reality of relationships with spiritual beings and deity are central. The rediscovery of a life with soul is made possible through the performances of religious ritual. Faunalia provides an example of this process. The Pagan rituals of Faunalia produce intoxicating emotional states that transform not only people's shared moral orientations but also transform their embodied sense of self-worth and purpose in life.

Sauvage

Sauvage is a 41-year-old single male who has attended Faunalia four times. He became interested in Witchcraft 11 years ago and has attended various Pagan events:

> Sauvage: Before this last Faunalia, my sense of myself as a Pagan was probably pretty limited. I felt as though I was not really connecting with that energy, all of that essence, all of that lifestyle. I happily expressed myself as Pagan, but I just felt that my life had got to a point

of being so full of other things that I rarely did anything that practised an understanding of Paganism.

For Sauvage to connect with the 'energy' of Paganism he felt he needed to practice as a Pagan. Calling himself a Pagan and spending time with other Pagans was not enough. He was looking for something that would transform him on a deeper level. This is not just about lifestyle, but about an experience of being Pagan that is felt and performed, mainly through ritual. Participants seek to transform themselves, to discover a life with soul, through shared ritual performance. Sauvage's experience of the Baphomet rite at the Pagan Mardi Gras was recounted earlier. His experience there encouraged him to attend Faunalia:

> **Sauvage:** At Faunalia there is an opportunity to explore things and unlock things. You do not get [that opportunity in other places], or I haven't found it. [The specific things] change year to year. It is a deepening of that initial thing I said about being confronted with parts of yourself. [During the ritual you are] in the moment linking those aspects of yourself, the intellectual, the spiritual. And being present with others, and having a sense of your own power as a result of that . . . To be able to dance with beings, with yourself, with your shadow, with your past, with others that you felt a bond to, or an attraction, or were trying to resolve something. I felt safe enough to just be who I was.

Sauvage's participation in the Pagan rituals of Faunalia allowed him to work with some challenging and hard-to-change aspects of himself. Through these experiences he was able to grow, to become more confident and to find a stronger sense of self. This transformation was made possible through his participation in rituals that work with 'energy'. While the effects of these transformations are cognitively articulated, it is the aesthetic, somatic, performed and emotional dimensions that are primary. As discussed in Chapter Two, rituals transform the way people feel through somatic and symbolic processes in which cognition and meaning are of secondary significance.

Sauvage also underlines the importance of the relational and communal aspects of ritual. His sense of self changes as he participates in relationships of 'mutual recognition' (Benjamin 1988). In the 'dance' with other participants he feels 'safe' to be himself. This relational experience of mutual recognition is central to the power of the rituals at Faunalia. In the rituals participants dance and perform various roles that touch on some aspects of themselves they are afraid to reveal. It may be that they have poor body image and fear being naked, or have a disability they feel always segregates them, or a fear of dying, or low self-esteem. In the rituals participants are 'recognized' and acknowledged by other ritualists while performing these feared and problematic aspects of the self. The recognition and acknowledgement by other participants leads them to find strength, wisdom and beauty in these aspects of themselves. Sauvage, who uses a wheelchair, notes that through being 'present with others' he was able to have a sense of his 'own power'. Paradoxically, a sense of strength and independence comes in the moment of dependence on others. This is precisely Jessica Benjamin's point about mutual recognition:

> The vision of recognition between equal subjects gives rise to a new logic – the logic of paradox, of sustaining the tension between contradictory forces. Perhaps the most fateful paradox is the one posed by our simultaneous need for recognition and independence: that the other subject is outside our control and yet we need him. To embrace this paradox is the first step toward unravelling the bonds of love. This means not to undo our ties to others but rather to disentangle them; to make of them not shackles but circuits of recognition. (Benjamin 1988: 221)

For participants at Faunalia, internal validation comes through external validation. This is the paradox that Benjamin describes as characteristic of loving relationships. The same process operates in rituals. The rituals at Faunalia are structured processes of mutual recognition. They facilitate the development of etiquettes or relationships that shape the way participants relate to each other and to themselves. The external performances transform participants' internal self-understandings.

When I asked Sauvage how Faunalia had shaped him 'overall' his reply emphasizes the relationships he experienced at Faunalia:

> Sauvage: I think it reinforced to me that there are other ways to be, and that there are some things that are really important to me about just being alive, and being connected with the people that I enjoy and respect and trust and love. That is important and that is precious and I want to keep that happening, and that is the essence of magic to me . . . [Another part of it is] being prepared to explore things that other parts of society would frown upon. To me, now, [the fear that society has of those things is] more symbolism than actuality. Being confronted with what the Baphomet rite does or can do, can trigger things for each person that has the potential to really bother them. If you are brave and you go there, you will have a pretty profound experience . . . I had got to the point where I really actually want to deal with those things. I want to look into myself and I want to explore that, and find out whether those elements can be addressed and whether I can deal with it in a healthy way.

Sauvage feels confronted by some of the aspects of Faunalia and the emotional aftermath that it can create. It is through engaging with the unsettling nature of these experiences that Sauvage is able to find a healthier way of living. The willingness to explore confronting and unsettling experiences is discussed in more detail in Chapter Four. Through the rituals he discovers some things that are 'really important' about 'being alive'. Sauvage has found a sense of confidence, resilience and agency through a combination of a sense of belonging that is 'extraordinarily rare' and ritual practices that have allowed him to explore some confronting aspects of himself and find healthier ways of living. The structures of the rituals at Faunalia support an etiquette of relationships both to self and others that facilitates a life with soul.

The sense of 'loss of soul' that marks contemporary Western society is in part a product of the rarity of events like Faunalia. Rituals and events such as carnivals, weddings, funerals, dance parties and a wide variety of other similar practices are either empty and formalistic, or too infrequent. In these moments people engage in performances that transform the way they feel about themselves. Such events are not always wonderful, and can sometimes be emotionally challenging or disruptive. The contrast between a Dionysian emphasis on emotions and experience and Apollonian emphasis on rational thought and control is useful here (Pan 2001). Dionysian rituals are often emotionally intense, irrational and ecstatic (Shilling and Mellor 2011). Many prefer 'the Apollonian world of rationality and light' (Benjamin 1988: 141). Yet, despite these concerns, it is at Dionysian events that many people discover what it is to feel alive, wise, strong, beautiful and to taste 'what life can be like if you can just embrace what you have inside you' (René).

Religion is not what you believe

Religion is as much about performances, bodies, relationships and emotions, as it is about beliefs, texts and verbalization. A life with soul is primarily found in ritual performances that shape emotions and relationships, not in cognitions and beliefs. For Phoebe and Sauvage the constructive effects of Faunalia begin with a change in the way they interact with other people. Constructive social relationships are facilitated both by the 'heart' friendships that they form and also by the greater confidence they derive from their ritual participation. Shilling and Mellor (2011) point out that for Durkheim, bodies and emotions, particularly intoxicating and powerful emotions, were not simply the province of addiction, spoilt identities and irrationality. Rather, Durkheim argues that 'societies and religions are constituted through the embodied intoxication of their members' (Shilling and Mellor 2011: 18). Durkheim thought that ritual intoxication generated commitment to beliefs and shared normative orientations. I suggest that rituals do not necessarily create commitment to beliefs, but they do create commitments to particular ethical practices and etiquettes of relating.

The accounts of participants at Faunalia demonstrate that their religion emphasizes embodied, emotionally engaged, communal, ritual performance. It is this that generates a sense of soul, a sense of a life well lived. Beliefs and ideas are discussed, but not central. Most participants engage in long conversational debriefings of various forms, which presume a certain set of beliefs. However, even these debriefing sessions do not usually involve discussions of the truth or falsity of beliefs. Participants are much more interested in emotional self-understandings and relational etiquette.

The point that 'belief is a Christian category' should not really need to be made, as Harvey (2013: 20) notes: 'because this has been said so many times that it ought to be unnecessary to say it too many more times.' More specifically, McGuire (2008: 20) argues that 'sociology's disciplinary focus on what people believe, affirm, and think, as indicators of their religion and religiosity, is based on Reformation-era theological ideas that privilege belief over practice'. Nonetheless, it remains common for 'religion' and 'belief' to be used synonymously in popular discourse and academic accounts (Riis and Woodhead 2010: 3). King (1999: 36) traces the understanding of religion as a matter of 'adherence to particular doctrines or beliefs' to the beginnings of Christianity. In Pagan Rome, religion and tradition were integrated such that allegiance to the traditions of one's ancestors involved the performances of ritual practices that honoured the Gods. Early Christian discourses 'drove a wedge' between tradition and religion, separating out religion as belief in contrast to traditional practice.

Bodies, practices and performances are central to the everyday practices of spiritual and religious lives (McGuire 2008). While recent Protestant religious thought has conceptualized the spiritual realm in opposition to embodied practices in the physical realm, McGuire argues that this theological assumption is not good sociology. Rather, she suggests: 'to the contrary, that spirituality fully involves people's material bodies, not just their minds or spirits' (McGuire 2008: 97). McGuire provides a rich range of examples drawn from medieval Christianity, through Mexican American popular religious practices, to southern evangelicals, to demonstrate that a wide range of embodied experiences, including visual images, sounds and smells 'heighten our spiritual focus and evoke meaningful religious experiences' (McGuire 2008: 99). The primary concern of most religious practitioners is not the truth or falsity of their theology, but rather the value of their ritual practices.

In the Pagan contexts of both ancient Rome and Faunalia it makes no sense to ask whether a religion is true or false. Such a question demonstrates a misunderstanding of the nature of religious practices (King 1999). In ancient Rome one could ask if 'one was faithfully adhering to a particular ancestral practice' (King 1999: 37). At Faunalia, ancestral practice is absent, and the primary question becomes one of authenticity in the pursuit of experiential self-transformation through ritual performance. Participants at Faunalia are primarily concerned with whether they are being true to themselves, while at the same time honouring the people and Gods they respect and love. This reflects the influence of the cultural politics of Western societies on contemporary religious practice (Asad 2003). The ethic of authenticity is discussed in more detail in Chapter Six. Harrison read an early draft of this book and in response to this paragraph suggested that the connection with a historical and ancient Witchcraft tradition through adoption of the medieval Witch's sabbat imagery could be seen as a way of connecting with ancestral practices. In this sense there is a moral imperative associated with the desire to faithfully adhere to the tradition of ecstatic shamanistic practices this tradition is understood to contain (Ginsburg 1992).

In the Pagan rituals of Faunalia, and perhaps for most religious ritual, what matters is the suspension of disbelief and the preparedness to accept the ritual on its own terms. Tanya Luhrmann (1989) made precisely this point in her ethnography of Pagan magical communities in England. As a Pagan, or 'magician' as Luhrmann refers to her participants, begins to practice and engage in ritual: 'the ideas of magical practice make progressively more sense, and seem progressively more natural; the magician becomes more likely to "believe" in their truth, by acting as if they were true and defending them in conversation' (Luhrmann 1989: 313). Luhrmann emphasizes the role of reading and solitary practice, which is certainly important for many Pagans. However, in the context of larger group rituals, the social dimensions become increasingly important.

Religion is both a matter of communal involvement and willing 'acceptance' of the ritual practice. Engaging in ritual in a way that is experienced and perceived as authentic is a social and relational practice. The key is to participate in a way that 'accepts' the ritual. 'Acceptance . . . is not a private state, but a public act, visible both to witnesses and to performers themselves . . . Acceptance entails neither belief nor obedience' (Rappaport 1999: 120). Pagans at Faunalia vary from 'hard polytheists' who believe that deities are real beings, through those who understand deity as archetypes in the Jungian sense, to those who describe themselves as atheist Pagans who understand deities as simply symbols of the natural world. Participants rarely concern themselves with debating the merits of these different understandings of deity. What matters is willing participation in the rituals.

The Christian practice of emphasizing individual belief is bound up with enlightenment and modernist obsession with cognitive knowing that ignores the communal and performative dimensions of religion (Arnal and McCutcheon 2013). McGuire (2008: 39) argues that medieval Christian religion privileged practice, not belief, and that the Christian focus on belief was a product of reformation movements to centralize authority and power. Bruno Latour (2010) differentiates the rhetoric of how modern people understand the world – which assumes that belief and objectivity are primary – from the practice of what moderns do. According to Latour, in practice modern people are equally as shaped by feelings, relationships and embodied practice as any other historical or contemporary culture. It is a modernist myth that they are rational, and not influenced by embodied practice. This is what Latour means when he describes modern people as having 'factish' gods – modern people create the idea of an objective disembodied 'fact' in the same way that other cultures create 'fetishes'.

Belief is integrally bound up with practices. Rather than deconstructing belief, Latour argues we should focus on what the actors are pointing at when they describe a deity or religious practice. To separate out belief from knowledge, action from understanding, is to miss the point of what is going on. The singular focus on belief is 'what allows one to keep the practical form of life, in which one causes something to be fabricated, at a distance from the theoretical forms of life, in which one has to choose between facts and fetishes' (Latour 2010: 20). It is in this sense that belief can be understood as a form of practice.

Participants at Faunalia do not reject belief. Rather, the experience of ritual, and its transformative effects, renders concerns about beliefs peripheral in almost precisely the way that Latour describes they are in non-modern cultures. This post-humanist hybridity of beliefs and practice is not universally characteristic of all Paganisms. There are some Paganisms that are much more concerned with beliefs (York 2003). The rituals at Faunalia provide an 'extreme case' (Ezzy 2002) example of the importance of the non-cognitive dimensions of religion. Participants are not concerned with whether a deity or energy is a fact. Rather, the deity and energy are fabricated through the ritual and become real, or their reality is manifest, in the subsequent experiences.

The Pagan rituals at Faunalia produce significant self-transformations, such as those described by Phoebe and Sauvage. Phoebe found her own voice, developed a sense of self-confidence and some valued friendships. Sauvage was reminded of the importance of good relationships and that perhaps he did not need to fear some things as much as he had been. The self-transformative consequences of the rituals at Faunalia are similar to the Charismatic healing rituals described by Csordas (1994). Csordas (1994: 70) argues that 'Charismatic healing creates a modulation of somatic attention that changes the way people respond to physical symptoms'. To understand Charismatic healing requires going beyond a simplistic analysis of cognitive belief to an examination of 'embodied imaginal performance' (Csordas 1994: 203). It is in the embodied performance, which is in turn imagined and cognitively evaluated, that the sacred self is constructed and transformed. At Faunalia it is not physical illness, but emotional self-understandings that are the focus of this transformative process.

Explaining these transformations requires analysis of the sensuous and relational ritual performances that are, in turn, bound up with ideas and understandings that some participants then examine intellectually. When asked about her beliefs, Marie describes a contrast between the modernist obsession with facts and the sensitivity to sensuous experience she derives from Pagan ritual:

> **Marie:** There's the old Cartesian notion 'I think therefore I am' and there's the notion that we cannot trust our sense experiences. And that is the basis on which modern science operates. [In contrast experiences at Faunalia] are all sense experiences. I have an open mind to them. I wonder at them and I think they create this wonderful sense of mystery about reality. Reality is quite mysterious.

Following Latour (2010) and Vásquez (2011) I focus on the experience of religion, and the things that make up those experiences. As Vásquez (2011: 7) puts it: 'the task of the scholar of religion is to study how embodiment and embeddedness in time and place enable and constrain diverse, flexible, yet patterned subjective experiences that come to be understood as religious.' This is a sociological task, in the sense that embodied and temporally embedded subjective experience is also socially constructed and communally experienced.

Lewis

Lewis is a 44-year-old who has been a Pagan for 18 years. He uses the term 'soulful' in his description of the first Baphomet rite at The Pagan Mardi Gras:

> **Lewis:** But that night was probably one of the most successful, most powerful experiences I have had in my life because of the entities that I connected with that night. To me it was very much out of this body, even though the body was very much used and explored. It was just an amazing place. It is very rare. It doesn't happen all the time. But that happened in the early hours of the morning. I partake the fruits and the magic, the subtleties of that aftermath, that energy that is created or conjured up throughout the night, it offers itself up in the most beautiful, most powerful, most soulful, most beautiful way you can imagine. You cannot put it in words. There are only a few of these [experiences] that come by in your life, and that is about it.

Lewis makes two important points. First, one of the things that distinguishes the rituals at Faunalia is their peak or extraordinary nature. This will be examined in detail in the discussion of liminality in Chapter Two. Second, Lewis points to the ineffable nature of these experiences with spiritual 'entities'. The point here is not to mystify the experience, so much as to emphasize the necessarily limited nature of words to describe all aspects of what it is to be human, and in particular to describe powerfully intoxicating religious experiences (Ricoeur 1985).

Nonetheless, Lewis uses words to point towards his experience, although he often talks in metaphors and parables. Song, dance, poetry, images and icons are also used to point towards these ineffable experiences. These forms of communication allow a complexity of meaning, and engage with the emotional, visual and embodied aspects of the experience. Both Benjamin (1988) and Irigaray (2001) use metaphorical language to describe erotic relationships because they are describing in words an experience that is felt, somatic and performed, and as such is difficult to describe in language. Words do, nonetheless, point towards the structure of these experiences. Participants at Faunalia similarly use metaphorical language to point towards their experiences.

The rituals at Faunalia change people through processes that are not primarily cognitive. It is often assumed that changing people's behaviour requires changing their thoughts, their cognitive self-understandings. For example, the psychoanalytic tradition based in Freud's work aims to articulate cognitively those symptomatic expressions of the unconscious, and as a consequence to find healthier ways of living (Benjamin 1998: 9). However, the transformations of self that occur at Faunalia operate at a level somewhere between the conscious and the unconscious. Benjamin (1998: 11) develops Freud's term 'acting' to describe embodied performances of perceptions and feelings. Acting is: 'a term that evokes not merely doing, but dramatizing, representing in deed.' Benjamin argues that acting and interacting are essential to contemporary forms of psychoanalysis: 'At the very least, acting constitutes a new intermediate position between unconscious and conscious, a different kind of effort at representation, which at once reveals and resists – to paraphrase what Winnicott says about destruction, it is only resistance because of our liability not to understand it, to become caught up in it' (Benjamin 1998: 11).

Ritual is an intentional form of acting, in the sense that Benjamin uses this term. The rituals at Faunalia engage with aspects of self of which participants are often only partially consciously aware. The symbolic and metaphoric nature of the ritual performances facilitates this engagement. Through the performance of the rituals participants engage with their half-conscious somatic and emotional self-understandings, and transform them. Similar processes operate in most rituals that are emotionally transformative, including both religious and secular rituals of various kinds. Effective rituals operate at a level that is somewhere between conscious and unconscious.

Religion as performative relationality

Rituals shape the ethics of relationships. Carl Einstein (Pan 2001) argues that myth and ritual have a performative mimetic function, drawing people into relationships of respect and care. Key to this function is the valuing of myth and ritual as ends in themselves, rather than as instrumental techniques to serve other goals. When poetry, myth and ritual are valued as ends in themselves, they mediate moral relationships, through the symbolic representation of shared moral orientations to 'the other'. When myth and ritual provide a mimetic experience of the difference of 'the other' they allow participants to discover ethical strategies for living with this difference.

Carl Einstein (1885–1940) was a German Jewish art historian and critic who also wrote about myth and religious ritual (Pan 2001). Einstein argued that 'modernity stems from the attempt to replace mythic structures of experience with scientific and rational ones that fail to recognize the unconscious forces of the psyche' (Pan 2001: 13). Rather than seeking a technical or rationalist solution to the alienation of contemporary life, Einstein argues for the importance of myth and ritual to organize and make sense of human experience. Einstein is here developing a tradition from nineteenth-century romantic expressionism that moral significance derives from aesthetic experiences and artistically medicated epiphany (Taylor 1989: 425). Einstein's ideas are important because they encompass myth and ritual, morality and aesthetically mediated relationships.

Einstein is particularly concerned to differentiate a 'properly functioning ritual' from the Fascist rituals of Nazi Germany (Pan 2001). The Fascist rituals create an etiquette of relationship that is oppressive and destructive. The Fascist rituals incorporate the other into the same, to use Levinas' (1985) language, either by requiring conformity, or by elimination. Once the Fascists assumed control and established a totalitarian state, Germans were required to participate in Fascist rallies. Those who resisted were punished or eliminated (Allen 1984). In contrast, Einstein argues the properly functioning ritual, like a work of art, brings the person into relationship with the other in a way that respects and represents that other as something independent and of value in and of its own right.

Ritual brings people into relationship. In this sense religious ritual can be also understood as an instance of 'mutual recognition' that Benjamin (1988) describes in erotic relationships. Benjamin points out that engagement with others who are different reminds us that we are passive in the face of people and processes that we cannot control: 'Whether we will or no, the world exposes us to the *different* others who, not only reflect our lack of control, but who also threaten to evoke in us what we have repudiated in order to protect the self: weakness, vulnerability, decay, or perhaps sexual otherness, transgression, instability – the excluded abject in either Kristeva's and Butler's sense' (Benjamin 1998: 95). It is precisely these themes that are explored in the rituals at Faunalia. The Underworld rite (Chapters Three and Four) focuses on suffering, vulnerability, death and decay. The Baphomet rite (Chapters Five and Six) explores the issues of sexual otherness, desire, pleasure and transgression.

The 'other' that is engaged with in ritually mediated relationships can also be an aspect or expression of one's self. This is the experience of many participants at Faunalia. Through the rituals they develop new ways of relating to their own fears, sadness, suffering, desires, bodies and pleasures. Because these aspects of the self are often only half-consciously apprehended, these are understood as aspects of the shadow self (see Chapter Four). From the perspective of the participants, a good ritual is one that is challenging and disturbing, because this means that it is providing an opportunity to work with these repressed or shadow parts of their selves. Sauvage puts it this way:

> **Sauvage:** I have got to the point where I really actually want to deal with those [unsettling and challenging] things. I want to look into myself and I want to explore, to find out whether those elements can be addressed and whether I can deal with them in a healthy way. In some ways for me it was a bit like meeting myself. It wasn't just like the shadow self. If you can imagine yourself split and there's another being or twin of yourself that does all the things that you don't do, or can't do. Internally there's a bit of a conflict with that, and there's a bit of a fear that they might jump out at some point when you're not ready for them. The path for me is to try and come together with that other being, and be friends with them. Or at least have some sort of rules of engagement. [Faunalia] allowed me the opportunity to do that.

The rituals at Faunalia allow participants to develop new ways of relating to parts of themselves that they find difficult or uncomfortable. Sauvage describes a form of 'splitting' of the self that is discussed in more detail in Chapter Four.

Both Benjamin and Einstein are concerned with the moral structures of relationship. Bringing their two theories together provides a subtle framework for understanding the rituals at Faunalia. Benjamin's theory is important because she focuses on embodied and emotional self-understandings and the process of mutual recognition. Einstein's theory is important because it explains how ritual and myth draw on aesthetics in mediating relationships, and the importance of collective experience. Individual aesthetic understandings are shaped by collective experiences of art and rituals:

> The work of art takes on a disciplinary function in which aesthetic form turns perception into a group event by compelling individual perception to adhere to a collective pattern. Rather than being free to develop idiosyncratic modes of seeing, the individual is compelled by art to adhere to the perceptual norms of a wider community. The closed form is the work of art's depiction of the communal totality into which the viewer is to be integrated. (Pan 2001: 133)

Art, myth and ritual draw participants into collective ways of seeing the world. They do this by drawing people into shared ways of relating to 'the other'. At Faunalia pleasure, desire, death and suffering are presented as inevitable parts of life. The rituals create aesthetically structured relationships to 'the other' of pleasure, desire, death and suffering. It is quite possible for these shared meanings to be resisted, ignored or found irrelevant. However, most participants allow themselves to be drawn by the ritual into an aesthetically mediated relationship.

In Einstein's terms, the rituals at Faunalia represent death, suffering, fear, desire and pleasure, as things of value in and of themselves. The rituals do not attempt to overcome, control or deny these aspects of life. They have a performative mimetic function that mediates moral relationships to the confronting nature of sex and death. The rituals encourage participants to discover strategies for living with fear, desire, pleasure, death and suffering in ways that respect them and lead them into a life with soul.

The rituals at Faunalia bring participants into relationship with deities such as Hades, Persephone and Baphomet. These deities have many confronting qualities. The rituals are designed to present these deities, and the aspects of life that they represent, to participants as an 'other' with whom participants enter into relationship. These deities do not simply represent the values and interests of the collective, as Durkheim (1976) would have it; they also represent an 'other' that confronts participants with often difficult aspects of their lives and the world around them. Participants engage these deities in collective rituals of mutual recognition.

Conclusion

Soulful lives are performed, embodied, emotional and reflected upon. To live with soul is to live a life that has meaning, purpose and a sense of a life well lived. This is achieved through performances that engage with the emotional and sensuous part of the self, which exists somewhere between the unconscious and the fully conscious self. Jessica Benjamin (1998) describes this as 'acting'. These sensuous aspects of the self exist in relationships, in the surfaces and spaces 'in-between'. Rituals are processes that explicitly work with and transform these aspects of the self in relationship. The next chapter examines these ritual processes in more detail.

Vignette: Therion

Therion is a 31-year-old male who is in a relationship. I interviewed him both before and after the festival, which he had attended for six years after becoming interested in Paganism 11 years ago. This vignette is drawn from his interview prior to the 2005 festival.[1]

I heard about Faunalia at 'Pagans in the Pub'.[2] I thought: 'this is going to be a big adventure'. I had gone to Confest,[3] which is not specifically Pagan but was sufficiently alternative for me to be able to [consider] the idea of going to a Pagan festival which had the reputation, even for the first one, of being a bit dangerous, a bit risqué, no holds barred magic. I met Harrison and, to some extent, our relationship at first was a bit prickly. But I met Phoebe and was instantly in love with her, as everyone does. So I thought 'right, I am going to go to this' [even though] I did not know anybody really in the Pagan community.

My first Faunalia was a wonderful adventure, at least partly because it was the beginning of that period when I started coming out of my shell. The Faunalias really were part of that process of becoming a more social and outgoing person. Going up and introducing myself to girls, and starting to flirt with them, everything was a big struggle for me. I got the sense that spiritually I was very much an unfinished person. My work spiritually was to become a more complete person.

It gave me a sense of being able to experience spirituality in a group environment. Being able to share my experience with everyone in a way that was tribal in nature and feeling like I was part of something, and never more so than during those rituals, to experience that sense of communality, experiencing all of that was an adventure.

[I felt] like a part of me that had always been there, the seed form, was just starting to sprout up. When I was at Pagans in the Pub previously I still very much felt like I was an observer. Discussing things around tables on an intellectual level, there was still that sense of reservation. Who are you and why are you here? After Faunalia, so many more people knew me and I knew them. There were people I could say hello to, walk up and start a conversation. That extended itself right the way through to other Pagan events.

I felt very emotional [leaving the first Faunalia]. I was very misty. But there wasn't a full letting go, but that sense of discovery of something kicking loose inside me. Yes. That went with me pretty much all the way home, and for the next week or so I was in a very different state, and I actually avoided going out. I just stayed at home to process everything. At that point in my life I was very unemotional. I had not yet opened up emotionally, because of an interesting emotional social development through childhood, and into adulthood. So that was part of it.

The Faunalias have been different each year. The first Faunalia was finding my feet, really, and the beginning of it. The second one was, for me, an experience of just throwing caution to the wind and really indulging my physical appetites and not feeling bad about it. Just having that indulgence. Lots of sex, and it was fantastic. I had not done anything like that before. Not in a concentrated weekend of debauchery. That was great! Not only that, but just being socially outgoing.

At that second Faunalia I was asked to play a key part in one of the main rituals. I was the sinister looking fellow in the robe. I had a lot of lines to learn. I lived up to the expectations and felt very good about that. I learnt it all, did it all on the night really, really well, and that ritual itself was amazing, as everyone who was there that year would agree. While there were a few people the previous year who had gone skyclad in the Baphomet rite, that ritual [in the second year] was the first ritual at Faunalia where the vast majority of people took their clothes off and raised energy.

[In the 'Dark Night' ritual[4]] time stopped while we were dancing around this cauldron filled with methylated spirits, and flames rising up. I saw a pillar of fire. I don't know how high it actually was, but it seemed, what, to go up 12 feet. I felt a corresponding energy run up my spine. It dropped down again afterwards. The inherent sensuality that I felt dancing in a circle with so many people, and the sweat, the oil, because there was body anointing and even the looks of the people who didn't join in with it, who didn't take their clothes off, who just stood around and watched everyone else and the awe on their faces, the way they just looked. It was a very, very intense experience.

I will always be grateful for doing the 'Dark Night' rite for that experience, for knowing that you can change things around if you want and it can work. It does not have to be air in the East, fire in the North, water in the West, that kind of thing. It all depends on what you are doing. It really took my mind out of what I would consider a self-imposed straitjacket, out of a dogmatic approach. Just because I had read it everywhere in books and, and have experienced the elements and the directions that way myself I thought that was how it was. But this ritual is a completely different setting. It worked and it shook my mind out of its straitjacket.

The next festival was less about my own personal experience and more about understanding and coming to terms with relationship issues. It made me realize that there were certain compromises that I had to make as part of that relationship at that point.

It was becoming apparent to me that I needed to do more work emotionally, that I very much was still a work-in-progress. I was becoming aware that I had learned to shut myself off emotionally. When faced with any kind of emotional pressure being placed on me for any reason, [I was] just tending to shut down emotionally rather than [take the initiative]. In any kind of emotionally threatening or emotionally confronting situation, as the rituals that are staged for Faunalia are designed to provoke, my tendency had always been to shut down. So realizing that I had to open up, and to take the initiative was an important thing. I was actually catching myself. [I would say to myself]: 'Well, no, you need to honour that emotion. It does exist for a reason. Work with it.'

[Faunalia] did give me an appreciation of the difference between my own emotional issues and things like dependence and co-dependence and insecurity and the contrasting thing of letting go of those things and just enjoying experiences and not trying to hang onto them. It was a continuation of that process of emotional development and integrated new experiences into my life.

I think the major risk of Faunalia is to simply treat it as a party and as a chance to indulge yourself, and gratify your physical appetites. It takes a certain amount of effort to go beyond that. It is easy to just fall back into that kind of space and that kind of awareness. To actually go beyond it and look inside yourself, and internalize the energies that are being worked with during the rituals, that is a step beyond. A lot of people take it. Some people don't.

Faunalia has opened up my head, messed around with the contents, put it back in and let me process for a year, then takes it all out again, messes it up a bit, puts it back in and each time I have grown a little more; or sometimes a lot more. I am a far happier person than I was when I first went in, just in myself, and it just seems to be as I have grown older, I am still very much a work-in-progress, as we all are. But I am not grappling with the same kinds of insecurities and issues that I was back then. I am happier as a person. I am secure to some extent in myself. Certainly far more than what I was. And I am just looking forward to seeing where the journey takes me. [chuckle.]

CHAPTER TWO

Ritual

Introduction

The experience of liminality is central to the rituals of Faunalia. The word 'liminal' is derived from the Latin *limen*, meaning threshold. It is a transitional phase in rituals and is a 'period and area of ambiguity, a sort of social limbo' (Turner 1983: 187). For example, at a funeral the person is dead, but not yet buried. Liminal spaces are unsettling, but usually in a constructive way. Liminality makes possible new ways of relating to ourselves, people around us and the world. The liminal nature of Faunalia is made possible both by the way that participants think about and understand the festival, and by the somatic practices, physical infrastructure and social relationships that constitute the festival.

'Liminality' was originally used by Arnold van Gennep (2004/1909) to describe the in-between or transitional phase of life-cycle rituals. For example, during rituals in which a person is made an adult member of the social group there is a phase where a person is separated from the role of the child, but is not yet fully an adult. Van Gennep argued that all life-cycle rituals, such as puberty rites, marriages and funerals, followed a tripartite pattern of *separation* from the old status, *liminality* and *integration* to the new status. Victor Turner (1969) extended van Gennep's concept to describe the liminal nature of a range of ritual performances. Faunalia is not a life-cycle ritual, but it is characterized by ritually produced liminality. Liminality is key to the production of the experiences that are valued by participants. While the main rituals at Faunalia are peak liminal experiences, the entire festival has a liminal tone.

A number of different aspects of Faunalia contribute to the liminal nature of the festival. This chapter is organized around these aspects: liminality is temporally constructed; material artefacts and infrastructure are integral to liminality; participants understand the festival as liminal; liminality is an embodied experience that transforms 'iconic consciousness' (Alexander 2008); liminality creates communitas and liminality is bound up with the morality of authenticity.

The sensuously rich and emotionally intense ritual performances at Faunalia engage symbolic resources to produce transformations in both moral orientations and self-understandings. The rituals are the primary source of the transformative experiences at Faunalia. Later chapters describe further dimensions to liminality that are experienced during the night-time rituals, including trance, dance, eroticism, macabre and melancholic themes, costume and other chaotic inversions. This chapter begins with a description of the general characteristics of Faunalia, including the overall structure and organization of the festival and the role of temporal factors and material objects in creating liminality. The second half of the chapter develops Turner's (1969) concept of liminality, bringing it into dialogue with the relational, aesthetic and embodied aspects of ritual introduced in Chapter One.

Temporal and geographical liminality

Many participants describe a sense of anticipation and excitement in the weeks leading up to Faunalia. Lewis reported that he was aware that: 'An event was approaching which is exciting.' Natasha noted that: 'I was quite excited to be going somewhere different.' One person described how in the week beforehand her partner would announce the number of days before the festival commenced. In their meditations and rituals in the weeks prior to the festival some participants began to work with deities from Faunalia, actively meditating on them and preparing themselves for the rituals.

The significance of this anticipatory excitement is perhaps best illustrated by a person who did not experience it. One person reported that he had 'forgotten' that he had paid and planned to go to the festival until a friend reminded him a few days before the festival was to commence. This same person was one of the few participants that did not find the festival particularly transformative or profound, describing the rituals in muted terms as 'nice'. The absence of anticipatory excitement for this person was one of the factors that contributed to an experience of the rituals at Faunalia as less transformative, and more mundane. For most participants, anticipatory excitement heightens the liminal nature and impact of the rituals at Faunalia.

The temporal structure and geographical location of Faunalia play an important role in the festival. Faunalia takes place over the Easter long weekend. Participants arrive on the Thursday night and leave on the Monday afternoon. This extended period of time makes possible both longer rituals that last through the night, and long periods of time where nothing organized happens. Both of these unusual temporal aspects contribute to the liminality of the festival.

The conscious act of 'separation' from the mundane world and the transition into a liminal time and space was clear in most people's accounts. For example, Adele reported that: 'As I was driving to the site I could feel the stress leaving me. Going out the window and leaving me.' Similarly, Calvin, a 32-year-old who was attending the festival for the second time in 2005 said:

> **Calvin:** I took the day off on the way up to get out of the mundane world, and arrive, have a chance to get set up, take that psychological deep breath and say, 'Ok, I am here', before the opening rite starts. [I made a] clear demarcation line of that Thursday. My life [in the city] stops Wednesday night and Thursday is my journeying into [Faunalia].

Sinead is a 32-year-old single female who attended Faunalia for the first time in 2005 after hearing a lot about it from the coven she had worked with for just over a year. She was glad to have left work early to 'move away from my work persona . . . [to] disengage from my current life'. She travelled by plane from another city, and then caught a train, giving the trip a 'holiday' feel. After an 'enjoyable wait' at the train station, Sinead was picked up by a shuttle bus arranged by the festival organizers. Another participant commented on the train trip: 'I remember the train trip. I was feeling really excited, wondering what the place would look like, what the energy would be.'

Similar processes of anticipation, travel, remote location and symbolic separation from the mundane world are described in a number of studies of comparable festivals. Introducing her study of Pagan festivals in the United States, Pike (2001: 12) quotes a festival organizer: 'There is something magickal[1] about simply *going* to a Festival. Especially if the journey is a long and rigorous one.' Tramacchi (2000) recounts the important process of anticipation and travel to an alternative liminal space in his analysis of the ritual structure of a 'doof' (rave-like dance parties in Australian bush settings). Similar processes are observed by Gilmore and Van Proyen (2005) in accounts of the Burning Man festival, and St John's (2000) account of Confest, an alternative lifestyle festival.

Prior to attending Faunalia, participants are required to sign an informed consent form that outlines the type of experiences they are likely to encounter at Faunalia. The content of this form contributes to the anticipatory excitement about the festival. Natasha, a 28-year-old who attended the festival for the first time in 2005, recalled the form:

> **Natasha:** The idea that I have about Faunalia is we go there to do ritual where amazing stuff can happen. We were told a lot of things before going. We had to sign stuff. We had to read stuff. It was saying you go

there, you are dedicated to your process. All sorts of crazy stuff can happen. Be warned. I'm thinking, great, I'm allowed to engage in crazy stuff. People are ready to accept that. I felt like I'm allowed to really process here. It's OK and it's safe.

The structure of the ritual provides a framework within which participants feel safer with the likelihood of the 'crazy stuff' that occurs at the festival. As Natasha observes, the consent form clearly marks the festival off as a space where 'crazy stuff' can happen. Liminality is marked by chaos, dissolution of normality and subversion of the status quo (Turner 1969, 1983). Such craziness does not happen before or after the festival. It is contained by the ritual boundaries set up around the festival. The ritual process protects the mundane everyday world from the threatening and dangerous aspects of the liminal state (Ezzy et al. 2009). The 'crazy stuff', chaos and alterity of the liminal phase of rituals are what create the potential for personal and social change (Turner 1983, St John 2010). 'Alterity' derives from the Latin for 'otherness' and refers to the unusual and radically 'not normal' nature of the rituals, practices, clothing and events at Faunalia. Anticipatory excitement both adds power to the liminal experience and contains the social inversions within the liminal stage.

The clear demarcation that Calvin notes at the commencement of the festival also occurs at the close. Therion, for example, puts it this way:

> Therion: Every time that I drive back from Faunalia, it is coming back, and that first set of traffic lights [brings about a] sense of being wrapped in psychic pollution again, especially all the cars, all the people. The advertising, the continual bombardment of things which you might consider mundane or profane. Having that removed for the five days of the event really helps me experience the sacred.

The combination of the extended time of the festival, remote location and travel, facilitate a particularly intense type of liminality. Events that last only one evening, such as many Pagan rituals, have a different temporal structure to events that last a number of days. Calvin observed that rituals that last only one night do not provide enough time to create the sort of experiences characteristic of Faunalia: 'There's a certain amount of time getting into the mind state, that sort of open state, that free state.'

The transformations of the routines of everyday acts of eating, sleeping and washing are important to the ritual process at Faunalia. These everyday transformations during the daytime anticipate and make possible the hyper-inversions of the night-time rituals. The daytime inversions take on a 'normality' of their own. For example, Leanan reported: 'The Saturday was a fairly normal Faunalia day. Eating, sitting around, drumming, talking, doing the work that had to be done, just the standard things.' In most other contexts these activities would be extraordinary: sharing a meal with 80 other people, talking intimately and openly about issues of substantial import, participating in a drumming circle and making preparations for a profoundly confronting and transformative ritual.

The liminal experience at Faunalia is associated with temporal disorientation. Some participants had difficulty recalling the order of events at Faunalia. For example, Leonie, a married 30-year-old who was attending the festival for her third time said: 'The days are a bit of a blur and I don't have many memories of the days. I remember long days of having lots of fun hanging out with like-minded people.' Sinead similarly said: 'It's hard to remember things in order . . . in my memory over the weekend, if you asked me if a debrief happened, I'd probably have a bit of a challenge [remembering].' Heath was a little more sanguine, perhaps reflecting the number of times he had attended, but still indicating the liminal structure of the festival: 'I just wanted to be in the bush and be among friends, and just forget my work and forget everything.'

The structure of Faunalia that facilitates this intense form of liminality takes a great deal of planning and care. An organizing committee runs the festival. In one year, two members of the committee attended a conflict resolution course and then shared what they learnt with the other members of the committee so they had the skills to deal with issues that arise during the festival. The organizers of the festival focus on participation and respect, doing a lot of work themselves. At the first Faunalia the caterers withdrew at the last minute and Phoebe, one of the primary organizers, and Rennie arranged the catering with assistance from some other people, so that they could go ahead with the gathering. 'Phoebe has kept an eye on the catering ever since then, to maintain as high a standard as we can for what we charge' (Harrison).

Anticipatory excitement, travel to and from the festival and the expectation of 'crazy stuff' at the festival all have important aesthetic, embodied aspects. Cognition is important – participants describe talking and thinking about travel and anticipation. These cognitive understandings come alive in the physical acts of leaving the mundane world, of travelling and of felt anticipatory excitement about the festival. The ritual process, as an embodied aesthetic process, begins well before the festival and finishes well after it. These temporal and geographical aspects of the festival are social processes that contribute to Faunalia working as a profoundly transformative set of rituals.

Material liminality

Liminality is as much a physical practice as it is a cognitive understanding. For example, when Turner (1969) discusses initiation rites among the

IMAGE 2.1 *Earth altar and drums at the central meeting area.*
Photo copyright Edan Mumford. Reproduced with permission.

Ndembu, the physical experience of the initiate as he or she is removed from the community and spends time in a distant secluded location is a key aspect of the ritual process that facilitates the experience of liminality. While the cognitive interpretation of the separation is important, the somatic experience of the physical geography is central to making the initiation a powerful transformative event.

Similarly, the physical geography of the grounds where Faunalia is held facilitates liminal experiences. The same site was used for the festival from the time of its commencement in 2000 up to the 2005 festival. The site is located on a large block of bushland. There is a central open meeting area with a bonfire and many chairs. The ritual briefings and debriefings were often held here. There is a kitchen with dining area attached where all meals were served. A large gymnasium is off to one side and bunkhouse accommodation is located at the other end of the meeting area. A three-bedroom house is used by the main ritualists and organizers as accommodation, a meeting place and to prepare for the rituals. Small altars are set up at each of the directions around the meeting area (see Image 2.1) and there is a sound system also here. Music is played at various times during the festival, and often utilized during the rituals. The Underworld rite made use of the central meeting area, surrounding bushland and the gymnasium. The Baphomet rite took place in a specially constructed site approximately 300 metres away in a secluded bush setting.

> Sinead: When I got there we put our stuff in the cabin fairly quickly. There was a committee member who was up at the main cabin. He told me which cabin I would be in and explained the kitchen roster system, where the bathrooms were, and that people were having a meeting later in the afternoon. He gave a bit of a rundown of how things were going to be that first day. And I found that particularly helpful and welcoming. There was some of my friends that were already there, and they were like, 'Oh, you're in Cabin Eight, it is down there.' And then really the rest of the afternoon was pretty much catching up with a few people that I am very close to who I had not seen for a while, [with] cups of tea and hugs. [I felt] really good. I felt a bit of support in case there would be anything that I was perhaps concerned about over the course of the weekend. There were a couple of people there that I very much felt that I could go to and speak to if I was concerned about anything.

First, note Sinead's comment that in the liminal space of the festival challenging things may happen, but she still feels safe. Many people expressed a confidence in the organizers to ensure the safety of participants. A number of people made comments similar to that of Sinead, that if something did happen with which they were uncomfortable, that there were people they trusted who would help them to deal with such issues properly. This sense anticipates the 'shadow work' that is described in more detail in the following chapters.

Second, note how the buildings and physical layout of the site are central to Sinead's description of the liminal nature of her experiences. Eating is communal, with people rostered to assist in the kitchen. People congregate around the tea and coffee facilities. Sleeping is in communal cabins, often with people who participants may have not previously met. The toilets and shower block were not gender segregated:

> Calvin: It is amazing how three or four days can change perceptions of what is normal. Even just from silly little things like the toilet shower blocks not being men and women. I was having a shower, two girls were talking at the mirror, doing their makeup or whatever it was, and I joined in the conversation at something they said. One of the said, 'oh, I wish I had known it was you in there, I would have come in and washed your back'. And I said, 'well, you can do it anyway'. So she came in and washed my back. And that was it. [There was] no sexual context whatsoever. Just purely a freedom. It is a body, it gets washed. It is fine to be like that. In that space there was no self-consciousness about my body or someone sharing the shower with

IMAGE 2.2 *Participants drumming and sitting around during the day.*
Photo by Philippe.

> me, even though her husband was on the camp. It was just completely
> natural and normal. Then coming back out into the world and driving
> by shopping centres and stuff on the way home and remembering, no,
> that is not the way the world is. That is what makes Faunalia special.
> You have got freedoms like that.

A deep sense of shame and fear mixed with an almost obsessive fascination
characterizes contemporary experiences of the naked body (Bordo 1995,
Featherstone 1982). The material infrastructure of an amenities block is
marked as unsegregated by gender. This challenges and inverts normal
understanding of bodies. Calvin's comment that it was 'just purely freedom'
should not be underestimated. There is a palpable sense of freedom from
everyday expectations that this observation expresses.

Physical objects are key to the creation of the ritual experience of
liminality. Physical objects such as costumes and theatrical props are
central to the rituals. At Faunalia there are very large bonfires that require
significant time to build. Most of the ritual equipment and the costumes
are handmade. The fabrication of ritual equipment, costumes, campfires
and the construction of sacred spaces plays a key role in the liminality
of Faunalia. They invert much that is taken for granted in participants'

everyday lives. The importance of these material aspects of religion has been observed by a number of theorists. Extending the analytical focus beyond belief and meaning, Vásquez (2011) points to the grounding of religion in material objects. McCloud (2011) combines Vásquez's analysis with Bourdieu's (1977) theory of habitus to conceptualize religious practice as grounded in materiality, along with embodiment and cognition.

Peter is a 54-year-old who takes responsibility for organizing the ritual sites. He starts preparations three months in advance of the festival, checking equipment, ritual gear and making new things that are required. Once at the festival, Peter sets up the physical infrastructure for the rituals, recruiting people to assist and delegating tasks in a way that actively creates community. Most people understand the importance of participation in these activities. Seemingly mundane tasks such as building a bonfire, or ensuring the fire hose will reach the ritual site, create a sense of anticipation that is an important part of the ritual experience of the whole festival. Calvin, for example, reported that: 'Helping out with setting up on the first day made me feel part of it.'

Harrison highlights the role of the physical infrastructure in creating altered states of consciousness during the rituals:

> **Harrison:** I think it is the atmosphere, the costumes, the expectation, and the light. The fact that it is in a forest and there is a great big bonfire, that all helps to put people into an altered state of consciousness. The fact that there are other people there including me and Phoebe that go into an altered state, also facilitates that altered state.

The experience of liminality at Faunalia depends on the material infrastructure of the campsite, the construction of ritual equipment, including bonfires, and the preparation of ritual sites. The ritual process of separation, liminality and re-integration is a social, this-worldly material process that contributes to the transformative power of the rituals at Faunalia. Communal eating and sleeping, wearing festive clothing, sitting around with friends discussing intimate topics are all collective, embodied, social practices made possible by material infrastructure.

Liminal culture: Between the worlds

Participants at Faunalia understand the festival as a liminal space where people are more aware of, or more directly in contact with, the spiritual and sacred aspects of life. Contemporary Witchcraft often utilizes phrases in ritual such as 'a time out of time' and 'a place out of place'. For example, many Wiccan circle casting liturgies include the statement that participants are now 'between the worlds'. Casting a circle creates a place 'between the worlds in which Wiccan religious activity occurs' (Bado-Fralick 2005: 126). Each of the major rituals at Faunalia includes a circle casting. Further, the festival itself is understood to commence with the casting of the circle during the first ritual that circumscribes the whole festival as a sacred space. The fire lit during the opening ritual is kept alight for the entire festival as a symbol of the sacrality of the festival.

The opening rite on the Thursday night, and the closing rite on Monday, define Faunalia as a sacred time and space. Turner (1983: 127) emphasizes that ritual separation is not only the physical movement into a sacred space, but must involve a ritual that 'changes the quality of *time* also, or constructs a cultural realm which is defined as "out of time," that is, beyond or outside the time which measures secular processes and routines'. The mythology and liturgy of Witchcraft, from which Faunalia draws much of its practice, provides precisely this subcultural framing of the festival as a sacred time and space.

Many interviewees articulated an understanding of the liminal nature of Faunalia. Leanan, for example, said: 'For me it is a world between worlds.' Heath, a 44-year-old who had attended all previous Faunalias said: 'At Faunalia there is a real transcending of time . . . It was like being between the worlds.' Similarly, Peter said: 'I like the atmosphere of Faunalia. Get rid of the mundane world for a while, go into a sacred space and create this energy.'

There is a two-tiered structure of liminality at Faunalia, with the main night-time rituals forming a second tier of more intense liminality. In some ways this parallels Turner's (1983) distinction between liminal and liminoid. The daytime at Faunalia is marked by play, choice and entertainment that Turner characterizes as liminoid. The night time rituals are 'a matter of deep seriousness, even dread' (Turner 1983: 146). However, the distinction is not really apt, because Turner's liminality is more closely associated with compulsory rituals of a tribal society, and is ultimately functional for social structure because the ritual serves to reinforce social norms. Turner sees the liminoid as mainly found in industrialized societies and being socially subversive.

While Faunalia as a whole does fit Turner's (1983) account of the liminoid, the night-time rituals are closer to his description of the liminal because of the intensity of the experiences and their transformative nature. Liminal rituals involve inversions, breaking of taboos and sharing of secrets. The aim is that: 'the novices are taught that they did not know what they thought they knew. Beneath the surface structure of custom was a deep structure, whose rules they had to learn, through paradox and shock' (Turner 1983: 145). I argue in the following chapters that there is a similar element of discovery of hidden knowledge in the main rituals of Faunalia.

Iconic consciousness

Experiences that engage the 'evidence of the senses' are central to Faunalia and to the experience of liminality. Lewis connected with 'entities' during the Baphomet rite at the Pagan Mardi Gras and Sauvage observed a 'sense of awe and wonder'. These experiences, ineffable, intimate and communal, are integral to discovering a life with soul. To question the empirical reality of these experiences, or the cognitive beliefs associated with them, is to misunderstand both the experiences and their reality. They are experienced as real on a somatic, tactile, emotional and iconic level. These experiences can be understood as forms of 'iconic consciousness' (Alexander 2008).

Iconic meanings are aesthetic, and less concerned with specifics and details. Iconic meanings draw us into a felt experience of immersion in the world and the depths of reality. Jeffrey Alexander (2008: 2) notes that in *The Birth of Tragedy*, Nietzsche 'plays with the contrast between surface and depth, clarity and mystery, challenging the modernist separation of aesthetics and morality'. Through a detailed analysis of the art of Alberto Giacometti, Alexander (2008: 6) argues that: 'The artist tells the truth about an object by using surface form as a device to draw us deeper, into what might be called iconic meaning.' This contrasts with the rational modern form of impersonal knowing that withdraws from engagement:

> In the course of everyday life, we are drawn into the experience of meaning and emotionality by surface forms. We experience these forms in a tactile way. They have an expressive texture that we 'feel' in our unconscious minds and associate with other ideas and things. These ideas and things are simultaneously personal and social . . . What I have wished to suggest here is that the expressive/aesthetic dimension is also fundamental in modern societies, that it communicates through material forms whose surface draws an actor inward to experience deeper moral and emotional depths. (Alexander 2008: 6, 10)

Beginning with Durkheim's (1976) analysis of mana and totems in the *Elementary Forms of the Religious Life*, Alexander argues that Durkheim's incipient understanding of 'feeling consciousness and aesthetic surface' can be developed into a theory of iconic consciousness. In particular, I emphasize Alexander's attention to the meaningfulness of this form of aesthetic experience that is not primarily concerned with cognition: 'To be iconically conscious is to understand without knowing, or at least without knowing that one knows. It is to understand by feeling, by contact, by the "evidence of the senses" rather than the mind' (Alexander 2010: 11). At Faunalia iconic consciousness draws people into relationships, tactile emotional relational experiences with other people, deities and 'energy'.

Alexander does not examine the implications of iconic meanings for religion. Nonetheless he points to the importance of the non-cognitive aesthetic experience of icons that is central to religious experience. Riis and Woodhead (2010: 42) suggest that: 'In religion . . . participants normally relate not to a symbol, but to that which it represents: to God, a saint, a spirit, and so on. Here "symbol" means not a carrier of a fundamental notion, but the "target" itself.' Emotions and aesthetic experience are integral to this because iconic consciousness brings people into a tactile, emotional, somatic experience of relationship. Or, as Alexander puts it:

> With icons, the signifier (an idea) is made material (a thing). The signified is no longer only in the mind, something thought of, but something experienced, something felt, in the heart and the body. The idea becomes an object in time and space, a thing. (Alexander 2010: 11)

Jessica Benjamin (1988) makes a similar point about the experience of erotic relationships. Mutual recognition arises in the intersubjective moment of relationship which is not simply cognitive, but also embodied, and performed. Benjamin (1988: 130) describes mutual recognition as an 'exchange of gestures' involving 'shared feeling and discovery' and 'the sensual capacities of the whole body'. Benjamin does not seek to displace cognitive representations of desire, so much as to challenge their dominance and to suggest alternative ways of experiencing desire that co-exist with them.

'Iconic consciousness' is both an embodied sensuous ritual practice, and a symbolic resource. It disturbs the distinction between ritual practice and symbolic resource that is set up in the definition of religion used earlier. This is because at Faunalia the symbolic resources are ritual practices. For example, Baphomet is the deity at the heart of Faunalia and is described in Chapters Five and Six. Baphomet is a symbol, with a history and attached meanings. Baphomet is also a ritual, which evokes half-articulated emotions and expressive and aesthetic relationships. When participants use the word 'Baphomet' it can refer to either, or both, the symbol and the ritual. Perhaps Baphomet is best conceptualized as a hybrid, in the posthumanist sense that Latour (2010) uses that term. Baphomet is a hybrid in this sense because he/she is both a 'being' who is understood to really exist and whose characteristics can be discussed, and Baphomet is a creation of a ritual who is experienced, and felt, and is beyond words.

The rituals at Faunalia, like the gendered dance of the bonds of love described by Benjamin, and the iconic consciousness described by Alexander, make use of the 'space in-between' (Benjamin 1988: 130) in which half-conscious perceptions and feelings are acted out. Religious rituals, and erotic relationships, are formed both in cognitive understandings and in the aesthetic and somatic practices of mutual recognition. These aspects shape moral valuations and etiquettes of relationships. To discover a life with soul is to discover moments that engage these semi-conscious aspects of the self in relationship.

Faunalia is a liminal space because the ritual practices privilege iconic consciousness. This contrasts starkly with the cognitive emphasis of mainstream Western culture. Describing his experience of the Underworld rite, Heath says: 'I was getting more and more out of my mind and more into the process, and . . . I was just really transformed.'

Liminality and somatic knowing

Ritual is 'necessarily embodied and social' (Grimes 2000: 4). In the liminal phase of rituals the aesthetic and somatic aspects of experience are central and cognitive ways of knowing the self and the world become less important. The liminal space is a space where 'acting' (Benjamin 1998) and 'iconic consciousness' (Alexander 2008) are deliberately prioritized and privileged. Although not referring to ritual specifically, Ahmed takes this a step further arguing that 'emotions are crucial to the very constitution of the psychic and the social as objects' (Ahmed 2004: 10).

The centrality of emotions and somatic knowing is clear in the interviews with participants at Faunalia. Therion, in the vignette, emphasizes his emotional responses to the rituals at Faunalia. He describes how Faunalia enabled him to transform his confidence in sexual relationships, his understanding of his own emotional responses to threatening situations and his emotional development within a committed relationship. There is clearly a cognitive dimension to these experiences, as Therion thinks through his experiences and discusses them with others. However, the primary emphasis is on the aesthetic and emotional dimensions of the experience. His emotions are integral to the process that constitutes Therion as a person.

Ritually re-enacted sacred stories 'seem to be allusive expressions of stories that cannot be fully and directly told, because they live, so to speak, in the arms and legs and bellies of the celebrants' (Crites 1971: 295). The rituals of Faunalia operate in this realm. They drive 'something deeply into the bone' (Grimes 2000: 124). Participants do talk about their experiences. However, most of what is significant is not articulated linguistically, but felt, danced and performed, understood as the 'energy' of the rite. Ritual debriefings last two or three hours on the day following a ritual. Participants take turns to reflect on their responses to the rites. People will sometimes choose not to talk about their experiences, while others who have difficulty articulating how they are feeling may say that they are still 'processing' their responses. Pike (2001) describing similar, although less-organized, rituals around a fire at a Pagan festival in the United States reports: 'Neopagans, it seems, construct their identities around the fire by moving back and forth between verbal and somatic ways of knowing' (Pike 2001: 189). These are, I suggest, specific liminal forms of the acting and iconic consciousness.

The 'somatic ways of knowing' that Pike describes are generated in a context that is overloaded with sensory information:

> The deluge of images and sounds, sage burning and incense, challenges festival fire participants' personal boundaries on a physiological level. As they walk differently and dance differently, festival goers claim that the body is transformed, and so they also say, is the self . . . Costumed, tattooed, jewel covered, and glistening nude dancers, chanting, drummers and other musicians, smoke, and flame, make festival fires a feast for the senses. (Pike 2001: 189)

Similarly, Tramacchi (2000) points out that the 'collective effervescence' experienced at doofs is generated not only by the use of trance-inducing drugs but also by a constellation of factors including the natural environment, the 'liminal quality of camping, psychedelic music, exposure to the elements, kaleidoscopic light shows, religious iconography, spatial decoration', the 'auditory driving' nature of the music and 'dancing all night' (Tramacchi 2000: 208). Unlike the more mundane forms of iconic consciousness described by Alexander (2008), the experiences at these events are profoundly transformative, chaotic and intense.

It is precisely these aesthetic and sensuous elements that generate the liminal character of rituals, as described by Turner (1969), elaborating on the work of van Gennep (2004). According to Turner (1969: 128), liminality, and the associated experience of communitas, 'transgresses or dissolves the norms that govern structured institutionalized relationships and is accompanied by experiences of unprecedented potency'. Liminality is a form of marginality that involves an inversion, or clash, of accepted cultural symbols and forms of action. 'Such marginal spaces in life are extremely powerful because when normal categorisations are abandoned, when there is willing suspension of belief, the outcomes are uncertain' (Ezzy et. al. 2009: 397). It is not simply the cognitive aspect of liminality that is powerful and transformative, but primarily its somatic, emotional and experiential nature (St John 2000).

Turner's conception of ritual, and liminality in particular, tends to underestimate the significance of the emotional, carnal and somatic dimensions. St John (2000, 2004) and Olaveson (2004) have both pointed to the 'clinically social' focus of Turner's work, noting that 'despite a late theoretical interest, Turner was not an anthropologist of the body' (Olaveson 2004: 88). Turner's framework can be extended to include a more balanced appreciation of the role of somatic knowing alongside his analysis of myth, cognition and belief. Drawing together the theories of Turner, Alexander and Benjamin, provides a sophisticated and sensitive framework for describing and analysing the rituals at Faunalia.

Community and communitas

'Communitas' is one of the key characteristics of liminality (Turner 1969). Communitas is a deeper sense of community in which relationships are more intimate and open. The experience of community, and communitas, at Faunalia has a two-tiered structure. During the daytime participants describe an experience of community that is 'tribal' (Heath). 'People are already walking in there with open hearts' (Phoebe). This tribal sense of community is created around the conversations where friends catch up, the collective meals and shared chores. Simple tasks, such as cleaning-up after a ritual take on a communal character. Lewis described his experience of cleaning-up after one of the rituals as a form of sacred male bonding: '[We needed to] tidy up the grounds. [So] we had a bit of a men's gathering. We had a bit of a chant. Which was great. It's good to have a brotherhood.' Ruth similarly reported that: 'The tribal sense at Faunalia makes me think differently.'

In the vignette Therion describes this two-tiered structure in which the experience of 'communality' was intensified in the rituals. He points to his sense of the group, that he was 'part of something', and his ability to share his experiences 'in a way that was tribal in nature'. During the rituals at night this experience of community is intensified: 'And never more so than during those rituals.'

Olaveson summarizes the conception of communitas, drawing on a wide range of Turner's work, as including: 'an unstructured or rudimentarily structured community of equal individuals . . .; an essential and generic human bond . . .; a set of egalitarian, direct, non-rational bonds between concrete and historical individuals . . .; and a deep inherently emotional experience or state' (Olaveson 2004: 89). Many of these factors are evident at Faunalia. Leanan's account of community at Faunalia highlights some of them:

> Leanan: We get a real community and you lose your sense of, not embarrassment, your sense of self-consciousness, and you just do things that are a little bit out of your mundane world character because you are so comfortable in the community that is around you. Everybody accepts everybody else for what they are. That is how I feel anyway. [I think people learn] tolerance, because there are a lot of different people from a lot of different paths, coming out in different ways. And [we] think how to help each other. There are a lot of people give a lot of help to others without being asked for it. . . . There was a lot of that caring going on this year.

Flora similarly describes her experience of community at Faunalia that reflects the characteristics of communitas: 'There is a deep sense of intimacy happening at Faunalia. A sense of trust and reliance on each other. The way you behave and the things that you discuss are so intimate, and it's so safe.' These experiences have clear parallels with communitas as experienced at other festivals. Olaveson (2004: 87) highlights 'the phenomenological experience most consistently reported by ravers of an intense sensation of inter-personal and sometimes universal connecting between participants, often described as "connectedness", "unity", or "love" . . . participants often experience profound feelings of communality, equality, and basic humanity.'

The experience of community and communitas at Faunalia is not simply an emotional sense of intimacy. It often has very real and practical dimensions. Sauvage has mobility challenges. He regularly experiences social exclusion due to his use of a wheelchair. Sauvage's experience illustrates the egalitarian imperative that many people experience at Faunalia. At the ritual briefing on Friday afternoon for the Underworld rite Sauvage heard that part of the ritual involved walking through the bush:

> **Sauvage:** I wanted to know how important it was to go on that journey, and I was sensing that it was significantly important. [I wanted to know] what would be involved, and the fact that there was a few of us at the event that had a range of issues that would mean that it was going to be difficult for them to move through the bush comfortably and with enough space in their head to actually absorb what the experience was all about, other than just navigating the terrain. I found it useful that they were able to really appreciate that, and were able to pinpoint that you really need to be a part of these things. [They said]: 'Something will happen here, you need to be here. Let's have a look at that. Here is what we can do. How do you find that?' And we had a whole discussion about how that might work. The fact that people were really OK to engage in that because it was important to them that people got the most out of the experience that they could was pretty fundamental and important to me. So I felt at ease going into that ritual. I didn't necessarily think it was going to be OK or easy, but I didn't think it would be overtly traumatic or that I would miss things. I could just be at a similar space to everybody else.

The experience of communitas is, however, temporary. Ivakhiv (2003: 98), following Turner (1969), defines communitas as: 'the temporary shedding of social roles, and the experience of unmediated and liberatory relations between people.' While some participants at Faunalia are members of ongoing communities and social networks, many live in geographically dispersed locations and only see each other intermittently. The care that Sauvage experienced at Faunalia does not necessarily continue outside

Faunalia. Although, the experience of such care had a profound impact on Sauvage and changed his perceptions about what was possible or reasonable to expect.

Conflict is also common at Faunalia. Personal animosities are formed and nurtured. Complaints about inappropriate behaviour also occur and are managed. Olaveson (2004: 87) points out that 'communitas has become a reified and all-encompassing "primal unity" that fails to account for the underlying and backstage diversity, tensions and multiplicity of competing voices in such phenomena'. It is important not to romanticize community at Faunalia. One person discussed a splinter group that formed one year in which a group of people kept to themselves and did not participate. In another year there was considerable conflict. Discussing the high levels of mutual support, generosity and community spirit at Faunalia, Harrison said: 'I mean, we do not get that every year. [There was] a very difficult year in terms of interpersonal interactions between people. There was a lot of niggling between people. I felt like I spent practically the whole festival running around hosing out emotional bushfires. I didn't really, but that is what it felt like.'

Faunalia is an erotically and emotionally charged event, but does not seem to experience any more or less conflict and inappropriate behaviour as a consequence. Throughout the festival, and particularly at the ritual briefings, the organizers emphasize the importance of mutual consent and respect in negotiating the often intense emotions that are generated, particularly during the Baphomet rite on the third night. Flora is in a monogamous relationship, and her partner does not attend the festival. She reported:

> **Flora:** I have had a few sexual advances from people. In each case they have been really good about backing off. I just said, 'Sorry, I am not in that space'. I think that is the beauty of the way the event is run. It is made really clear every day, every moment, that everything must be fully consensual, every interaction, every negotiation, everything must be fully consensual. So, as I said, I have been approached by men and women, and I have said, 'No, I am sorry, I can't go there'.

The standards of moral behaviour at Faunalia seem similar to those found at most other large social occasions such as music festivals, weddings and church services. Most people act respectfully, some are amazingly generous and a few people act selfishly and inconsiderately towards others.

In the broader Pagan community there have been occasional cases of sexual abuse (Ezzy 2013), but these are no more or less than might be expected in any community, and Pagans have been proactive about exposing such abuse and encouraging people to report it to police. Several people mentioned that they had heard of some inappropriate sexual behaviour in previous years at Faunalia. One participant discussed a male who was pushy about asking women to hug him, and another incident involved an unwanted kiss. These were dealt with at the time, with people making complaints to the organizers who mediated a resolution. One organizer said that four people had been asked not return to Faunalia after inappropriate behaviour of various kinds. For the 2005 festival, Ruth, a 25-year-old single female, reported: 'I did not encounter any lecherousness or [inappropriate] stuff, which was really nice. There were a couple of guys that [I did not] go that close to, but nothing uncomfortable, which was really good.'

Faunalia is marked by an experience of communitas. The experience of emotional nurturing, generosity and tribal intimacy is significantly different from that of the mundane worlds of everyday life. Faunalia is still a human community, with animosities and individuals who act inappropriately. However, the festival generates an experience of communitas that people value because it is radically different to their experiences of mundane everyday life. Perhaps one of the reasons this experience is so valued is 'in middle-class life in Western societies it is difficult to find rituals that provide much experience of communitas' (Driver 1991: 165). The experience of communitas is even more intensely felt during the altered states of consciousness that the night-time rituals produce.

Liminal, but not a passage rite

Turner (1983) notes that in van Gennep's (2004/1909) original account, rites may take two forms: life-cycle rituals and calendrical or seasonal rituals. Van Gennep's analysis, and most subsequent work, has tended to focus on life-cycle rituals. However, these two types of rituals have quite different characteristics. Life-cycle rituals and similar passage rites change a person's status, moving them 'a stage further along life's culturally prefabricated road' (Turner 1983: 128). However, 'for those taking part in a calendrical or seasonal ritual, no change in status may be involved' (Turner 1983: 128). In contrast to passage rites that are irreversible, 'calendrical rites are repeated every year by everyone' (Turner 1983: 128). These different types of rites have different outcomes: Initiatory rites tend to humble the initiates before elevating them to a new permanent status. In contrast: 'seasonal rites (whose residues are carnivals and festivals) elevate those of low status transiently before returning them to their permanent humbleness' (Turner 1983: 128).

Pagan festivals such as Faunalia are similar to raves and other electronic dance music events in that they can be considered as contemporary descendants of seasonal rites. In such rites there is no transition to a new or higher status. Rather, the festival places people in a liminal status for a time, and returns them to their pre-ritual status at the termination of the festival. St John's (2010: 225) comments about electronic dance music apply equally to Pagan festivals: participants do not seek passage to a new status, and evidence of a 'telos of participants' is lacking. 'It appears that these dance "rituals" may be more efficacious in transporting participants *into* a liminal community than effecting transit to a well-defined externally recognized social condition' (St John 2010: 226).

It is the ritual process, and particularly the somatic practices, that create this temporary experience of liminality at Faunalia. In her insightful analysis of a Wiccan initiation ritual, Bado-Fralick (2005: 143) describes van Gennep's theory of ritual as 'a simple unilinear directional movement', and suggests 'a major shift away from van Gennep's theories' (Bado-Fralick 2005: 64). Her shift away from van Gennep's ritual theory involves an understanding of ritual as a multidirectional process in which ritual is about learned somatic practice that integrates people into community. Bado-Fralick is correct to suggest that van Gennep's threefold transitional model is a somewhat simplistic linear understanding of the ritual process (Grimes 2000). However, I argue that rather than moving away from it, what is required is an integration of somatic practice into a more complex understanding of ritual, including a consideration of seasonal rituals. St John (2000, 2010), among others, provides this more nuanced approach to the ritual process that recognizes the complexity of contemporary rites and underlines the significance of somatic experiences.

Authenticity and ritual

Pagan festivals such as Faunalia shape participant moral orientations in a way that parallels the social production of morality that Durkheim and Turner identify. Turner suggests that calendrical and seasonal rites return participants 'ritually prepared for a whole series of changes in the nature of the cultural and ecological activities to be undertaken and of the relationships they will then have with others' (Turner 1983: 128). Modern Pagans do not typically sow or harvest crops, although a few do live on farms. However, they do engage in the contemporary urban parallels of these practices: going to work, attending social events and working out relationships with friends and colleagues. Faunalia, and other similar festivals, return participants to mundane life with a renewed understanding of, and preparedness for, these mundane activities.

Durkheim (1976) emphasizes the moral outcomes of religious rites, pointing out that both the corroboree and church integrated people into moral community. The intense emotions, or 'collective effervescence', generated during religious rituals sustains the religious ideas that serve to provide social integration (Durkheim 1976: 218). Pagan community does not have the organizational structure of either an indigenous tribe or a church, with participants reflecting the contemporary social trend towards individualism and dispersed social networks. However, the religious rites of Faunalia clearly have an impact on the moral stance of participants. For Therion, in the vignette that precedes this chapter, as with other participants at Faunalia, the moral transformation wrought during the rituals turns on working towards an 'authentic' self (Taylor 1991). Authenticity contains a moral ideal of how we 'ought to be' that focuses on the pursuit of self-awareness for its own sake. The rituals of Faunalia facilitate a moral project of self-discovery. Therion says: 'I got the sense . . . that I was very much an unfinished person. My work spiritually was to become a more complete person.' This is consistent with many analyses of the New Age and other individualistic forms of contemporary religion (Heelas et al. 2005, Heelas 1996).

The emphasis on self-development and authenticity is different from the selfish individualism that some have identified in contemporary spiritualties (Heelas 2006). Following Taylor's (1991) analysis of authenticity and Heelas' (1996) and Sutcliffe's (2003) discussions of contemporary spirituality, I suggest the form of authenticity pursued at Faunalia is relational in the sense that the focus is on finding new forms of self in relationship. Social life is inherently relational, and the discovery of self is made through our relationships with others (Taylor 1991, Benjamin 1988). Similarly, 'ritual is not about itself, but about relation to not-self' (Driver 1991: 98). Thus, the pursuit of authenticity at Faunalia has significant consequences for the moral practices of participants as they relate to people around them. This point is examined in detail in Chapter Six.

There is not one consistent moral trajectory associated with Faunalia. Therion observed that some people at Faunalia do treat it as a hedonistic opportunity to indulge their physical appetites. Others clearly use it as an opportunity for therapeutic self-development. Dingo is a 41-year-old single male who had been practicing as a Pagan for 20 years, but attended Faunalia for the first time in 2005. He was involved in various forms of social activism and was disturbed by the apparent lack of ongoing community and the lack of ongoing obligations to each other and various social justice issues. His assessment of Faunalia was that: 'The festival is primarily self-indulgent and therapeutic.' Dingo's criticism is consistent with Letcher's (2000) observation that much of contemporary Paganism is not very concerned about the environment or social justice issues, and in this sense he is correct. However, I think it is too simplistic to caricature Faunalia as a culture of hedonistic avoidance, similar to Reynold's (1999) critique of raves. Such observations underestimate the moral trajectory of these events as liminal spaces of inversion that often result in moral self-transformations that have a broader social significance (Turner 1969).

They also oversimplify the variety in the moral trajectories of participants. Celeste, a 27-year-old single woman, puts it this way:

Celeste: I would like [people] to understand that Paganism is not just about sex and death. I think a lot of people think that that is what we do. But I want people to realize that everything is sacred. The Earth is sacred and sexuality is sacred, and the way that we relate to other people is also sacred. And you cannot just piss about and desecrate those links that you have with yourself, with other people and with the Earth. You have got to treat them all with respect.

The ritual liminality at Faunalia reinforces a morality of authenticity that, in turn, sustains and transforms moral relationships in other aspects of people's lives. Contemporary festivals do not have the society-wide transformative impact that rites have in tribal societies. Nonetheless, the emphasis on authenticity at Faunalia is a moral project that is central to contemporary society (Giddens 1991, Taylor 1991). In some ways the morality of authenticity explored and reinforced at Faunalia functions as a form of social glue, helping participants to constructively participate in society when they return to the everyday world.

According to Durkheim (1976), for an individual to transcend the morality of self-centred individualism and animal passions this requires the interests of the group to be represented to the individual. Through their participation in rituals and shared beliefs about the totem or god, they understand and respect the moral concerns of the social collective. Durkheim's account is problematic because of its ahistorical, static and overly integrated conception of culture, reflecting his primarily functionalist social theory (Bell 1997). Further, according to Durkheim, morality is derived externally to the individual, as he or she is socialized into obedience to functionally required normative behaviour that benefits the collective. This assumes that people somehow become human, and then have to be socialized into being moral. Durkheim's model of morality is asocial, assuming that selfish individualism is a product of a lack of socialization (Shilling 2005).

In contrast, theorists such as Benjamin (1988) and Levinas (1979) see morality as integral to personhood. Selfish individualism is a particular structure of relational practice, rather than a state that is prior to the development of morality. Personhood and morality are inherent in relationships, and morality is moulded and shaped through the practice of these relationships. In his relational theory of morality Emmanuel Levinas (1979) argues that Western thought asserts 'the primacy of the self, the Same, the subject or Being' (Davis 1996: 40). Making the self or the individual the starting point is imperialistic in the sense that it ignores the role of relationships in creating humans. The 'other' of the relationship, alterity, is suppressed or integrated into the project of the self. In contrast, a relational understanding of being human, and religion, begins with the self in relationship. As Martin Buber (1958: 12) puts it: 'In the beginning is the relationship.'

Levinas pursues an ethics 'without foundation, without imperatives or claim to universality' (Davis 1996: 3). Ethics does not emerge through a common harmonious relationship. Nor does ethics emerge through adherence to normative obligations imposed by a social collective. Rather, ethics emerges through relationships that involve respecting the strangeness, the confronting difference, of the other. For Levinas ethics begins with an attempt to welcome the other as other, and to take responsibility for the other as other. As Kemp (1997: 3) puts it: 'He considers ethics as a vision of the Other who makes an appeal to me to take care, and thereby his ethics becomes a questioning of what I can do in order to make possible the good life of the Other.' Further, for Levinas the ethical concern for the other is disruptive of one's own self-understandings and self-sufficiency (Bernasconi 1997). Ethical relationships do not lead to a peaceful sense of one's identity. Rather, they disrupt an individual's sense of self-satisfaction because ethical relationships lead to an 'attentiveness to the vulnerability of the other' (Bernasconi 1997: 90). The following chapters pay particular attention to the way ritual generates moral transformations. Rituals deliberately bring participants face to face with confronting aspects of both self and others, including sexual desire and death.

Religious ritual shapes moral etiquette. At Faunalia somatic practices and carnal inversions experienced during liminal rites are key mechanisms that facilitate a moral project of the pursuit of authenticity, transforming the self-in-relationship. The transformations are less transformations of cognitive self-understandings, although such transformations do occur; rather, the primary transformations are emotional, aesthetic, somatic and relational.

Conclusion

At Faunalia temporal, geographical and material factors are key in creating liminality. These are experienced sensuously and emotionally, as well as cognitively and interpretatively. Liminality is understood as a 'time out of time' that creates an experience of communitas – a deep sense of intimacy of trust. Faunalia, like other festivals, is a descendent of seasonal rites that do not involve a transition in status, so much as providing an experience of liminality that reinvigorates participation in mundane life. At the heart of this reinvigoration is the pursuit of an ethic of authenticity. The following chapters provide more detailed accounts of these aspects through an examination of the two main rituals at Faunalia.

Rituals dramatize social tensions in a community (Bell 1992). Turner (1969, 1975) clearly demonstrates this point in his accounts of the

Ndembu rituals such as the *Ihamba*, *Chihamba* and divinatory practices. According to Turner, the social inversions of liminal rites simultaneously legitimate and modify the social order, providing responses to the social tensions they dramatize (Bell 1992: 40). The two main rituals of the 2005 Faunalia dramatize the fear and anxiety around sexual desire and death. Performing these rituals transforms the somatic awareness of participants. They identify barriers to the pursuit of an ethic of authenticity, and in so doing find a life that is more meaningful, a life with soul.

CHAPTER THREE

Death

Introduction

The Underworld rite is performed on the second night of Faunalia. This chapter describes the ritual, largely in the words of participants. In the Underworld rite participants come face to face with their mortality and the suffering inherent in some life transitions. It is unsettling, painful and difficult to confront suffering, sadness and one's own death. In the ritual, the pain is honoured, the fear is confronted and the awareness of a life lived 'towards death' becomes just a little more bearable.

The sequestration of death in Western societies sustains a general discomfort with death, dying and mortality. As McNamara (2001: 1) suggests: 'Dying is something most of us would rather not think about.' Many people are embarrassed to talk about death (Kellehear 1996). The Underworld rite confronts this discomfort and fear. The rite changes the way people feel about death, dying and loss. Most participants report that after the ritual they are less afraid of their own mortality and better able to deal with experiences of loss and suffering.

Ritual provides an etiquette of relating to events and experiences that are otherwise difficult and uncomfortable. The power of ritual derives from the liminality of the experience that operates at the level of 'acting' (Benjamin 1998) or 'iconic consciousness' (Alexander 2008). Rituals change the way that participants feel as well as changing the way they think. Rituals work through somatic performances that are bound up with cultures of cognitive and somatic knowing. These experiences allow participants to develop life-enhancing responses to some of the central challenges of contemporary life. As Armstrong (2005: 3) puts it: 'mythology . . . is not about opting out of this world, but about enabling us to live more intensely within it.' This is illustrated in the chapter through a detailed recounting of a ritual descent into the underworld.

Preparation

Participants emerge from their bunkhouse accommodation, tents and caravans, on Friday morning to participate in a self-serve breakfast. The food is vegetarian and alcohol use is discouraged, although a few people did imbibe during the party on the final night. Most of Friday is spent sitting around chatting in the dinning room, or outside around a bonfire in the centre of a large open space approximately 80 metres across. In the early afternoon there is typically an optional workshop on Tantra, Pagan activism or some other topic. People are recruited to assist the organizers of the ritual for that night in various ways. Some trenches are dug, a path cleared through the bush and the gymnasium decorated. For most people the day passes slowly, with a relaxed party or holiday atmosphere.

During the afternoon a large gateway is erected in the outside meeting area. It serves as a stark indicator of things to come. It is over two metres high with a large wooden board at the top, 30 centimetres wide and two metres long. The gateway reminds participants of the ritual that is to come that evening, and heightens expectations. The words carved on this gateway are from Dante's (1949) *Inferno*:

> Through me the road to the city of desolation. Through me the road to sorrows diuturnal. Through me the road among the lost creation. Nothing ere I was made was made to be save things eterne, and I eterne abide. Lay down all hope you that go in by me. (Dante 1949: 117)

Late in the afternoon there is a compulsory ritual briefing. Anyone who wants to participate in the ritual is required to attend. The basic rules of the festival are reiterated: participants should aim to treat each other 'excellently'. Participants are reminded that when people are in trance states they can be very open and vulnerable. Any inappropriate behaviour should be reported to designated people. After these and other injunctions the organizers of the ritual for that evening provide an outline of the theme and main events of the ritual. The aim is to provide participants with enough information so that they can participate with informed consent, but not too much information to spoil the ritual – surprise is a key element in most rituals at Faunalia.

The theme of this night's ritual is death. There will be various ordeals. For example, at one point participants must sing a song or recite something of their own choosing. It is emphasized that if anyone feels uncomfortable at any stage that they have the right and responsibility to say 'stop, I don't want to do this'. Participants are warned that the ritual will be long, slow and probably quite cold, so they should dress for warmth.

> **Sinead:** Once we had the briefing in the afternoon about what exactly the ritual that night was going to be all about, I tended to retreat into

my shell a bit. We were told that we were going to be marked for death, and that we were going to go on a journey of transformation into the underworld. I spent a great deal of time that afternoon thinking about that ritual and what it meant. I found that I went into the state of mind as if I was going to die, quite easily. [I had a serious accident] back in September. The last seven months has been very significantly reduced work hours. So I have had a lot of time to think [short laugh]. Having a fright like that does remind you of your mortality. We are not indestructible. Within the last two years I have ended my relationship, I have moved house and I have started a new job, so I have undergone a lot of change, a lot of death. Over the course of that afternoon I spent a great deal of time reviewing my life. This whole notion of being marked for death [raises the question] am I ready for death? Have I done the things that I wanted to do? Do I regret the things that I have actually done? One of my mottos is to not [sigh], not regret the things that you have not done. To actually try not to have regrets about it. So it was a good process to go through that afternoon and think about – OK, well, what do you really regret? And the main thing that came up was being lazy and procrastinating about several key areas in my life.

Louis, who wrote the ritual, said that the main sources for the rite were *The Odyssey*, The *Orphic Hymns*, The *Homeric Hymns*, Dante's *Inferno* and *The Aeneid*. The ritual was inspired by the Eleusinian mystery rites. The Eleusinian mystery rites were 'the most revered of all ancient mystery cults' (Bowden 2010: 26). Celebrated for over a thousand years, the ritual focused around the myth of Persephone's descent into the underworld. Louis said that he had tried to capture the spirit of the ritual. The aim was to have a powerful experience, not to be worried about whether details were historically correct or not. He wanted it to be an ordeal, people to be bored during it and for it to be unpleasant. He did not want to make it fun. He pointed out that the ordeals were low key and mostly symbolic. He also hoped that the rite allowed people to learn the myth of Persephone's descent into the underworld.

In Greek myth Hades is the name of the underworld – a dreary place where all mortals go when they die (Burkett 1985). Hades is also a god, the ruler of the underworld. The myth of Persephone's (also called Kore) journey into the underworld is recounted in a variety of compendiums of mythology that Pagans often read, and on various internet sites. There are various versions, but the central story is that 'Kore-Persephone was a virgin goddess of extra-ordinary beauty. But Hades desired a wife, and schemed to carry off Persephone' (Rose 1959: 91). Hades abducted Persephone while she was collecting flowers in a field. Demeter, a fertility goddess, became concerned about her daughter Persephone, weeping when she could not find her. The Earth responded to her grief and became infertile. In response to the desolate Earth Zeus sought to return Persephone to Demeter. However, while Persephone was in the underworld she ate a pomegranate seed, which meant that she was bound to the underworld. A compromise was reached: 'Persephone was to remain in the house of Hades for a third (or a half) of each year, spending the rest on Earth with her mother' (Rose 1959: 92), and this resulted in the seasons of winter and summer. During her travels, Demeter had been involved in the creation of the rituals of the Eleusinian Mysteries. Once Persephone was returned Demeter fulfilled a promise to the Eleusinians and restored the fertility of the Earth.

At the heart of this myth is an understanding of the interweaving of agricultural cycles of growth and death with the lives of humans. Performing a ritual based on this myth becomes a way for participants to engage with the meaning of their own mortality. Not everyone at Faunalia was familiar with the details of this myth, and it is quite probable that some had never heard of it before participating in the rite. This did not seem to worry organizers. Cognitive framing is less important than somatic experience and emotional self-transformation.

While the ritual's theme was death, the emphasis was understood by participants to be about self-transformation and renewal. The journey into the underworld is followed by a journey of return. Leanan put it this way: 'Although it was quite deep and meaningful, and quite a dark ritual, it was not dark either. At the end it is rebirth anyway which is transformational.'

The evening meal was served around dusk. The ritualists were served first and then they went off to prepare. Most participants sat around chatting, drinking cups of tea and coffee. Around nine o'clock in the evening (it is difficult to be precise because few people wore watches and there were few clocks) participants began to appear in the dining area in their ritual attire. Most were dressed in loose black clothing, wrapped in capes and robes. People also congregated around the large fire outside, in the centre of the site where the ritual was to begin. There were messages from the ritual organizers suggesting the ritual might begin soon, but the general understanding was that participants just had to wait until they were ready, and that would take them as long as it took. This anticipation prior to the ritual is a key part of what makes the ritual itself work. Eventually, perhaps around eleven o'clock, the ritual began.

Opening the door to the underworld

The ritual begins quite similar to most Witchcraft rituals. The quarters are called, symbols of the elements are taken around the circle and deities are invoked. The dark theme of the ritual soon began to express itself. The circle is cast widdershins. As noted in the Introduction, a widdershins working is understood to be associated with darker, more challenging deities and aspects of the self. Jars are carried around the circle containing incense and wine (common to most Wiccan rituals), but also materials rarely seen in ritual, including sheep's milk, blood (purchased from a butcher), honey and barley. These are all poured into a large cauldron and stirred into a potion with accompanying chanting. The deities are invoked by reciting sections from the *Orphic Hymns*. The deities include Hecate, a goddess of the underworld, Hades, Persephone and Demeter. Ritualists representing each deity appear as they are invoked wearing lavish costumes and makeup. Ruth, one of the younger participants at Faunalia recalled the invocations of these deities:

> **Ruth:** The underworld journey was amazing. I am a kind of addict when it comes to ancient Greek mythology, so it was right up my alley. [I felt] part of something ancient. Using the *Orphic Hymns*, [even though] they were greatly shortened . . . that was cool.

Each participant is given a one-dollar coin[1] with the injunction 'look after this'. Ritualists walk around the circle with some anointing oil and mark

IMAGE 3.1 *Philippe and Michelle costumed as Hades and Persephone.*
Photo by Philippe.

each person on the forehead with their thumb saying 'You are marked for death'.

> René: When they said, 'You are marked for death', I went, 'I am not ready. I don't know if I want to be marked for death, hang on a minute' [laughs]. Stop the train, I want to get off! It got my stomach and my solar plexus going, and I am sitting there, going ooooh, this is deep, this is intense, am I ready for this? What does this mean for me?

Blood is a liminal substance (Douglas 1996). It makes people feel uncomfortable. That is one of the reasons for using it in the ritual. Being told you are 'marked for death' is similarly confronting. Participant responses begin as cognitive reflections, illustrated by Sinead's response to the ritual briefing. The deeper into the ritual participants go, the more the responses become embodied, emotional and 'somatic', as illustrated by René's responses above. Louis describes the next part of the ritual:

> Louis: The necromancy is part of the rite that involves opening a gateway to the underworld. Most people who enter the realm of the dead go there and do not come back. The point of the necromancy is to make a gateway to enter through which we can also return. First, there were three knocks on the ground. Like knocking on the door of the underworld. Then we dug a trench. Then they poured the potion into the trench. It contained sheep's milk, water, wine, blood, honey and barley.

The gateway to the underworld is declared open and the ritualists disappear out through the gateway erected earlier. Those who remain begin slowly circling widdershins around the fire. At this point the ritual has been going for approximately an hour. The mood is sombre and reflective. Sinead recalls the next events:

> Sinead: The most powerful image was when we were all round in the circle and the drumming started up. Just the way it was being done, shifted me to an interesting place where I felt some sort of tribal aspect. I started dancing to the drumming, moving in the circle along with everybody else. Then there was this moment when Harrison came swirling [stressed] through the centre of the circle. He was in black, and he whirled up to somebody who was one or two people away from me, a man, who was also in black, and drew them into the tantric circle. He did that with about four or five other men. There was about six men that started off whirling. They looked like Sufis in the centre of the circle, all in these black robes. Then there was this drumming that was just affecting me on this other level. It was such a powerful image for me that it literally [hand hitting fist] affected

me straight away, because it was [hand hitting fist] straight into the rite. Then gradually people started joining the centre of the circle, and I watched the crowd gradually 'intermove' – is the best way I can describe it – the eighty people begin to move in a circle around the fire. After a little while, the abductions started happening. There was screaming and yelling, and people being dragged off.

Two men dressed all in black, including hoods and facemasks, came back through the gateway into the circle and moved among the participants. Suddenly they placed a hessian bag over someone's head. They grabbed her under the arms and dragged her out through the gateway into the underworld. She screamed as she went. At regular intervals of around a few minutes the men in black would return, weaving in and out of the participants and take another person. Ruth remembers her abduction in this way:

> **Ruth:** I was kidnapped, I am guessing, maybe half way through. [The] bastards took me completely by surprise [laughs]. They were intending that. I was in an altered state at that stage, and then there is just this sackcloth coming over my head and I wasn't feigning the shaking and shrieking thing. Oh well, actually, the screaming I did [fake]. I went for the best operatic screaming too. Why not? But I was completely thrown by that. I remember one point just seeing everybody as simply dead and nameless. Just these shuffling souls. I had chosen for that rite not to wear glasses. And I also had my face ochred. And [I was] feeling the drying, crackling ochre on my skin, and falling into my lips and my eyes. And the dust that was coming up from all the people walking around the fire and the heat, it really was like tasting only ashes. It really did trip me into an underworld space.

Ritual at Faunalia is serious playful performance. Ruth's description of the moment of her abduction captures precisely the seriousness, and the intentional theatricality, of her participation. Her scream was both acted: 'I went for my best operatic screaming', and real: 'I wasn't feigning the shaking and shrieking.' These two statements are only apparently contradictory. Participants engage with the ritual, suspending disbelief, and by so doing access parts of themselves that are not fully conscious that they find difficult to experience or 'work with' in mundane realities. They are 'acting' in Benjamin's (1988) sense, dramatizing their experiences through performance.

With abductions occurring approximately every three minutes this meant that some of the 65 participants[2] wait for nearly three hours before being abducted. Participants continue to circle around the central fire, waiting. The mood is sombre, marked by occasional macabre jokes and laughter. The regular abductions place participants in a constant state of anticipation. For some participants this part of the ritual is the highlight. The waiting and the constant awareness of impending abduction/death lead to some profound self-reflection:

> **Sinead:** I started thinking there are a lot of people here to be taken. Pretty much the whole way through I just kept waiting for it to happen and hoping it would happen, but it didn't happen quickly at all, and I was actually one of the last five people to be taken out of those eighty people. It was a very long time being in around the circle. For me, that was the experience of the ritual. It wasn't going to the palace at the end. I had my experience by that stage. The death aspect. The time spent around that circle waiting to die and watching people go, and watching people, after a period of time, be almost desperate to go. I was within that ritual state, I was bringing that into a broader perspective. When you are senile and eighty, and your friends are getting picked off one by one, is this what it is like? Is it people sitting round in an old people's home waiting to die, and being almost jubilant when they actually do? Some of these people that were getting taken towards the end were [jubilant]. They didn't have to move around the fire any more. They [laughs], they were going to wherever they were going. So, to me, it was having that long period of time to contemplate how it might be. What I took out of it was the sense that death is something we have no control over.

Being kidnapped was a profound experience for many people. Once through the gateway they were spun around a few times and then guided along a path for perhaps 30 metres.

> **Lewis:** And as the kidnapping began, I was just running around the circle, and there was the moon right above me. They started kidnapping and they were taking them away. I had all this bamboo and I was stomping, sweeping and whacking the ground as they were getting taken away, and I was whacking near their heels and whipping the ground as they were being dragged away. I really enjoyed that actually. [There was] all this dust. Bamboo's got a great cracking sound. Then you can hover [it] above their head, and even rattle and cracking this above their head. It just disturbs their reality. Disorienting. The whole process is about disorienting the people who are getting kidnapped.

Lewis's actions with the bamboo were not scripted. At Faunalia the script is only a guide. Ritualists improvize in order to enhance the experience. One of the ritualists who challenged people at one of the ordeals reported that he 'absolutely loved that role'. He could not remember his lines very well, but that did not seem to matter. 'I played with the role. I could read their eyes and see if they were quite nervous.' Another ritualist said: 'It was really beautiful seeing the different range of expressions. We had a lot of fun with people's responses.'

The ordeals

The first ordeal was that of 'Earth'. Participants, with hessian bag still in place over their heads, were guided to a trench, asked to step into it, kneel down and then lie down. The trench had been freshly dug that afternoon and was perhaps 30 centimetres deep. Participants experienced it as a grave:

> **Leanan:** And then when you get to the first gateway to the underworld, this is where you get buried. They said 'Would you lie down in the grave', and they made a gravel tin digging sound and they throw a handful of dirt over your face. I had my eyes open inside the bag, and the dust came through into my mouth and into my eyes, and I thought, 'Shit, I am really going to die here!' [laughs]. It was only a few seconds, I am sure, but it felt like such a long time. I am a bit claustrophobic. I could have said at any time, let me out, but I did not want to, I wanted to go through with it properly. So I did. But it felt like a long time, and the dust in my eyes and the dust in my mouth and whatever, it really did feel like you were going to die. It was a real experience of the heart. I remember walking up the path, and wiping my eyes [laughing] to get dust out. I enjoyed it, and it did mean a lot. Mum was dying and I have just retired, so it was very transitional. When I went through the burial, I was thinking that it was like going through a gateway and leaving a part of your life behind, and moving along to the next part and looking forward to it, but dreading it, because you do not know what is going to happen. There is an uncertainty and a hope and a dread, and then, oh, it is [pause for 2 seconds] very mixed emotions, very ambiguous, yeah, feel ambivalent really. I think it helped me get through this period of my life anyway. I did get some strength from it because I learned that, yes, you can lie there and get buried and have stuff thrown in your face without going into a screaming fit.

Dingo reported a similarly powerful experience:

> **Dingo:** The hessian bag was over my head, and they began to sprinkle dirt over my head, which went through the hessian and into my eyes and up my nose and in my mouth. Every time you take a breath in, you get this huge cloud of dust. That was awesome. Just the sound of the shovel going into the dirt near your head. It really was very powerful.

IMAGE 3.2 *Honeybarb costumed as a Guardian.*
Photo by Philippe.

Later participants are advised to close their eyes before the dust is sprinkled over their faces in the hessian bag. Next the participant is asked to stand up, the hessian bag is removed, and they are confronted with a guardian in a white facemask who gives them a few words of wisdom. A guide then takes their hand and leads them on to the next ordeal.

> **Ruth:** I was actually apprehensive about the rite to begin with. Just such an [pause of 2 seconds] unambiguous rite of death. But after being led down and laid in the grave, it was an amazing sense of release there. Being taken was the peak of the anticipation, apprehension, and [then] being dragged, led along the path. Then being raised up out of the grave – it was like everything fell, all of the dross, all of the worries just fell off. It was really, really amazing.

A guide takes the participant's hand and leads them on to the next element of Water:

> **Ruth:** The next one was Charon the ferryman. Oh God he reeked like lavender and tea-tree but the ambience he created there was just creepy, freaky, cool. It was fantastic. I was feeling very bare, just completely

stripped of all kind of pretences. Even though I was wrapped up, I think I had pants and a turtleneck on under my robe, and I had gloves on and a scarf and a beanie, and a cloak over that. I still felt very naked. But not in a frightened kind of way.

The ritualists deliberately work with all the senses: taste, touch, aural, visual and smell. Charon is the boatman in the Greek mythology who takes the dead across the river Styx and into the underworld. At his ordeal there is a trench filled with water. Beside the trench stood Charon in costume and heavy makeup. Charon challenges the participants, asking if they have the fare for the boat trip:

> **Dale:** I had fingerless gloves on at the beginning of the rite. I wondered what to do with the coin. I have got no pockets. So I put it in my glove and didn't think about it for the rest of the time. When I was taken to the ferryman and he said to me 'Have you got a coin?' [I said] 'Coin? Oh, that's right, yeah!' I had to remember where I put it. 'Here you go.' [laughs]. [Then he said] 'You may pass.' He got me there, because I'd totally forgotten about the coin aspect.

Another guide led participants on to Cerberus, the canine guardian of the underworld, representing the element of Air.

> **Ruth:** Then it was the puppy after that, Cerberus. I sung a medieval song. It pleased the puppy. That was nice.

> **Sinead:** I have to say the encounter with Cerberus was terrifying. I was really, really scared. Because they sped it through right at the end by the time I got to Cerberus, to Air, I had caught up with somebody, and we went through the Cerberus ordeal together. We were told [at the ritual briefing] that everybody had to sing something to calm Cerberus. The guardian picked me, and put me on the spot to do the calming thing. Then I looked at Cerberus and he was so real. There was this ferocious growling and the way he was moving was quite animal-like. I remember being quite alarmed at the noise and the ferocious barking and growling. I was dead set scared. It took me a little while to gather my thoughts and sing my little song. But [short laugh] oh, I did it in the end.

Having completed the ordeals of Earth (the grave), Water (Charon) and Air (singing to Cerberus), the final ordeal was of Fire. Another trench was filled with fire and Hephaestus, the Greek God of fire, stood beside it. He again challenged participants:

> **Sinead:** I have to say that seeing Hephaestus painted up the way he was, was quite powerful for me because it looked to me like there had been a shift in him, and I really appreciated that. In all four ordeals the

intensity that the ritualists delivered to me and the experience that I had been through, that was very, very strong.

The underworld

Participants finally arrived at their destination in the underworld (also referred to by some participants as 'the palace' and 'the house of the gods'). In the underworld Hades and Persephone were cuddling in a corner 'as an expression of their love', according to Louis. There was a central cauldron with a methylated spirits-fuelled fire in it and four altars spread around the area. Despite the underworld's supposed dreariness, this space was quite festive:

> **Ruth:** Coming into the house of the gods was yummy and sumptuous. More because of the heat than anything else, I took off a whole bunch of my clothes [laughs], and had just my basic robe on. I was drumming for a while and dancing around the lit cauldron. For me it was a pretty kick back, cruisey energy, just warm, nestley, comfy. It was fitting, and really comforting after the trials. Being rather tired I scampered off to bed not long after [laughs].

Once everyone was in the underworld, Hades and Persephone arose out of their corner and came to a central podium where the myth of Persephone's descent and return from the underworld was recounted. Participants were invited to come to the podium to be told the mystery and drink from the waters of the underworld. Participants were given a choice of drinking from the waters of Lethe, to forget, or Acheron, to remember. The waters of Lethe contained absinthe, with the option of green cordial if the participant did not want alcohol, and the waters of Acheron contained guarana, with the option of red cordial.

> **Natasha:** I chose to forget. Why would you want to remember? It is all just data. Gone. Let it go. I could not believe anyone wanted to remember.
>
> **Sauvage:** [When we were given the elixir] I chose to remember. It was many things. I had a sense that I have probably gotten a useful tool set of wisdom through my life. It would be a bit too pointless to just forget about that and start again. It felt like I was not honouring my experience, and if I chose to not remember, it felt like I was discarding what I had been through.
>
> **Sinead:** [Once I got into the underworld] I hit the wall [and was very tired]. The scene was quite beautiful. There were people moving

around. It felt quite crowded. I think that was because I had been outside for so many hours, and moving around quite freely, and then suddenly I am in this space with straw on the floor and wall-to-wall people. I knew roughly that there were four altars. I really only went to one of them. I had really had enough by that stage. I would have been there, you know, it would be forty-five minutes tops. It would not have been an hour. I burnt a sigil, danced around the cauldron for a bit. I had the elixir. I sort of walked around a little bit, and that was it. I checked out [laughs].

Participants gradually drift off to bed and a few remain until dawn. The emotions generated by the rituals are so intense that many people sleep only a few hours a night. Others take longer to recover:

Sinead: The next day. I did not want to get out of bed. I had moved and moved and moved and moved and moved around that fire until my feet could move no more. I had really drummed and danced and spun and everything. I was lying in bed curled in a little kind of 'C' shape [short laugh] under about two sleeping bags.

Embodied liminality

The Underworld rite described here creates a profound liminal experience that for most participants is immersive:

René: At no point did any mundane thought or thoughts of the outside world, or my kids, or my life out there ever intrude for a minute, which was quite a thing for me because normally my brain is working overtime on my life issues and stuff. So for those four, five, six hours, I was completely out of time and space.

This sustained immersive liminality is achieved by a complex set of factors: the liminal nature of bunkhouse accommodation, a bush setting, wearing different clothes, not following 'normal' mundane routines during the day, having ample time to sit and reflect, staying up all night, waiting in anticipation to be taken, dancing around an open fire, drumming, participating in a sophisticated theatrical performance, being abducted, being confronted with one's mortality, lying in a trench experienced as a grave, being challenged in various ways, unusual sounds, smells and tastes. All of these factors work together to create the depth and intensity of the ritual as an immersive, embodied, emotional and cognitive experience. This is consistent with the observations of both Pike (2001) and Tramacchi (2000) about immersive liminality described in Chapter Two. Grimes (2000) suggests:

> Death rites never provide answers. In fact, celebrations often spring up around questions that are by their very nature unanswerable. Ritual is a way of performing, thereby becoming identified with, our most troubling questions. (Grimes 2000: 257)

The Underworld rite at Faunalia is emblematic of a common understanding in Pagan cosmologies that humans have limited agency. The web of life is woven about the individual, but the individual also participates, to a greater or lesser extent, in the weaving of their lives and the lives of others (Harvey 2005, Orr 2007). The living out of this tension between agency and fate, is one of the most troubling questions for Western individuals (Giddens 1991, Taylor 1991, Bauman 1993). Participants' embodied orientation towards death is a very poignant case of precisely this tension. I asked René how the rite had changed her attitude towards death:

> René: Yes [it changed the way I feel about death]. I was sitting there in the circle thinking 'I am not afraid to die.' I don't embrace death, but I am not afraid to die. [The ritual] showed me that I did not have that fear any more.

Note that this change is an emotional transformation in René's somatic self-awareness. René reports she is no longer afraid. Ruti (2006: 135) argues that: 'The paradox of existence, for both Heidegger and Lacan, is that it is only by accepting insecurity that the human being can begin to live in an inspired manner.' Insecurity is not just a cognitively framed understanding of risk. It is also a somatically experienced emotion, often only half-consciously articulated. The rituals at Faunalia enable participants to accept the uncertainty of their mortality, or at least, they become less uncomfortable with it. Death is always going to be something they would rather avoid, but it becomes less fearful.

The cultural framing of these somatic experiences is important. For many participants, the idea of reincarnation helped to make sense of their experiences:

> René: When the time came for me to be taken through the gateway, it was like I was aware of revisiting old friends. That was not the first time I had made that journey. So although a part of me was going, how will I be received this time, I was also going, I have walked this way before and I know that I am going to make it through here. I did not feel any fear.

From the opposite point of view, one person said that because she did not believe in an underworld, the ritual's effects were limited:

Adele: The concept of an underworld is not part of my personal belief system. My concept of death has nothing to do with an underworld. My concept of death is just your spirit dissipating into the ether. Because I do not buy into a concept of an underworld, for me it was not a particularly touching ritual.

Adele had not attended Faunalia before and only had limited ritual experience. Luhrmann (1989) suggests that as Pagans develop more ritual experience their beliefs slowly 'drift' to be consistent with the beliefs of their fellow practitioners. The disconnect between Adele's beliefs and the ritual performance may reflect her relative newness to Pagan ritual practice. It may also be that for rituals to 'work' both the somatic experience and the cognitive beliefs must 'mesh'. Or, at least, the cognitive interpretations must not undermine the ritual, which is what appears to have been the case for Adele.

Participation in Pagan ritual does not require naïve belief. Rather it requires the willing suspension of disbelief, and 'acceptance' of the rite, so that participants can engage in the embodied, passionate experience of a myth retold. Grimes (2000: 282) argues: 'in effect, we need a renewed mythologizing of death and the dead, one that does not require naïve belief, but depends on dramatic storytelling and bold, performed images of Old Death.' This is precisely the sort of ritual that is performed at Faunalia.

Pike (2001: 189) observes that her fieldwork at Pagan festivals generated somatic memories: 'My memories of the festival are not simply of the events I saw and conversations I shared with other participants; they are sensual memories embedded in my body as well as written in my field notes.' Many participants make similar observations about their own experience. Leanan, for example, observes: 'I came away knowing that I have got strength that I did not have before, or a stubborn strength that I did not know I had.' This is a memory of an emoted bodily response to the challenges and confronting experiences of the Underworld rite.

Not everyone who attends Faunalia leaves with positive feelings. Pike's (2001: 195) observation about Pagan festivals in the United States apply equally well to Faunalia: 'Some men and women come to festivals intentionally to work on healing emotional wounds, while others find that festival going and involvement in Neopaganisms opens up wounds and forces them to seek healing.' Similarly, while the participants at Faunalia are committed to ethical stands of mutual respect, they are equally as likely as any other group to be fallible in the performance of these ethics. However, it is clear that the majority of participants find Faunalia a transformative and positive experience. Sinead, for example, said: 'Faunalia helped me to develop trust and self-respect because of the respect with which I was treated by others.'

The Underworld rite is a deliberate form of 'acting', which brings participants into performative relationships with half-conscious fears and anxieties associated with death and major life transitions. The performance of the ritual allows some participants to find these fears and anxieties to be slightly more bearable. As Armstrong (2005: 57) puts it, in her recounting of the Persephone myth: 'the confrontation with death led to spiritual regeneration . . . it could not bring immortality – only the gods lived forever – but it could enable you to live more fearlessly and therefore more fully here on Earth, looking death calmly in the face.'

Religious ritual provides participants with an emotional confidence in the face of the complexities and uncertainties of living in a world in which we will all, one day, die. Religion also helps participants to frame the world cognitively by providing a worldview within which to locate themselves. It is the combination of the ritually generated somatic memories with beliefs and other symbolic resources that enable participants to find a life with soul.

CHAPTER FOUR

Shadow

Introduction

In the Underworld rite participants reluctantly accept death and suffering as inevitable parts of life. They do not seek to overcome or escape from these difficult aspects of life. They do not look to a life beyond death. They embrace death as a part of life. Through the ritual participants discover a new strength to face suffering and the inevitability of their own mortality. The Underworld rite does not focus on changing participant's cognitive beliefs or understandings. Rather, the ritual changes participants' emotional and aesthetic orientations. The rituals at Faunalia engage with the somatic dimensions of experience, transforming participants' relationships to 'shadow', hidden or repressed parts of their lives.

Shadow work at Faunalia

The creators of Faunalia deliberately design the rituals to be confronting. The confronting and unsettling aspects of the rituals are understood in terms of the Jungian concept of the shadow. Six of the interviewees specifically refer to working with their 'shadow' during ritual. Jung's writings are an important 'symbolic resource' that participants at Faunalia draw on to make sense of their experiences.

Harrison: [After the first Faunalia] Phoebe and I started moving in a different direction magically towards a more ecstatic and darker, [by which I mean] more in terms of the Jungian shadow side of ourselves, and working with the dark archetypes. [We also developed] a more ecstatic approach, with less structure and more intuitive too.

The rituals of contemporary Witchcraft and Paganism vary along a continuum. At one end are those that are more formal and follow established liturgies. At the other end of the continuum are those that are more ecstatic, intuitive and improvized. The ritual practice of key participants at Faunalia tends strongly towards the ecstatic end of the spectrum. Ecstatic ritual practice places greater emphasis on aesthetic and somatic knowledge, and is more likely to engage in 'shadow work'.

Sinead attended Faunalia for the first time in 2005. She indicated in her interview prior to the festival that engaging in shadow work was one of the things she hoped to achieve at Faunalia:

> **Sinead:** I have been doing a bit of work on shadow stuff myself. I read *Owning Your Own Shadow* [Johnson 1991] last year, and it struck a bit of a chord with me. It is a personal hope that I will be able to work with some of those aspects of myself at Faunalia. From what I have read, from what people have said to me, the environment is certainly conducive to that. It is also supportive for people who may have challenging stuff come up . . . I am looking forward to taking off the corporate, work, career type handle, even though it is very much a part of me and I love what I do. I am looking forward to taking that off and accessing the less public [laughs] aspects of myself.

Robert Johnson's (1991) book *Owning Your Own Shadow: Understanding the Dark Side of the Psyche* is recommended by the organizers of Faunalia as preparatory background reading for the festival. Johnson (1991: 4) defines the shadow as 'that part of us we fail to see or know'. Most commonly the shadow is understood as emotions, such as fears, obsessions and projections, that shape people's behaviour without their conscious awareness. 'By shadow I mean the "negative" side of the personality, the sum of all those unpleasant qualities we like to hide, together with the insufficiently developed functions and the content of the personal unconscious' (Carl Jung quoted in Zweig and Abrams 1991: 1).

Jung's conception of the shadow is a 'symbolic resource' that frames and shapes participants' experience of ritual at Faunalia. Participants' cognitions and emotions are mutually influential on each other. I argue that ritual at Faunalia primarily works at the level of somatic consciousness, shaping half-articulated emotional experiences. This is made possible, in part, because participants consciously approach Faunalia as an experience of shadow work.

There is a powerful moral dimension to the shadow. This can operate in two ways. First, the shadow can simply be those parts of ourselves which we avoid and find uncomfortable to acknowledge consciously as a product of our particular biography: 'For example, while one person may find it difficult to acknowledge anger, domination, or lust, another may find it equally difficult to experience or express sensitivity, gentleness or compassion'

(Daniels 2005: 73). Second, the shadow is often linked to morally dubious or unacceptable aspects of the self that reflect public pressure to shape ourselves to that which we perceive to be socially acceptable. In this second dimension the shadow reflects more general social and cultural processes. While these two dimensions of the shadow often overlap, it is not always the case.

Developing a Jungian psychotherapeutic perspective, Connie Zweig and Jeremiah Abrams (1991) first used the term 'shadow-work'.

Through *shadow-work*, a term we coined to refer to the continuing effort to develop a creative relationship with the shadow, we can:

- achieve a more genuine self-acceptance, based on a more complete knowledge of who we are;

- defuse the negative emotions that erupt unexpectedly in our daily lives;

- feel more free of the guilt and shame associated with our negative feelings and actions;

- recognize the projections that color our opinion of others;

- heal our relationships through the more honest self-examination and direct communication;

- and use the creative imagination via dreams, drawing, writing, and rituals to own the disowned self. (Zweig and Abrams 1991: xxv; original emphasis)

While Zweig and Abrams mention rituals, their book *Meeting the Shadow* focuses almost solely on Jungian-inspired psychotherapeutic practice and has little or no mention of religious practice and ritual.

The shadow is understood as being in opposition to 'light' that is often associated with consciousness. 'Jung defined the shadow as personifying "everything that the subject refuses to acknowledge about himself [or herself] and yet (which) is always thrusting itself upon him directly or indirectly"' (Earl 2001: 285). The shadow is largely outside of conscious awareness and control.

I argue that the ritual 'acting' at Faunalia allows participants to engage in 'shadow work' through embodied performance, even though their experiences may not be entirely articulated linguistically as part of the cognitive, conscious self. This understanding draws on Jessica Benjamin's (1998) psychoanalytic analysis of 'acting' as an 'intermediate position between unconscious and conscious', Victor Turner's (1969) analysis of liminality in ritual, Carl Einstein's (Pan 2001) understanding of ritual as creating aesthetically mediated relationships and Alexander (2008) conception of 'iconic consciousness'. In this chapter I do not examine Jung's theory of the shadow in detail. Rather, I focus on the ritual experiences of participants that are interpreted as 'shadow work', and the social processes that shape these experiences.

Ritual is quite different to the therapeutic practice of psychoanalysis because its primary aim is not the transformation of cognitive self-understandings. Benjamin (1998: xiv) notes that Freudian psychoanalysis aims to 'bring the inarticulate subject to speech'. This is different to the aim of rituals such as those at Faunalia, which aim to transform emotions, somatic habits and iconic consciousness through participation in ritual. Cognitive understandings are transformed, and some aspects of the shadow are brought to consciousness, but this is only part of what is important to participants, and the transformation of cognitions is not the vehicle through which transformation is achieved. The primary aim is to work symbolically with those aspects of the self that may be in the shadow. Participants at Faunalia hope that through working ritually, aesthetically, performatively and symbolically with the shadow, it will cause less harm and interpersonal tension.

Huskinson (2004) points out that Freud and Jung have quite different understandings of the unconscious. For Freud the unconscious is a reflection of the conscious mind, its repressions and residues, and has no independent autonomy. Freud prioritizes the consciousness of the ego. In contrast, Jung's thought has many similarities to a Nietzschean understanding that the contents of the unconscious are 'wholly unlike those of consciousness and are ungraspable by the ego' (Huskinson 2004: 1). From this perspective the unconscious can function autonomously from the conscious mind. Nietzsche's approach, as noted earlier in the discussion of iconic consciousness: 'recognizes other sources of knowledge considered irrational, such as emotion, imagination and intuition' (Huskinson 2004: 1).

This has major implications for the aim of therapeutic practice, and for understanding ritual, because symbolic language in which meanings are not fully articulated can be an important part of personal development:

> The difference between the sign and the symbol is significant in that the former is a conscious construct – a fixed reference that conceals something knowable – whereas the latter is in part conscious and in part unconscious – a dynamic living entity that expresses something that is not fully graspable. (Huskinson 2004: 1)

Enlightenment culture is uncomfortable with irrationality[1] and half-conscious forms of understanding characteristic of aesthetic and iconic consciousness. Enlightenment culture, like Freud, 'prefers the Apollonian world of rationality and light' (Benjamin 1988: 141). Benjamin argues that the idea of a self free from irrationality is a product of splitting in which the image of the 'good father' is split off from the dangerous mother. Benjamin challenges the view that only masculine rational authority can prevent the loss of self in a femininity of 'undifferentiated infantile bliss' (Benjamin 1988: 147). She sees this view as an ongoing outworking of the unresolved opposition in the 'Western tradition – between rationalism and romanticism, Apollo and Dionysus' (Benjamin 1988: 147). Rather, the symbolic feminine, like 'real mothers in our culture', contributes to the creation of independence. It is the maintenance of the tension between independence and dependence that is the basis for a strong self. Benjamin argues that the healthy, strong self engages in relationship with both the rational and irrational other, seeing both of these as parts of self and other.

Benjamin does not discuss the concept of the shadow. However, her psychoanalytic approach contains some similar concepts, emphasizing tension, paradox and acceptance of irrational aspects of the self. The process of mutual recognition, that Benjamin describes as holding the self and other in tension involves including both same and different, rational and irrational. This can clearly be applied to participants' relationships with deities such as Hades and Persephone. Similar processes of balance and tension in relationship are discussed by Jung and Nietzsche. Both Nietzsche and Jung see the self as a combination of Apollonian and Dionysian aspects. Huskinson describes a Jungian and Nietzschean approach in this way:

> I shall argue that, for Nietzsche and Jung, the goal or height of human health and potential is the realization of the whole self, which they refer to as the 'Ubermensch' and 'Self' respectively. This achievement is marked by creativity, which is achieved by the cultivation and balance of all antithetical psychological impulses – both rational and irrational – within the personality, and it is in this sense that I shall refer to the whole self as a union of opposites. (Huskinson 2004: 3)

When participants at Faunalia say they are engaging in 'shadow work', they are drawing on a tradition of thought that is represented by people such as Jung, Nietzsche, Jessica Benjamin, Richard Kearney, Carl Einstein and going back to the classical Paganism of the Greek tragic poets. In this tradition of thought the opposition between Dionysian and Apollonian, rational and irrational, feminine and masculine, aesthetic and scientific, self and other, are reformulated. The two opposing tendencies are held in tension. The experience of tension or paradox is the place where healthy responses to death, suffering and radical otherness are to be found. 'When the opposites fail to synthesize, or when only one opposite in the pair is present, Nietzsche and Jung warn of impending psychological damage' (Huskinson 2004: 3). Shadow work is both an engagement with repressed parts of ourselves and an engagement in relationship with others who represent and evoke such shadows. The rituals at Faunalia facilitate this process.

To interact with the shadow side of one's self takes courage (Earl 2001). It is challenging and difficult. However, it is also rewarding:

> **Harrison:** I think my willingness to face difficult paths and to face other challenges comes from the feminine side of me. Particularly if you take the Jungian thing that the feminine sense is a buried sense that you have to bring out and nurture. Because that was not a natural way for me to be. The ability to face those difficult things . . . the idea of doing unpleasant things or being brave was not particularly appealing. But I think doing magic and putting myself in positions where I was forced to look within and see what was really in there and all the shit as well as all the good bits, the more I did that, the more courage I got to do it, to look within and find out what was in there and accept it. Not [to] allow it if I didn't think it was appropriate, but to accept that it was there and to accept myself even if it took courage. That courage generalized into other areas, [such as at] work.

Harrison's reflections draw together a number of the themes of this chapter. He accepts parts of himself that are unpleasant, although that does not mean that he allows them to dominate. He seeks to understand his feminine side as integral to himself, and as empowering, pointing to his magical and ritual practice as enabling this sort of self-discovery. He also argues that these changes have had a broader positive impact on how he lives his life. The shadow work of his magical practice has been an important part of Harrison's pursuit of a life with soul.

When I asked Sauvage whether he thought there were any dangers in attending Faunalia, he turned the question around, pointing to the dangers of a life without soul, when there is no 'ghost in the machine' (by 'ghost' I think he is referring to a life with soul, as I am using the term, rather than a Cartesian dualistic understanding of the self). His comments contain a mixture of implied shadow work, with those parts of himself that he had 'boxed' and 'archived' and a discourse about the discovery of authenticity, the true essential self (this theme is taken up in Chapter Six). The danger, for Sauvage, was in not working with those shadow parts of the self:

> **Sauvage:** There are dangers in life. There are dangers in not living. There are many dangers. One of them is to get some glimpse of your capacity and your potential . . . [and not] do it or you do not explore it. In my lead in to this year's Faunalia, I think that was some of what I was trying to deal with. There were so many parts of myself that I had just boxed and archived that there was not much left. I was functioning and I was operating in the world as you do, but there was no ghost in the machine. [It means that] you do not become that useful to other people, you are not being who you are. You do not feel safe to be who you are, so you become something else, [a] reflection of what others

want you to be. So you are never driven by your essence. That is the danger.

Sauvage's last few sentences describe Benjamin's concepts of mutual recognition and domination. Domination occurs when the individual becomes simply a reflection of what others demand of them. Mutual recognition requires both self-assertion, 'to be who you are', and relationships, 'become that useful to other people'. Sauvage's pursuit of an authentic self is not a rationally autonomous self, but an aesthetically mediated self in a relationship of mutual recognition. Whether it is through the rituals of Faunalia or by some other means, the danger for Sauvage is the inability to find relationships of mutual recognition that make it possible to live an authentic life.

Mortality and monsters

'Strangers, gods and monsters' speak of a 'fracture within the human psyche' (Kearney 2003: 4). Kearney suggests the temptation is to repudiate, ignore and ostracize the confronting strangeness of fears and monsters. Instead, he argues that we need to accommodate the unfamiliar and terrifying otherness of monsters and strangers: 'It is also my conviction that the project of enlightenment will remain unenlightened until it comes to terms with the strangers, gods and monsters that it has all too often ostracized or ignored' (Kearney 2003: 7). Kearney develops an approach that he terms 'diacritical hermeneutics' that draws on, and extends, Levinas, Derrida and Kristeva.

The process of 'splitting' involves separating the self into two parts, with the othered, confronting, repressed or fearful aspects of the self split off in opposition to the rest of the self (Kristeva 1991). Fears and anxieties about dying, for example, are split off and hidden away, resulting in avoidance of events and relationships that might confront us with the reality of death and dying. Benjamin (1998) argues that splitting itself is not problematic, so much as the way the devalued or feared aspects of the self are engaged:

> Splitting, then, need not be conceived in opposition to some normative ideal of the whole self, but rather as the initial form adopted by the self with respect to contradictions in feelings or apprehensions; it can either be transformed in relation to the outside other or reduce the other to a locus of the self's disowned parts. (Benjamin 1998: 97)

Structures that radically divide 'self and other' as 'good versus bad' or 'included versus excluded' are, according to Benjamin, likely to lead to

IMAGE 4.1 *Vinde costumed as a 'Fury'.*
Photo by Philippe.

problematic relationships. The aim, Benjamin suggests, is to engage the feared and split parts of self in relationship. The etiquette of relationships that Benjamin describes as creating domination and oppression in erotic relationships has many similarities to the etiquette of relationships that Carl Einstein describes in ritually mediated relationships, and which are oppressive or destructive of the other (Pan 2001). To avoid domination and oppression both Benjamin and Einstein argue we need etiquettes that involve an acceptance of the other as a valued other in and of its own right.

Sauvage describes an occurence of 'splitting' in his experience of the rituals at Faunalia: 'If you can imagine yourself split and there's another being or twin of yourself that does all the things that you don't do, or can't do . . . The path for me is to try and come together with that other being, and be friends with them. Or at least have some sort of rules of engagement.' The rituals at Faunalia help Sauvage find an etiquette for relating to those split off parts of himself, to find some 'rules of engagement'.

The 'other' that is engaged with in ritually mediated relationships is often an aspect or expression of one's self. This was the experience of many participants in the Underworld rite. Through the rite they developed new ways of relating to their own fears, sadness and suffering. These are understood as aspects of their shadow selves. 'Strictly speaking, the shadow is the repressed part of the ego and represents what we are unable to acknowledge about ourselves' (Conger 1991: 84). From this perspective a good ritual is one that is challenging and disturbing, because this means that it provides an opportunity to work with these repressed or shadow parts of their selves.

It is possible to come to a détente with the awareness of our mortality. Kearney suggests that this can be achieved through 'a working-through of loss and fear by means of cathartic imagination and mindful acknowledgement' (2003: 8). The act of mourning is a way of learning to live with the seemingly unbearable aspects of being human. While Kearney's discussion in this quote relates to the experience of evil, it applies equally to our experience of death, dying and suffering, as Kearney himself argues below:

> One of the wisest responses to evil is, on this count, to acknowledge its traumatizing effects and work them through (*durcharbeiten*) as best we can. Practical understanding can only redirect us towards action if it has already recognized that some element of alterity most always attaches to evil, especially when it concerns illness, horror, catastrophe or death. No matter how prepared we are to make sense of evil we are never prepared enough. That is why the 'work of mourning' is so important. (Kearney 2003: 103)

Kearney goes on to emphasize the role of narrative imagination that allows the unspeakable pain of suffering to be rendered in poetry, testimony, literature and other forms. This allows us to wrestle with such monsters, and render them less fearful, and to engage with them in an ethical and transformative way.

Speaking and narrative are important at Faunalia, particularly in the ritual debriefings. However, following Carl Einstein and Victor Turner's analysis of myth and ritual, I suggest that rituals primarily engage understanding on an aesthetic, somatic and iconic level. When René was 'marked for death', she did think about it, but her primary response was emotional and embodied: 'It got my stomach and my solar plexus going.' Leanan similarly reported that when she was lying down in the mock grave: 'It was a real experience of the heart.'

Constructive and soulful relationships are achieved through letting the 'other be other', so that the 'self may be itself again' (Kearney 2003: 8). Rather than demonizing the other, horrified and fearful, Kearney argues that we need to engage in a 'hospitable' acceptance of the difficult, fearful and confronting nature of the 'other'. The task here is to avoid projecting our own fears on to the other, so that we are 'less likely to live in horror of the dark. For the dark is all too frequently a mask for the alterity of our own death' (Kearney 2003: 18). This is the paradox of mutual recognition: to both acknowledge the other, escaping from our repressed and projected fear of the other, but also to not assimilate ourselves into the other, or the other into ourselves:

> The other's difference must exist outside; not be felt as a coercive command to 'become' the other, and therefore not be defended against by assimilating it to self. It is here that the notion of recognition as mediated not only through identification, but through direct confrontation with the other's externality, makes a difference. (Benjamin 1998: 95)

When we fear, exclude and deny the other as an extension of the process of splitting, we are also denying aspects of ourselves. In particular, Kearney (2003), drawing on Kristeva (1991), points to the 'shadow of our own finitude' (Kearney 2003: 76). 'The phantasmatic double which returns to haunt us again and again, through the mists of troubling strangeness, is ultimately nothing other than our fear of death. This spectre of our own mortality . . . is something we cannot bear' (Kearney 2003: 76). Martha Nussbaum (2004: 17) similarly suggests that: 'human beings cannot bear to live with the constant awareness of mortality and of their frail animal bodies.'

The Underworld rite provides a controlled moment of awareness of participants' own mortality. This awareness is 'held' in the ritual process of liminal transition. The rite separates participants from everyday experiences and consciousness. They are drawn into a liminal state, where the inevitability of death and of suffering is revealed. It is in this liminal moment that participants engage in an intimate relational encounter with the stranger, the 'monster', of human mortality, of the inevitability of death. However, this moment is only transitory. The ritual ends, and participants are returned to everyday consciousness, but with a renewed and transformed understanding of death and suffering. It is the need for transformed understandings of death that leads Grimes (2000: 282) to call for rituals that provide 'a renewed mythologizing of death and the dead'.

One of the reasons that some Pagans, among others, find Faunalia unsettling is because people are afraid that they may be overwhelmed by the shadow. They fear that acknowledging death and suffering may somehow give grief and suffering more power in their lives. Discussing the characters of Jekyll and Faust, Stevens (1991: 28) makes the point that: 'The anxiety which haunts all such stories is not so much a fear of being caught as fear that the evil side will get out of control.' However, to work with the shadow does not mean that participants embrace all that the shadow represents.

A number of participants voiced fears that the ritual might generate emotions that would 'get out of control'. One person was afraid of having an anxiety attack when lying in the grave. Another was afraid she might be overwhelmed by emotion as she recalled the recent death of a loved one. However, in both cases the participants' fears were not realized. While they did experience anxiety and grief, they were able to complete the ritual and as a consequence felt their fears lose some of their power. René makes precisely this point when she says about her experience of the Underworld rite that it 'showed me that I did not have that fear [of dying] anymore.'

From this perspective, it is not dying, in and of itself, which is problematic. Rather, difficulties arise when people become so afraid of dying that it causes them to act in problematic ways. They may be unable to talk about death and dying, or they may be deeply traumatized by the death of one they love. As John Sandford (1991: 21) puts it: 'So the shadow, no matter how troublesome it may be, is not intrinsically evil. The ego, in its refusal of insight and its refusal to accept the entire personality, contributes much more to evil than the shadow.'

In other words, the fear of engaging with the shadow is intrinsic to the nature of the shadow self. To some extent this is healthy. It is not good to be continually overwhelmed by grief. However, when grief and mortality become repressed, this can be problematic. Ritual provides a way of safely engaging with grief, suffering and the awareness of our mortality. It provides some 'rules of engagement' (Sauvage). The ritual process controls the moment of awareness so that it does not overwhelm the participant.

Engaging with the shadow means to discipline or negotiate with those urges, fears and desires that exist within the shadow (Whitmont 1991). Repression involves refusing to acknowledge desires and fears as part of our being. Shadow work acknowledges those fears and desires and then chooses how to respond to them, either by accepting them, or by disciplining and negotiating with them. The acknowledgement of a desire or fear does not mean that individuals then feel compelled to act on them. Quite the contrary.

Pagan moral ontology

Classical Greek literature is another 'symbolic resource' that contemporary Pagans at Faunalia draw on to inform their ritual practice. It contains a moral ontology that reluctantly accepts death and suffering. Reading such literature, and contemporary exponents of similar ideas such as Nietzsche, does change some participants' self-understandings. Cognitive changes to beliefs about death and suffering are bound up with embodied, somatic and aesthetic forms of consciousness

Pagan moral ontology accepts death and suffering as inevitable and unavoidable aspects of a good life. The Greek myth of Persephone's descent into the underworld explains death and suffering as ordained by the Gods. Demeter's grief causes Winter, but Demeter is also a goddess of fertility and agriculture. Persephone must spend half her time with Hades and half her time with Demeter. The implication is that if suffering and unpleasant choices are part of the life of the Gods, they are also part of the life of humans. While some participants at Faunalia believe in reincarnation, none mentioned a belief in a realm where suffering ceases to exist. Paganism is a this-worldly religion which embraces, celebrates and ritually enacts both the joys and suffering of an earthly life.

Nussbaum contrasts the view of the Greek tragic poets with the Platonist and Kantian commitment to rational self-control defined by: 'the aspiration to make the goodness of a good human life safe from luck through the controlling power of reason' (Nussbaum 1986: 3). 'Luck' translates the Greek *tuche*, which refers to the passivity of humans in the face of greater powers that shape human fate. Drawing on the ideas of the classic Greek tragic poets, Nussbaum argues humans are both agents and passive recipients of what life gives them – they are inevitably at the mercy of luck. This means that suffering and death are inevitable and integral parts of the good life. It is impossible to completely escape from them, or completely control them.

This understanding is similar to Nietzsche's injunction: *amor fati* (love one's fate), also derived from the Greek tragic poets. 'The Nietzschean lover of fate not only endures what is necessary in life, but chooses to welcome this necessity even when it frustrates, disappoints, or causes pain' (Ruti 2006: 214). Ruti suggests that Nietzsche's vision tends towards elitism in his demand for absolute indifference to those aspects of life that are beyond our control. Rather than loving our fate, Ruti suggests it is better to say that one should reluctantly accept the path of sorrow:

> What Nietzsche shows us is that this course of individuation remains incomplete without the individual's ability to process pain. Even if existential lightness is the good toward which the noble moves, Nietzsche makes it clear that this lightness can only be attained through a familiarity with the sadder and more solemn side of existence. This implies that to the extent that our culture insists on contentment, and tries to weed out the slightest trace of sadness, it might actually be hindering the psyche's ability to reach its full potential. (Ruti 2006: 217)

According to Ruti's psychoanalytic view, humans should accept sadness, suffering and death, as an inevitable part of life. Indeed, mental well-being may be linked to the ability to incorporate suffering rather than attempting to overcome it: 'Melancholia may be a necessary precondition of the psyche's ability to grow in the sense that a psyche that has never known sadness is not necessarily a well-rounded or fully realized psyche' (Ruti 2006: 158). Drawing on Melanie Klein's psychoanalytic theory, Alford

(1997: 72) similarly argues that the healthy experience of suffering does not so much embrace it, as reluctantly accept it: 'Reluctant acceptance [is] the path that passes through sorrow, mourning, tears, and grief'. This involves mourning our own mortality, and that of those we love, but also involves a reluctant acceptance of 'a world that is filled with malevolence, suffering, and loss, a world of almost incalculable sorrow' (Alford 1997: 72).

The Western obsession with rational solutions to all problems, assumes that suffering can be eliminated, and that happiness is the ideal state. A number of commentators on the current epidemic of depression and related mental health disorders in the West have argued that it stems in part from a pathologization of sadness (Ahmed 2010, Horowitz and Wakefield 2007, Blazer 2005, Karp 1996). Sadness used to be considered a normal part of a healthy life. It has been transformed into a mental health issue that requires treatment. Allan Kellehear (2007) suggests our discomfort with death and dying has led us to treat those who are dying with less respect than they deserve. Morgan and Wilkinson (2001) further suggest that while sociology has often provided social explanations for suffering it has failed to address the existential and ethical dimensions of the experience and meaning of suffering.

Contemporary culture has lost many of the symbols that made sense of the existential and ethical dimensions of suffering and death. Fred Alford (1997) suggests that Alasdair MacIntyre's *After Virtue* (1981) should be read as arguing that contemporary culture has not simply lost the narrative unity that is the basis for values and virtue. Contemporary Western culture has also lost the sense of tragedy: 'It has lost the narrative resources to make sense of the experience of victimhood, above all the dread of what it is to be truly human' (Alford 1997: 80). The Underworld rite provides symbols, a myth and a ritual experience that engages with these existential and ethical dimensions of suffering and death.

> Suffering and hardship cannot be avoided; death is inevitable; virtue is not always rewarded. Justice may not be done in the short turn, although eventually wrongs will be righted, even if many innocent people will suffer. There is no hope of universal redemption. (Lefkowitz 2003: 235)

Most of the Pagans at Faunalia share a world view similar to that of classical Greek Paganism describe by Lefkowitz. The world view offers a constrained form of hope, a way of making sense of our place in the world and what we can 'reasonably expect' of our lives. This vision may seem somewhat pessimistic and fatalistic, but this is only half the story.

The classical and contemporary Pagan world view is one of constrained agency, rather than pessimism. Lefkowitz (2003: 235) notes that for the classical Greeks: 'even within the confines of their fate, mortals still have choices.' It is precisely a sense of constrained agency that some participants at Faunalia report discovering in the Underworld rite. Perhaps one of the most significant examples of constrained agency is how people respond to the inevitability of their mortality. In contrast to the fear and frustration that many people experience when faced with death, participants at Faunalia report a circumspect acceptance.

Sinead, who was one of the last to be taken on the Underworld journey reported that what she took out of the rite was: 'the sense that death is something we have no control over.' The context of this statement suggests that for Sinead this is simply something that one must accept. She is not angry about this, nor is she entirely happy. Rather, it is something that she reluctantly accepts, perhaps with a shrug of her shoulders. Sauvage gives a sense of his experience of waiting to be taken into the underworld that goes beyond fatalism to a celebration of the life that we have. As he was waiting to be abducted he was at first envious of other people's experiences, but then began to see things differently:

> **Sauvage:** I thought, well, you do what you do. Everybody is living. Everybody is experiencing what they are experiencing, so just lay back and be a part of it. Laugh with those that are laughing and chant and scream when the need arises, and in between that, just breathe deeply and be aware of your own mortality. And wonder when it will come. I really loved the way they just weaved in and grabbed somebody and weaved out, and nonetheless, we were all just there.

Sauvage takes stock of his situation and chooses to embrace it. Pagan moral ontology encourages precisely this choice in the face of the certainty of suffering and death. The Underworld rite gave people a confidence to live with the awareness of their mortality and the experience of suffering in their lives. Pagan understanding of time tends to be less teleological than Christian and enlightenment understanding (White 1967). Pagans tend to focus on celebrating the present, the cycles of the seasons and the events of this life, rather than being concerned with what might happen in the future.

Classical Greek culture is a 'symbolic resource' that many contemporary Pagans engage with in the development of their rituals. Several people demonstrated an awareness of this literature. Louis, who wrote the Underworld liturgy, had read extensively in the classical Greek sources. Ruth noted that 'ancient Greek mythology [is] . . . right up my alley.' Classical Greek literature contains a radically different moral ontology to that of both Christianity and enlightenment thought. Reading this literature may have changed some people's self-understandings. However, it is the ritual performance that engages with the emotional and somatic aspects of consciousness that has a more significant impact for most people at Faunalia.

Emotional authenticity

Finding a life with soul allows people to bear seemingly unbearable suffering. There are many aspects of life that can be experienced as unbearable: the failure to live up to traditional family expectations, the choice to leave a marriage and the sadness of the loss of a loved one. The rituals at Faunalia contribute to the ability of participants to find creative and resilient ways of responding to these aspects of their lives. As Harrison puts it:

> **Harrison:** [Participants need] the understanding that it is OK to be afraid, but that there are ways of relating to [fear], that may be more creative than just avoidance. They need to have the confidence in their own ability to face their fears and deal with them . . . with a certain amount of support.

Harrison's argument echoes the Lacanian (1977) understanding utilized by Ruti (2006). For Ruti, to live a life with soul is to have the ability to live with 'lack' – the sense of alienation that is impossible to resolve:

> The goal of analysis for Lacan is not to fill or cover over the subject's sense of alienation, but rather to translate this alienation into something that can be meaningfully articulated; 'healing' is therefore not about suturing the subject's sense of lack, but rather about teaching it to transform this lack into a manageable psychic reality. (Ruti 2006: 15)

In this understanding the world is inherently dissatisfying, alienated and marked by 'lack'. 'Lacan's response is to insist that it is only by embracing its lack, and by learning to cope with its alienation (and the suffering that this alienation may generate) in constructive ways, that the subject can begin to realize its potential' (Ruti 2006: 209).

Faunalia provides participants with emotional resources to live with their fears. Phoebe described how other members of the Pagan community would avoid her after the first couple of Faunalia festivals. She and the other organizers of the festival were confused by this response, but then began to understand what was going on:

> **Phoebe:** We realized from the feedback to the first and second Faunalia that their views were that way. But that is OK, that is OK. It did not stop us from going [to Pagan events]. I think it is fear, but that is like with life. You fear what you do not understand. In many ways Baphomet and Faunalia are precisely about expressing and experiencing those fears, aren't they? Now Baphomet is a representation of those fears. So it is not surprising. I have always said, Faunalia is not for everyone.

Phoebe feels excluded by some other Pagans. She suspects this is because of her involvement with Faunalia. She accepts this as part of the way things are. It is 'ok'. She still participates and engages with the broader Pagan community. Baphomet helps her make sense of this experience. She understands that people are afraid of what they do not understand, and that this might cause them to be reticent. Phoebe has learnt to cope not only with her own fears but also with the fears of others as these impact on her.

Faunalia confronts participants with a wide range of emotions: fear, sadness, suffering, desire, pleasure, aggression and passion, to name a few. The Lacanian emphasis on 'lack' does not cover this breadth of emotions. However, the process is similar. In each case, the rituals at Faunalia encourage participants to understand and accept their emotions, to make them manageable, so that they can live with them in constructive ways and fulfil their potential. Harrison describes his work with his emotions in this way:

> **Harrison:** When I was younger, I went through a stage where I pretty much learned to cut off from my feelings. The only feelings I really allowed myself to feel was horniness and aggression. When I started doing magic I learned over a long period of time to allow myself to feel other feelings. To feel anxious and to acknowledge that. To feel fear and acknowledge it. To acknowledge that I was not a particularly physically brave or courageous person and to be OK with that and still learn to do things. To not let that fear stop me from doing things. To learn to love, to open up to love and the danger and the potential for pain that that can cause, and that that is OK. A sense of compassion. I do not have much of an intellectual grasp on the idea of compassion but I do empathize with people, and I try and acknowledge that without getting swamped by it.

Participants at Faunalia typically aim to acknowledge their feelings, but not to be controlled by them. Dale made this point when discussing fear, as expressed in a mantra he repeated to Cerberus during the Underworld rite: 'I must not fear. Fear is the mind killer. Fear is that little death that will consume us. I must face my fears and let it pass through me.' The quote is from the science fiction novel *Dune* (Herbert 1965: 123). The first line suggest that fear is something that Dale does not want to feel: 'I must not fear.' However, his practice is more complex, as the last line encourages him to face his fear and let it flow through him. Lewis made a similar point about sadness and fear as he sat for an hour with his girlfriend during one of the rituals:

> **Lewis:** You know, I sat down and listened. She would cry and I would be there. Evoking, bringing it out, bringing out the cry, the cry is your

nurture, it is your mother. To say that, hey, this is very important to do this, and just let it come out, let it manifest. Bring out your fears. Be kind to yourself and nurture yourself because you are validating these feelings. They are real.

Participants aim to engage with their feelings in a similar way to which they engage with Pagan deities. They honour them, respect them, evoke them and learn to live with them. They do not feel compelled to always obey them, but neither do they seek to banish them or destroy them. In doing so, they consider themselves to be embracing their 'authentic' emotional self.

Conclusion

The challenge of the Underworld rite is to develop an etiquette for relating to mortality and suffering. This etiquette is developed through an aesthetic, somatic, iconic form of knowing that is somewhere between conscious and unconscious. Death is experienced, and represented to participants by a mock grave, Charon (the boatman who takes them into the underworld), Cerberus (the dog who guards the gateway to the underworld), Hephaestus (the god of fire), Persephone, Hades and Hekate. These represent the challenges of death, dying and suffering. Through the ritual, participants discover ways of engaging with these challenges. These relational encounters, made possible through the rituals, shape people's orientations towards, and understandings of, each other and the world.

Myth and ritual draw participants into shared ways of seeing the world. They do this by drawing participants into shared ways of relating to 'the other'. In this case, death and suffering are presented as inevitable parts of life, the subject of reluctant acceptance. The Underworld rite creates aesthetically structured relationships to 'the other' of death and suffering. It is quite possible for these shared meanings to be resisted, ignored or found irrelevant. This was the case for Adele, as described in Chapter Three, for whom the ritual did not work because, in her understanding, she did not believe in an underworld. However, for most participants the reality or not of the underworld is a peripheral concern. They allow themselves to be drawn by the ritual into an aesthetically mediated relationship with suffering and death.

Ritual at Faunalia is a collective and aesthetically mediated experience of 'mutual recognition' (Benjamin 1988). Participants recognized death and suffering as parts of life, but at the same time, define themselves as separate and autonomous from them. The ritual provides a way of making sense of, and living with, the inherent tensions in this relationship. René's response to being 'marked for death' is a good example of this process: 'I went, "I'm not ready. I don't know if I want to be marked for death, hang on a minute" [laughs].' Once she was in the circle, waiting to be abducted she was 'still quite reticent to go through the process.' As she watched people being 'stolen from the circle' she began to examine her own feelings about death. She chose to go through with the ritual, and in that choice found that she was not afraid of death any more: 'I do not embrace death, but I am not afraid to die.'

In Carl Einstein's (Pan 2001) terms, the Underworld rite represented death and suffering as things of value in and of themselves. The ritual did not attempt to overcome, control or deny death and suffering. The ritual had a performative mimetic function that mediated moral relationships to the confronting nature of death and suffering. It encouraged participants to discover strategies for living with death and suffering in ways that respected them.

The rituals at Faunalia bring participants into relationship with deities such as Hades, Persephone and Baphomet. These deities have many confronting qualities associated with death, the inevitability of suffering, and sexual otherness and transgression. The rituals are designed to present these deities, and the aspects of life that they represent, to participants as an 'other' with whom participants enter into relationship. These deities do not simply represent the values and interests of the collective, as Durkheim (1976) would have it; they also represent the shadow self that confronts participants, often with difficult aspects of their lives and the world around them. Participants engage these deities in a collective ritual of mutual recognition.

Vignette: René

René is a 33-year-old single parent with two children under ten years. She lives in a regional city and is studying health science. She first became interested in Paganism about five years ago when she was in her late twenties.

I was making aromatherapy gifts one Christmas and investigating stuff on the internet. I kept coming across these witchy sites, talking about Wicca, talking about Witchcraft. Reading a little bit about those was like reading something about myself. So instead of me finding something where I was trying to squeeze myself into it, this could have been written about me. At that point a light bulb went on in my head, and I thought, 'I need to learn more about this'.

Through the internet I got onto a couple of mailing lists and e-groups, and started making some connections with other people who considered themselves Pagan. I kept finding so many things that I had in common with them, and so many of their practices really fitted in with the place I wanted to take myself to.

The first time I ever came face to face with other Pagans was a Pagans in the Pub meeting. Everyone was bringing along books that they were talking about, and we met upstairs in a pub. We sat around talking about Pagan literature, which I knew nothing about. I had rocked up in a white shirt and a purple skirt, and looking very blonde and out of place, and they are all in black with their big pentagrams, and I am sitting there thinking, 'What the hell am I doing here? Who are these people?' It was a whole new world opening up to me and redefining how I thought about people and my experiences, my thought patterns.

A lot of the old stereotypes were suddenly being blown wide open. I was having to rethink how I looked at people and how I experienced people. [I began] looking at people as individuals, rather than according to some label. Being able to look at someone who calls themselves a Witch or a Pagan, and not finding any negative connotation with it. They were people just like me who believe just what I believe in, but they happened to call themselves something different.

René began attending a local coven. The dancing and the drumming and the energy was something I had never experienced before. It was a mind-blowing experience for me. To actually start with energy on that level, that was pretty much the first time I ever did feel the energy rise. [Practising Witchcraft changed me] quite profoundly actually.

I had not been spiritual for about ten years prior to that, and suddenly I was rediscovering myself as a spiritual being. [I was] raised Catholic. [In my] early twenties I read some of Barbara Theiring's works. I walked away from her books, going, Jesus was such a phenomenal person, but that is what he was, a person. As soon as I stopped believing in Jesus as God, I had to go, 'well, that means I am not a Christian, so what the heck am I?' I lost my label at that point. I was married not long after and had a baby, so my life got caught up in the mundane and I really did just put all matters of the spiritual on the shelf. I did not go there at all.

[Through Witchcraft] I rediscovered my spirituality. I rediscovered my connection with spirit and that sense of being part of something much bigger. Not just being part of the physical or mundane.

[Rediscovering my spiritual self through Witchcraft] ended my marriage. My marriage had been troubled for several years. I was married for seven years all up. The last three years of that, we were in significant trouble. Reconnecting to spirit, opening my mind and my heart to something bigger than me, and looking for deeper meaning and greater purpose – basically I realized that I was worth more than what I was putting up with. Which is not to say that my husband was a bad person. Just that we had grown apart on our pathways and our time had ended with each other. But I was still holding on out of fear and out of insecurity. All these other things, and getting connected with energy again, made me realize that I was not being true to myself. I was not treating myself properly.

Once I had come to that conclusion . . . I ended our marriage. That has been one of the cleverest things I ever did. I was terribly unhappy, and the growth that I have experienced on a personal level since then has just been huge and has taken me in all sorts of fabulous directions.

René quickly took on a leadership role in her coven. [As a consequence] I was given the opportunity to act as the priestess in a ritual where normally that would be taken on by someone far more experienced. Even though it took me some years to really fully develop those skills, the experiences I had along the way, [such as] as being a vessel for deity, were personality changing for me. That was part of the process and the healing as a woman after the breakdown in my marriage and going through this kind of 'no self-esteem whatsoever' to being able to say 'I hold the divine within me'. I gained a new respect for myself. I really started to grow as a person. I became stronger and I became braver, and I treated myself with more respect.

Right from the word go, we worked skyclad, which was very challenging for me. A woman with no self-esteem and a lot of body image problems being asked to work skyclad? It is one of those things where, when you are brave enough to make that step, you realize that the hurdle is actually bigger in your mind than it is in reality, once when you get to the other side of it. It encourages you to not be so afraid of taking a risk, or of things that appear to be bigger than they are.

Six months after beginning to practice as a Witch, René went to her first Faunalia. She was asked to play a key role in the opening ritual. [I was] really confronted by the base energy stuff and the sexual energy that was happening, [and] the whole Baphomet, the whole reclaiming of the Witches' sabbat. This was all so alien to me, and I had never worked with energy at that level before. I found it really confronting. Even on that first night. I had only worked skyclad with four people in the room. Now I am faced with the prospect of standing on an altar, naked, with 80 people in the [circle]. It was terrifying, absolutely terrifying. I was not sure if I could go through with it. I felt so inferior to so many of these other fabulous people who had so much more experience and knowledge than me. I am this rank amateur who knows nothing. And yet, here I am going to be priestess for the night.

[Our ritual] went off really smoothly and everything just fell into place. Then it was my turn. Everyone else was still robed at this point. So it was my turn to strip down and to get up behind the veils. There was just this complete sense of isolation. I could not see anything, I could not hear anything except the music, and that sounded so far away from me. Every part of me was shaking. I just opened myself up to it. I just let myself go with it. When they finally parted the veils and let me step down through them, these fabulous women were coming up to me, asking me for a blessing. It was such a humbling and amazing experience because I had been the vessel for deity to come through and touch these people, despite my own insecurities, despite my own inexperience, and it was such an amazing experience for me. It profoundly changed me. When that [deity] energy fills you, you feel beautiful and you feel strong and you feel wise and you feel wild and it just fills you on every level. It gives you a taste of what life can be like if you can just embrace what you have inside you. It goes 'Wow, I am special, I am amazing, I can do this stuff!' Then for other people to also recognize that and to tell you. That little inferior part of you that's going: 'Oh, I am fat and I am old and I am past it and I am hopeless and I am a failure.' That voice doesn't have the same strength any more. Eventually, the more you work with these powerful energies, that little voice fades away and you just do not hear it any more. And then, the way you carry yourself and the way you treat yourself, and the way other people perceive you, it changes.

It is important to see the truth in yourself but not get to that point where you want to stamp your foot and demand special attention or anything like that. It is a humbling experience as well to be able to share that with other people, to bring through energy like that and share it. It is as much outside of yourself as it is inside of yourself.

[After that experience at my first Faunalia] the next time I stepped back into ritual, I didn't step in with my tail tucked between my legs. I stepped in with my chin up. The more confidence with which you approach something, the better you are at it. As a ritualist, it made me much more confident.

I think it changed the way I related [to my kids] because it helped me to grow and become more confident as a person, to trust my own judgement, to respect my own vision, to give myself the same benefit of the doubt that I give other people. Yeah, it made me a stronger parent. It gave me more strength to parent [in the way] I believe is the right way. It gave me the impetus to go out there and learn new skills, and not just sit hiding in the corner, to actually acknowledge that I needed better parenting skills and to go out there and find them. It also stopped me feeling guilty about the fact that my marriage had broken down. I had taken all the responsibility on myself. I was happy to acknowledge my share of the responsibility, but I was not prepared to take it all on. I stopped making excuses for myself and disempowering myself with regard to my children and with regard to me. Because I was more able to take a stand and say what was OK and what was not OK for me.

[At my second Faunalia] we had no firewood, there was not enough food at that Faunalia, a lot of people went hungry or did not get fed at all. It was not the best organized event, that one.

The Baphomet [rite] was very, very challenging for me. Some of it because of personal stuff going on . . . [Also] because the Catholic in me was really struggling with it. It was not something I had found any personal resolution of in my past. The first couple of Baphomet rituals that I did, I thought were stupid, because I thought, 'this is just dumb'. That whole thing about fighting against the whole Catholic thing. How dark is that? I had a lot of this stuff going on in my head. Then getting caught up in the energy, and doing things like kissing women, which I had never done before. That came out for me in the Baphomet. It was a really safe place for me to explore my own sexuality and experience some things that normally I would not get to experience, and then go away and think about how that impacted upon my life and upon my psyche.

[At] this most recent Faunalia . . . I had no trouble. I had had two years away of learning and growing, and doing more magical work and developing as a person. When I came back to it this time, even though I was expecting to do my old thing of taking 24 hours to get into it and then being OK, and feeling challenged by the Baphomet, none of that happened this time round. Because I had worked through that stuff. I'd not realized I had until I actually was confronted with it again and found that it is something that I have been able to move through, thanks to the previous years' Faunalias. I have been able to let go of the issues that were remnants of my childhood and remnants of my upbringing. That has been quite powerful for me because I feel like I have taken yet another step forward as an adult. And come out of it, come out the other end.

Baphomet was terrifying in the first instance. Baphomet symbolized everything that I was taught to hate in my childhood. The whole goat's head. I remember [the Baphomet priestess's] body paint was very black, the whole lower part of her body was black. The big goat's head and the flame on the head, and the energy, the huge energy that she carried with her, it was terrifying. I was so confronted by it. I felt like a little girl and I am hanging onto friends, going, 'oh God, I am not sure I am ready for this'.

The Faunalia energy, it is challenging. It is always profound. The things that develop out of it. It is almost like life says, 'Are you ready for this?' If you are ready for this, then you have got to go out there and make it happen, and not just [hope it will] fall into place. Make it happen and then you will be able to reap the benefit. Going into it mindlessly, you just do not reap the benefits, but going into it in a directed and proactive way means that what comes out of it on the other side is so much more powerful in your life.

What do you think the world needs to know about Faunalia? The world needs to know that sometimes judging things without experiencing them is one of the dumbest things you can do. Closing a door before you have even looked to see what is on the other side of it. Shutting the curtains on the view that is through the window without looking at the view first [and then criticizing the view] is just closing your mind.

[Faunalia] offers an experience of group ritual that I think is very, very rare. Raising energy with three or four people in an intimate coven setting is magical. When you get eighty people together, raising energy, it is so amplified, that feeling. Faunalia is an opportunity for people to experience energy on a grand scale.

There is danger in it when it is not handled correctly. You would not give a child matches. Matches are not inherently dangerous, but if they are used inappropriately or by someone who does not know what they are doing with them, they could get hurt. Energy is like that too. Energy is just as much a weapon as it is a benefit. When somebody goes into a space like Faunalia, and they are either unprepared, too inexperienced or too closed to the possibility of what is available to them there, then I could see how they could get damaged. But the thing about Faunalia is that it has safety mechanisms in place to help people make that transition safely through no matter what their level of experience, to be able to embrace the energy and embrace the ritual without coming to any harm. But again, you might go through Faunalia unscathed and be fine, but not be emotionally prepared for the energetic consequences on the other side. There is potential for harm in anything. We can never really judge whether or not it is going to be a good lesson or a bad lesson. If the world puts Faunalia in your path, it is there for a reason.

Faunalia has been some of the major highlights in my magical career. It has been a development of some awesome friendships that I have found and connections that go beyond ordinary friendships. It has been a source of personal development for me to work through major inhibitions, to work through major hang-ups and emotional dramas of my own. It has given me the scope to grow as a person. It has given me the scope to grow as a priestess. It has given me the opportunity to have experiences of energy and of magic that are unlike anything else that I have ever had. I hold the Faunalia experience very, very dear to my heart, and that despite any overflow of consequences. Despite my own emotional [responses], [I am sometimes surprised and think] 'oh my God, that happens [laughs] when I am there'. I just feel so grateful and blessed to have that opportunity to grow as a person.

CHAPTER FIVE

Baphomet

A Witches' Sabbat

Male and female witches met at night, generally in solitary places, in fields or on mountains. Sometimes, having anointed their bodies, they flew, arriving astride poles or broom sticks; sometimes they arrived on the backs of animals, or transformed into animals themselves. Those who came for the first time had to renounce the Christian faith, desecrate the sacrament and offer homage to the devil, who was present in human or (most often) animal or semi-animal form. There would follow banquets, dancing, sexual orgies. Before returning home the female and male witches received evil ointments made from children's fat and other ingredients. (Ginsburg 1992: 1)

The Baphomet ritual performed at Faunalia is inspired by a desire to reclaim, and re-Paganize, the myth of the Witches' sabbat described by the early modern Christians. Drawing on historical accounts, the organizers recreate a contemporary Pagan version of the ritual. The idea has similarities to Margaret Murray's (1921) thesis that the Christian inquisitors discovered an ancient fertility religion. According to Murray, contemporary Witchcraft is a direct descendent of this ancient religion. Carlo Ginsburg (1992) presents a subtler version of the thesis. He argues that European shamanistic folk practices were reinterpreted by Christian inquisitors as evidence of the existence of a Witches' sabbat. Ginsburg contends that it is implausible that the elements of the Witches' sabbat described in the trials were entirely an invention of the inquisitors' imaginations. Although the Witches' sabbats were a fantasy, he suggests that they were based on a systematic Christian misinterpretation and diabolistic reinterpretation of a pre-existing set of folk beliefs and practices. Silverblatt (1983) presents a parallel argument that Spanish colonizers of the Andes sought to reinterpret indigenous culture as Witchcraft and Satanic. While there has been considerable academic criticism of Murray's work, and to a lesser extent Ginsburg's, the idea that the Witches' sabbat describes an ancient Pagan religious practice is taken up in a number of texts on contemporary Paganism, the most notable being the influential work of Starhawk (1979).

A quotation in the Introduction describes Harrison's motivations for creating the Baphomet rite. It is worth quoting again:

> **Harrison:** I wanted to create a rite that would challenge people's prejudices. There was a certain element of shit stirring and iconoclasm. At first it was going to be a mere Pagan revel with just a few elements drawn from the [medieval Witches'] sabbat. It would be evocative and Pagan and ecstatic. A lot of modern Paganism in my opinion is way too sanitized and inoffensive and not challenging to the status quo. I wanted to have an experience that was an emotional experience, that was moving and wonderful and magical. I got some ideas from the legend [of the Witches' sabbat. I said to myself] I will use that bit, but not that bit.

Where the Christian inquisitors sought moral self-development through the repression of the body and its pleasures, participants at Faunalia seek moral self-development through the celebration of the body and its pleasures. The Baphomet rite challenges the fear of these aspects of what it is to be human. The Christian inquisitors feared the bestial this-worldly aspects of human nature. Sex, dancing and other pleasures of the flesh were sinful. The Baphomet rite takes these pleasures, including their symbolic representation in Baphomet, and embraces them as integral aspects of what it is to be human. The ritual sacralizes bodies, sensuality, dancing and eroticism, at the same time as sacralizing fear, the animal nature of humanity and intense emotional experiences. These are all sacred aspects of Baphomet. Put another way, participants say that the ritual allows them to explore their shadow selves, finding courage to face their fears, rediscover their repressed sexual selves and develop respectful and healthier ways of relating to these aspects of themselves.

The Baphomet rite is at the heart of Faunalia. Other rituals have come and gone, but Baphomet has always been central to the festival. The deity Baphomet dates back to the medieval Knights Templar order, who were accused of blasphemously kissing the behind of Baphomet. The most commonly reproduced image of Baphomet is the nineteenth-century occultist Eliphas Levi's representation which has some similarities to the Devil of the Rider Waite Tarot cards. The deity is a hybrid on many dimensions: both male and female, human and beast, goat and bird, creator and destroyer. Baphomet represents ambiguity and complexity, a disturbing deity that symbolically resonates with the carnivalesque liminal space of Faunalia.

This chapter describes the Baphomet rite. The following chapters analyse the rite. This chapter provides a rich and evocative account of the rite in the words of the interviewees.

Pre-briefing and preparation

Saturday, the third day of the festival, commences slowly and quietly. Breakfast is at half past eight, but many arrive much later, showering before breakfast. In both the unisex shower/toilet blocks a bowl of condoms, dams and lubricants sits near the washbasins under a sign that says: 'Faunalia encourages safe sex, please use these.'

The ritual debriefing for the Underworld rite from the night before is scheduled to start at half past ten. As noted earlier, it is difficult to be precise about times because few people are concerned about noting the time. At the debriefing everyone is again encouraged to talk to one of the committee members if they have any issues or in any way feel uncomfortable with anything that has occurred. The debriefing lasts for about an hour.

After lunch a group of men and a few women walk up to the Baphomet ritual site, approximately 300 metres south of the main arena. Unlike the first Faunalia, the Baphomet rite in 2005 took place in a site among some trees further down the hill. It takes a long time to construct the ritual site. Great care is taken to ensure everything is in place, that fire safety equipment is ready and all other precautions are taken to eliminate hazards. Hessian is strung up between stakes and trees to enclose the circle, the ground is carefully swept to remove anything sharp and a central fire and four peripheral fire pots are set in place. The final touches include the addition of the ritual altar and the placement of other ritual items, although only the key ritualists are involved in this activity.

Later that afternoon participants are called to the pre-ritual workshop. The organizing committee insists that everyone is present. Each part of the ritual is clearly described to ensure everyone has enough information to make an informed choice about whether to participate. Some details are not disclosed to maintain the surprise element. Every participant is handed a length of white cloth and told to keep it with them for the ritual. Some tie it in their hair, others around their wrist or ankle. Almost no one has a pocket or handbag in which to place it. The absence of pockets and handbags is a poignant indicator of the liminality of Faunalia. Keys, money and other similar accoutrements of everyday life are not required at Faunalia. During the pre-briefing Harrison takes participants on a guided visualization where they imagine attending a Witches' sabbat. Sinead recalls this experience:

> **Sinead:** When we did the workshop briefing with Harrison, that was quite
> an interesting experience because he took us on a guided meditation

IMAGE 5.1 *The Baphomet ritual site in an early stage of preparation with Sean Scullion.*

Photo copyright Edan Mumford. Reproduced with permission.

of going to a sabbat gathering. I was very much going with it. That did start the visualization of the rite for me.

Evening is now approaching, and after a brief break and a light snack in lieu of the evening meal, the ritualists go off to prepare. Everyone else begins to put on their robes and other costumes. Despite some lingering tiredness from the previous night's exertions, participants soon find the anticipation and excitement infectious:

> Sinead: There was body painting. I got a blue crescent painted across my chest. I had also a blue crescent on my forehead as well, and blue snakes curling up my arms. I wore an Isis necklace that I am very fond of and a purple shimmy with lots of coins on, which I actually wore into the Baphomet rite. So I was topless with just a shimmy and the body paint and the necklace. I felt really comfortable with that.

The body painting becomes a group activity, with various people joining in to assist with painting. One person is painted as a cat. Sinead had modelled nude for life drawing classes as a student, so felt comfortable with the idea of performing the ritual naked. However:

> **Sinead:** Having said that, it was slightly challenging being in a big, open dining hall with blokes slathering themselves with mud and making lots of noise and [for me to] walk around in the nude with snakes on my arms, but everyone else was doing it.

Nudity at Faunalia tends to be restricted to the Baphomet rite and the period of preparation immediately prior to the rite. Although participants mentioned other moments of nudity, such as encounters in the shared amenity blocks and occasional nudity in the other rites, most people are clothed for most of the festival. In this context nudity takes on a liminal character that emphasizes the alterity of the Baphomet rite. As Sinead puts it: 'it was slightly challenging.' If nudity was common during the festival, the nudity of the Baphomet rite would lose some of its power as a liminal ritual practice. Lewis was one of the nude men having his body painted:

> **Lewis:** Carthy and I covered our bodies in [white] clay. We looked fantastic. I really enjoyed that. I love that earth sort of stuff. We dried outside with the fire cracking all the wet clay on our bodies. [We are also] creating atmosphere. We howl, chant, and then basically the night begins.

The erotic nature of the Baphomet rite is a topic of conversation for several people. Marie attended Faunalia with a group of people from her coven:

> **Marie:** There were at least two or three conversations where as a group we sat down and talked about the issue [of sexual expression during the ritual]. I think that was really healthy because it enabled people to feel that they could enter into the rite to a point where they were comfortable with it. Hopefully everyone then came out feeling that they had been respected and had explored their own boundaries to whatever extent. For some people that just meant standing during the Baphomet rite and watching. For others it meant participation.

Some couples explicitly negotiated boundaries of acceptable sexual activity during the rite. Dave, for example, had been holding hands with one woman during the weekend. It was his first time at Faunalia and he was unsure of what to expect of this woman who had been to Faunalia a few times previously. Dave asked her: 'What is likely to happen for you [in the ritual]? Are you likely to want to go off and have sex with somebody else? I want to know what to expect, so I can prepare myself for that. Because, I am monogamous. I can only have sex with one person.' The woman replied: 'Look darling, I will probably kiss and hug other people in the ritual space, but you are my chosen partner for the festival. But if you want to go off and do whatever, well that is up to you.' To which Dave responded: 'No, you are my chosen partner for the festival.' Not everyone negotiates boundaries in this explicit way, but it is common to discuss the issue.

The anticipatory excitement of this period of preparation and waiting is an important part of the rite. Dale noted both the build up of tension, and the movement into a more sensual somatic awareness that the preparatory activities create:

> Dale: There was a lot of tension before the rite. I had a shower, and I put makeup on, put my nail polish on. Black of course. I just love getting ready. [Once] I am ready, I go up to the fire, and you get warm, and you watch everybody else getting ready. I love the paint-up that goes on with it. There is this vibrancy of creativity coming through. It is a full, very thick feeling, it is wonderful. You are seeing these works of art being built on [people's bodies].

Participants assembled around the central fire waiting to be summoned. Some people started drumming while others danced. Gradually the space becomes crowded with costumed, painted and scantily clad participants, warming themselves by the large central bonfire. The waiting builds the excitement: 'And I was standing around just going, ooh, ooh yeah, pretty nervous, this is going to be full on' (Jenny). There is occasional conversation as participants prepare themselves, but for many the preparation time is the beginning of entry into a light trance state: 'And we were standing there watching the fire, and looking at each other, sinking into the right mind space' (Calvin).

The procession and elements

Eventually the participants are summoned. It is probably close to 11 p.m. They walk slowly down a path towards the ritual site. Some people drum as they walk. A chant that had been taught at the pre-briefing is repeated. One of the ritualists, who was waiting at the ritual site, describes it this way:

> Calvin: There is roughly eighty people coming up the path with their chant. That procession, feeling it approach was like a wave of 'here comes Baphomet'. In a way, it was like the feeling near the top of a roller-coaster. You are at a roller-coaster, you get in and you go up this really steep hill. It gets slower and slower as you go. Just near the top there's that moment of 'take a breath, it is too late to get off now, here goes, just ride the wave'.

Sinead was part of the procession and recalls a similar feeling:

> **Sinead:** I felt a really strong sense of expectation within the crowd, an energy within the crowd that was almost threatening to erupt. There was this 'mischievousness' is the best way I could describe it. All afternoon people had been cracking jokes, and high jinx going on, and it just seemed to me like there was this energy coming into the gathering, and it was building that afternoon. Then when we started to actually proceed down to the site, a couple of times it felt like the energy would almost erupt.

The visual effect of the path through the forest marked by candles is 'very striking' (Leanan). As participants approach the ritual site they pass between ritualists representing the elements of Earth, Water, Air and Fire. The elemental ritualists challenge each participant. For example, at the Fire element participants passed between two people fire twirling. 'The fire twirling was just stunning. Walking down and seeing that fire twirling was just beautiful. [An] absolutely powerful memory' (Sinead). Once they arrive at the ritual site they go through the main entrance, are welcomed and form a circle inside the hessian perimeter.

Dave and his partner entered the circle together: 'Then we went into the ritual space. My partner left her robe outside the ritual space and we both went in skyclad.' Many participants disrobe as they enter, some disrobe later in the ritual and some remain clothed for the entire rite. Leonie, for example, reported: 'Unlike some other years I kept my gear on this time. I really liked what I was wearing and I felt really good about doing that. I just see how it goes and decide whether to go naked or not.' Standing around a large bonfire with a group of 80 people who are mostly naked has a powerful impact. Even long-time participants at Faunalia and other alternative subcultures will have only rarely been in similar groups. It is profoundly liminal.

The inside of the ritual space is visually and sensorially overloaded. Late at night under a starry sky participants stand naked around a massive central bonfire surrounded by four peripheral fire pots. The site is enclosed by a hessian wall about two metres high, with banners in each cardinal direction:

> **Natasha:** [The Baphomet rite] was incredibly impressive. The atmosphere – God! I had never been anywhere as beautifully set up. And there is something about the Pagan [aesthetic], with the hay, the fires, the circle, the chanting, the people, the symbols, the cloaks, the costumes, the mud, that ancient Western magic thing that felt wonderful.

The ritual is commenced by two women and two men: 'it was interesting watching a couple of guys in see-through negligees is the best way I can describe them, and there were two women and two men. To watch them move around the circle in these feminine garments was quite beautiful.' The circle-casting utilizes many elements from the Western Witchcraft tradition, calling the quarters, creating the circle of power and other elements. However, this circle-casting is very different because it is performed widdershins and because of the centrality of Baphomet.

Trance

Most participants enter a trance state during the Baphomet rite. This ritually induced altered state of consciousness begins earlier in the evening, building during the circle-casting and reaches its climax during the ritual. The experience is deeply emotional and somatic. It is a form of 'iconic consciousness.'

> **Dale:** I really can not talk about what I do there [in the Baphomet rite] because I really do not know.
>
> **Heath:** In Baphomet I am not in my head. I do not know [where I am]. My unconscious comes through. It is a feeling rite. It is all about feeling. If you questioned it, then I do not think you could get into it.
>
> **Leonie:** Baphomet is awe inspiring. In the early part of the ritual I go into a trance. I am there and I am not there. Sort of out of my body.
>
> **Sauvage:** What do you want to know about Baphomet? Oh, I wish you were there [pause of 5 seconds].
>
> **Phoebe:** Once the energy is there and we are going through the ritual, I have a scattered memory.

Turner's (1969) concepts of liminality and communitas describe something of this experience. It also reflects the Dionysian chaotic formlessness described by Nietzsche and the sense of aesthetic experience of that which is beyond words, as described by Carl Einstein (Pan 2001). Ian explicitly linked his experience of trance to being more aware of his subconscious. He also describes some of the techniques he uses to attain trance:

> **Ian:** [In trance] people say they shift outside their body. For me it is just a moving over. This part of me is being shifted [over], and then another part of me takes over. Everything is much more clearer in a way. When you are in trance things are clearer because all our subconscious elemental kind of ideas and energies and things are fully see-able, are fully contactable. [I get into trance by doing] things – everything from breathing, deep meditation, or I'll do some form of ecstatic dancing. Before I start to go into a ritual, I'll start rocking my body and doing

light breathing. That will slowly start building me up into trance, so then I can effectively slip in [to trance in the ritual].

Similar techniques to those described by Ian are often used by many of the ritualists at other times. They are practiced at entering a state of trance. However, at Faunalia, and particularly in the Baphomet rite, the ritual environment – the enormous amount of preparation, the costumes, investment of time, rural location, the huge bonfire and the eroticism – makes it much easier to enter into trance. Natasha linked her trance experience to 'surrender' and Sinead linked hers to 'letting go'. The trance state involves a surrender to the somatic and iconic parts of self. This is facilitated by the ritual process. The ritual process also provides a structure to this experience, which might otherwise be overwhelming. The ritual takes participants into altered states of consciousness, provides a structure for their experiences while there and then safely returns participants to everyday consciousness.

Most interviewees found it extremely difficult to recount the order of events during the Baphomet rite. They experience ritually induced trance states that also mean few people attend to the details of the ritual performance. No one provided a detailed description of the early parts of the ritual. However, two chants did stick in a number of people's minds. These chants were part of the ritual after the circle-casting but prior to the appearance of Baphomet.

The bindings and beast chants

One chant focused on the pieces of white cloth that had been handed out at the ritual briefing earlier in the day. Participants held the pieces of cloth tightly around their own wrists in a symbolic binding. They then chanted: 'ignorance and oppression, fear and guilt.' This chant was repeated for some time and increased in intensity. Eventually, in their own time, participants threw their piece of cloth into the bonfire in a symbolic release from the binding influence of ignorance and oppression, fear and guilt. This binding ritual was followed by a prolonged chant of 'let the beast without awaken the beast within'.

> **Ruth:** The huge sense of liberation was like nothing I had ever experienced, nothing that I thought anyone did any more. The part of the rite where we hold our hands bound is always quite a profound part of the rite for me because no matter how much work you do, how long you live, there is still ignorance, oppression, fear and guilt rocking along. The breaking free from that, I think it is most explosive the first time. But it has not changed in the depth of profundity for

me. There is a dualism here, of the self, and also socially. On one hand there are limitations that you place on yourself through fear or wanting to be proper, good, nice, and whatever, and through that not desiring the experience of your essential self. The beast self, if we are going to go with Baphomet imagery. Then on the other hand you have got the social conditionings of, you should be this, look like this, act like this, you know, job, house, lifestyle, all that kind of thing, that really chafes. Being able to ritually toss it away is really great [small laugh]. I think even though you are going back into the same society afterwards, it is hopefully with at least more awareness of what is going on, and with more freedom to choose what to buy into and what not to. Being aware of yourself and the way you honestly feel about situations, relationships, people, environments. Going with what is right for you rather than what is perhaps expected of you. You don't always win friends that way but you get a lot better and more healthier, and the friends you do have tend to be a lot better.

Ruth's observations echo those of Sauvage in Chapter Four. I interpret these as illustrations of Benjamin's (1988) concept of mutual recognition. Self-confidence and healthier relationships with other people arise when individuals are able to escape from the oppressive and dominating forms of relationship in which they are merely echoes and reflections of what other people expect of them. This requires a confidence to separate self from other at the same time as acknowledging the dependence of self on others. For Ruth, Baphomet represents the inner shadow self with which she seeks to develop a more sophisticated relationship. Social pressures limit and constrain Ruth's 'essential' self. The ritual allows her momentary release from these pressures. Sinead provides some similar observations in her recollections of the two chants:

> **Sinead:** The bindings was quite interesting because we did the chant and then there was the let the beast without awaken the beast within. We did the actual binding. I was chanting with intent to be released, and I tried to throw the bonds off. I was quite early in throwing off and into the fire. But I threw it with such gusto that it sailed way over the fire and landed on the other side. It didn't even go in the fire. So I actually had to kind of go round the other side and deal with it. I was thinking 'tell me something I didn't know'. It is not going to be easy for me to, to be released from the binds. I definitely think that I am ignorant in some ways. Things like world affairs and there are a lot of subject areas that I feel that I should have spent more time learning about. It is my attitude towards not knowing about them that binds me. I beat up on myself for not knowing. [I should know because of my job.] That was on my mind a bit. I like to think I do not suffer that much from guilt but the Catholic is so ingrained in me. I do a lot of

apologizing to people, and I don't even know I am doing it sometimes. As I was chanting [I was thinking] it is time to let that go.

The guilt and shame described by Sinead are aspects of her shadow. They shape Sinead's actions in ways of which she is half conscious. 'Shame is fundamentally a feeling of loathing against *ourselves*, a hateful vision of ourselves through our own eyes – although this vision may be determined by how we expect or believe other people are experiencing us' (Morrison 1998: 13; original emphasis). Another way of putting this is to say that shame is failure of mutual recognition. We loathe ourselves because we believe other people also loathe us. To be released from the power of these processes is not easy. Morrison and Sinead emphasize that shame and guilt operate at an emotional and somatic level. It is through actions in this realm that Sinead hopes to obtain release from the shame and guilt that binds her.

Baphomet appears

Leanan: When Baphomet appears in the ritual, that is always a moment when everybody is awakened more. You look forward to it.

Harrison recalled the invocation of Baphomet from the first Faunalia. In that ritual he was the priest who invoked Baphomet and his actions had a significant influence on the pace and tempo of the ritual:

Harrison: It was an amazing experience as a priest of the ritual. I could feel the energy. It was like riding a tidal wave. I am trying to stay on [the wave], and I am trying to stop the wave from crashing. It was fucking nice. I felt as if the energy was just likely to go 'Poooow!' And I am [thinking], 'Wait! Wait!' 'Keep it up there, but wait, wait, wait for Baphomet.' Without saying it to everyone. Baphomet was covered [behind a cloth] so no one could see her. So I am going through the ritual, and then Baphomet comes out. There is a magic between the priestess and I when we work together. I am invoking Baphomet, and seeing the costume for the first time, the black wings and the goat mask and the torch burning, and the huge wooden cock sticking out from her groin. It went off. 'Pooow!' We danced and tranced into ecstasy. Then we all collapsed and the ritual finishes. We were just sitting round. It was freezing cold. Clumps of people huddling like penguins, rotating around to be near the fire for warmth, and sitting and sharing the wine, and it was really gentle. Everyone was just sitting around. There was no sex in the circle that year, just a very communal feeling.

In 2005 Baphomet was similarly attired and was hidden behind a curtain. The goat mask of Baphomet has a torch between the horns that is lit just prior to Baphomet appearing. The mask is a beautiful, handmade, work of art and looks exceptionally realistic. The wings and other aspects of the costume are also visually stunning. At a key point in the ritual Baphomet is summoned and appears. For the 2005 rite there were two invoking priests. Jenny, a first time participant, recalled it this way:

> **Jenny:** [The invoking priests] were like these guardians of the Baphomet. [I watched them] summon her and watched her be summoned. There are a lot of people within the circle who were yelling out things like, 'Baphomet', and you would hear mutterings, and people were doing their own kind of things. It happened so quick too. Everything was so quick and there is so much to take in that it is hard to remember exactly what went on in parts.

The 'mutterings' and yelling out 'Baphomet' by participants are not scripted. People make many such small contributions in ways that they feel are appropriate. The ritual does have a structure and script, but this is reworked and improvized during the performance on the night.

Sinead also recalled the arrival of Baphomet, and like most other first time participants, found it difficult to recall the order of events. Once revealed, Baphomet moves around the circle communing with participants. The experience of communing with Baphomet is emotional and profound. After reading this, Phoebe commented that Baphomet does not speak, but only verbalizes grunts and groans. Phoebe suggested that messages are telepathically communicated by Baphomet to participants. Communion often involves holding hands and a meeting of eyes:

> **Sinead:** The next main image is of Baphomet coming out. Remembering some of the things that went on in sequence is a bit difficult. I remember watching the red curtain. I remember thinking, based on what I have been told before, this person is going to come out with a strap-on dildo and with a goat mask on. When she emerged, I was just rooted to the spot because I believe I was watching a full-scale possession, because the way she moved was not as a human being marshals their own body. She was having difficulty walking. I remember just watching and thinking there is something else in there that is feeling that body. I was thinking this is real, full-on. So that was quite a powerful image for me. As she moved around the circle, I looked into the face. [I felt] a little bit scared. But also exhilarated at the same time. Because it was sort of like, oh shit, oh cool [short laugh]. I was wondering who she would pick out. I started thinking, oh God, is she going to come up to me. Because I started to see her sort of move around people.

Jenny: Baphomet came around the circle. When Baphomet got to me, I saw her. She actually walked past me and stopped, turned around and went, 'Oooh', and came back and grabbed my hands and it was explosive. I was shaking and crying and two people [stood] beside me. I felt hands come on my shoulders, and it was like, holy fuck! I do not know these people, they are supporting me, they can obviously see that there is some deep shit going on here.

After Baphomet has been around the circle of participants, (s)he blesses a chalice of red wine which is taken round the circle and shared by participants. For most participants this will be the first time they have drunk alcohol that day. Most people only have a few mouthfuls, but the effect is probably noticeable given that they have only eaten a light meal in the late afternoon and it is now the early hours of the morning.

Sauvage feels he has 'a bit of a bond with Phoebe'. Although he has not attended all the Faunalias he did attend the first Baphomet rite at the Pagan Mardi Gras and the first Faunalia. 'Having witnessed the passage of her involvement in Baphomet since the first one, I admire her enormously.'

Sauvage: Generally when Baphomet comes around the circle, when we make contact, I normally feel Phoebe with Baphomet there. There is still that concern element a bit. There is also caring. Which is good. The concern and caring is Phoebe. But this year I felt more Baphomet. Can I explain the . . . [feeling]? When Phoebe came around and we grabbed hands, I felt like what she was saying to me was, 'Wow! Something is in here. Have a shot'. And just went bam! There was this energy, and it just felt, well, a lot bigger than what it had done in the past. There was definitely a struggle. That was my sense of it. There was more of a struggle going on between Phoebe and Baphomet. But there was enough management there for her to go, 'Hey, check this out'. She gave me some zaps. But I sensed that she was not giving me a full load because it was probably way too big for us.

Phoebe's vignette at the beginning of Chapter Seven provides more detail of her experience of working with Baphomet. During the ritual Phoebe enters a trance state in which Baphomet shares her body: '[there is] the one container, but the two of us inside it' (Phoebe).

While there are some other semi-scripted aspects to the ritual, such as the feast of the beast, and the ending of the rite, from this point onwards the ritual becomes much more free-form and improvized. Music begins to be played and people dance, some sit in a corner, others stand. People have a variety of interactions. Most participants are naked, in a state of trance, deeply emotional and have an extraordinarily heightened sense of excitement. Many of those who had not disrobed at the commencement of the rite decide to disrobe now.

Calvin: A lot of people come in wearing minimal, if any, gear. Most people seem to lose their gear at about the stage that Baphomet's done a circle, and it becomes freeform dancing around the fire. We were all in the chaotic part of the ritual . . . [and for me] it became a dance with Juliette.

Eroticism

Participants' responses to the second half of the Baphomet rite are complex. For example, Leonie is in a relationship with a non-Pagan partner who does not attend Faunalia. I interviewed her both before and after the 2005 ritual. In the interview beforehand she reported that she had a wonderful time at her previous two Faunalia festivals, however: 'The Baphomet ritual seemed a bit fake. It seemed an excuse to fuck. There did not seem to be anything else to get out of it.' Most participants have a very different understanding of the sexual activity that occurs during the rite. The sexual activity is secondary, an expression of the sensuality and openness that is the primary focus of the rite. In the second interview after the 2005 festival, Leonie gave an account of the Baphomet rite that was more consistent with other participant accounts:

Leonie: Because I am in a relationship and not there for the sex, Baphomet for me has a party feel and is an opportunity to be with friends. I would dance for a while and then sit down with my friends. It was very intimate and erotic, we were lying all over each other. So I would do that for a while and then dance for a while. I cannot dance for very long because of my back . . . I have a shocking body image, a very poor image of myself. In Baphomet I feel fabulous and gorgeous about my body. At other times of the year when I might be feeling bad about my body, I remember how I feel at Faunalia and that can help with my body image and feeling good about myself. It also shapes my general attitude toward myself.

This transformation of deeply held self-evaluations is an example of the power of the Baphomet rite. While some people do have sex during the Baphomet rite, most interviewees noted that to focus on this aspect of the rite is to misunderstand what is occurring. Leanan observed that the people who have sex during the rite are typically already partners.

Leanan: To the outside world, I think some things that happen in circle would tend to be seen as an orgy, but it is not [an orgy]. It is basically partners who want to get aroused by whatever is going on there, make love, and whatever they want to do. You don't have to look. Each person does what they want to do. I am more an internalizing person,

I tend to go more into a meditation or a trance, or maybe go and play the drums or something, or dance around. This year I was more quiet and withdrawn. I just enjoyed the drums.

Flora is 39, has attended a number of Faunalias and has a non-Pagan partner who does not attend Faunalia: 'I have got to be really, really, really honest here. I behave myself, I was sleeping alone.' With some exceptions, discussed below, the majority of the people I interviewed were similarly 'sleeping alone' or attending Faunalia with their partner with whom they were monogamous.

Erotic energy is central to the Baphomet rite. Baphomet is a very sexual and sensual deity. However, the expression of this sexual energy is very different to what is normal in mundane life. Marie captures this experience:

> **Marie:** In the ritual we were expressing raw lust. Just expressing raw lust. We start by dancing. We start by dancing with each other. As we dance, we explore. We explore by reaching out to others, and if other people are responsive to that, then going further in that exploration. It might be touching, it might be caressing, it might be kissing, it might be more sexual and more intimate. It might be with one person, it might be with a group of people. It might be whatever happens spontaneously within that experience. It is simply honouring and allowing that aspect of our primal sexuality to be free.

A deep sensitivity to how the other person is responding to an invitation to erotic intimacy marks the Baphomet rite. Dingo noted this trust and openness:

> **Dingo:** In the Baphomet ritual there was a lot of trust. Everybody went there being very open, with their hearts open . . . I was really comfortable right throughout the ritual. I really did not care whether I got an erection or not. Seeing people fucking in circle, and transsexuals, and gay people, men and women. I have never experienced anything like that. That was awesome. It seemed very appropriate for the space because Baphomet is a very sensual ritual. Very much about raw sexual energy, and also mutually consenting. People were being careful about each other's boundaries. Even the community prankster was behaving himself.

This deep sensitivity to other people's boundaries is something that is reinforced in the ritual briefings. However, this ethics of care does not arise simply from enforced normative expectations, although if they are breached, they are policed. Rather, for the vast majority of participants, the emotional openness they experience in the Baphomet rite generates a deep sensitivity to the people with whom they interact. The ethics of the Baphomet rite is discussed in more detail in the next chapter.

Experimenting with erotic emotions and sensual interactions is the primary focus for most people in the second half of the Baphomet rite. Therion noted that the ritual provides a space where the social restrictions of everyday life do not apply. Participants are 'being more physically affectionate and emotionally open, playful and uninhibited about [their] bodies.' Such interactions may simply involve a caress, or a kiss, and nothing more than this. A kiss or a caress in the liminal space of the Baphomet rite can still be profoundly transformative. René noted that 'getting caught up in the energy' of the rite led her to: 'doing things like kissing women, which I had never done before.' Dale reported a similar experience of same sex intimacy that was quite unusual for him:

> Dale: I went up to Harrison and he was just – oh! And he gave me the biggest hug. And I turned around and looked at him square in the eyes, and I just gave him this biggest kiss that two men could ever have. It was just the climax of the evening. It was wonderful. It was totally full. I could not put more anymore into there. It was just mind-blowing.

For both René and Dale, the rite is a context within which they can safely explore transgressions of deeply held self-understandings. In this case, the possibility of same-sex attraction. For Celeste, the experience at the Baphomet rite profoundly changed her self-understanding on this account:

> Celeste: Faunalia was pretty multitudinous because finding a bunch of people who thought in much the same way I did, both in terms of their attitude towards spirituality and mainstream religion, and also that everyone is pretty open about sexuality in Faunalia. They [some people at Faunalia] might be monogamous and heterosexual, they are straight but they are not narrow. They are perfectly committed to their partners, and that is great, and they are lovely people. But they are also really open to the fact that not everyone is like that, and there are no assumptions made and there is no 'this is right and that's wrong'. That's really great because everywhere you go, so many assumptions get made about you on a daily basis. Faunalia is really open to re-thinking. It made me able to go, oh, this marriage thing is really not what I want, and I am not going to be in it any more. The Baphomet rite . . . really opened things up. There was the whole thing [kissing] with Claire there as well. It just freed me because I thought, 'I am really not prepared to spend the rest of my life trying to be this person that I am really not'. [I had been trying] to do what is considered the right thing to do. It actually took me a really long

time to work up the guts to tell Dave: 'Look, I can't be married to you anymore. This is really not going to work for me.'

At some stage during the early hours of the morning, one of the ritualists decides it is time for 'the feast of the Beast'. Calvin reports his experience of this:

> **Calvin:** Part way through there is a feast scene where four people lay down and fruit is placed on them. Then other revellers eat it off them. Obviously the four people are naked at the time. The person coming around with the plate looked at me and said, 'you can help. Lay down if you want'. So I thought OK, why not. I lay down and she tipped this cold fruit salad all over me. Which in itself was enough of a shock. As soon as the first or second person started biting into the fruit and therefore biting me, which unsurprisingly is concentrated more in sensitive parts of your body, to your area around your genitals, my awareness just went twenty feet up into the trees. I know that people were eating food off me but in a way I was in the trees rather than down where I physically was.

Marilyn and John

Marilyn is a 28-year-old attending Faunalia for the first time with her partner Joe. She is an experienced participant of various alternative subcultures and spiritual practices. During the second half of the Baphomet rite she had an intimate encounter with John, who I also interviewed, and who also recounted the experience:

> **Marilyn:** My partner was there, but we didn't have a sexual connection happening. So I was just being lush with everybody. Then I connected with Luna and she just started kissing me. Really full on. Really dirty, and she is an amazing kisser, wow! So we just journeyed with that for a bit . . . and that was wild. We both experienced part of Baphomet energy together. Yeah, that was crazy. I have kissed a few women before but that is only because my lover at one point, had three other lovers as well. We all kind of kissed at one time. But it wasn't really good. It wasn't happening. But this was great. It wasn't like a woman kissing a woman. It was Baphomet. It was like Baphomet kissing Baphomet. It was really different. She was very animal-like.
>
> And after that I just started kissing people a bit [laughs]. My partner seemed to be really cool about it. So I had this kind of cute guy and his wife. They were there, lushing out. They reminded me of a dream I had. So I asked. I felt very shy actually. If I could just play

with them for a bit, and they said OK, and it was OK, and everything was OK. Then it was a bit awkward, it was strange. I had never really experienced orgies or anything like that, the touching skin, hooh, it was strange. It was very liberating, it was very luscious. I could not believe that when I was with that couple, my partner came and fed us all grapes. I just felt so free, and freedom is so important to me. I was there just for long enough and connected to them and then I moved on, and danced out any passion that was built up from that, and danced that out.

John: The next thing this woman walks up to my partner and I. [She] just says to my partner 'Can I join in?' My partner and I were still caressing and everything else. My partner said yeah, we will let her join in. The way it happened, it was with my loved one, and there was not going to be a problem. In the back of my mind [I wondered] if there was going to be any problem with her partner. But I think after the four years I have known him, I think his reaction would not be anything detrimental. He was in his own space anyway. I think it was just the fact that this woman just wanted to be with somebody, and she chose us. There it was. It was absolutely wonderful. [We were] working with energies and there was this blend of androgynous energy flowing between three people. We have experienced this ménage a trois a few times now, and we have been developing it and are seeing where it goes. At the festival it just became a point where – aahh! – like, those 'ah ha' moments you look for?

We were not male or female. It was completely different to our male/female thing. When the three of us were there, it was a very androgynous thing. I didn't know whether I was male or female. I do not know what other people felt, but I was just there, and I felt both male and female. I had a real energy of Baphomet within me. This process of dissolving and reforming, *solvé coagula*. You become one, you become whole. It was wonderful. We were able to share that energy within the threesome. It was the most exhilarated I have been for quite a while. [To know] I have been there, at that level, in that situation, and then walk away with it, knowing the experience was one I will remember and will never try to pursue again. That was wonderful. What did I get out of it? Androgyny, understanding what the inner spark of life is all about.

This encounter between Marilyn, John and his partner was clearly very erotic. However, both Marilyn and John understand it as something more than this. For Marilyn it is a moment in which she 'felt so free'. For John it was a moment of spiritual exhilaration in which he experienced androgyny and the spark of all life. John describes it in terms of the alchemical formula *solvé coagula*, a theme discussed in Chapter Seven.

Lewis

Lewis is a gentle giant, a chaotic and unpredictable trickster at Faunalia, who is, at the same time, loved and trusted. At some point during the second half of the Baphomet ritual a spiral dance began to take place. Spiral dances are often performed at Pagan events and involve people holding hands and dancing in a circle, weaving in and out and back and forth. At the end of the dance Lewis knelt on the ground and became the centre of attention as he swayed and threw a lot of dirt in the air and made loud growling and beast like vocalizations.

> Lewis: There was a spiral dance, we were going round the fire, and it was a fantastic fire. We were weaving in or out in this spiral. All of a sudden it stopped. It was like a scorpion tail going 'clook' in the ground. From that point I kneel to the ground with a few others. We were howling, we were getting in a swaying type motion. We were vibrating a lot of sound. Then the chanting stopped, but I continue with the vibration, and then I started to sway. You are rocking, you are swaying your body. You are building up a momentum. This is what I naturally do. Working with energy, you are merging from physical, you start to stomp your hands in the Earth and you are circling up dust and dirt. Then you start covering the body with the Goddess dirt.
>
> [Then] I jump into the Earth. My body disappeared. I became in the Earth. [From] the Earth suddenly arms come out and scoop itself, and wash and cleanse its body with the Earth. This whole feeling of covering the body with the Earth, it actually continued to such a point I think I created a bit of a dust storm. I think from the feedback of people, they started to get a bit worried. I heard there was a few people that actually wanted to contain me, because they did not know what the fuck is going on here. My partner said, 'No, let the mother-fucker go'. People started telling me, that they were watching this experience, this entity being wild, and being in this whole energy and I do not have the language to just [clicks fingers] keep explaining it. So this momentum went on for some time, and I think one of the ritualists came over and he put a bit of dust on me just as part of showing humour and leaving me alone. Which is good. You leave it alone. And that is what it is about. You leave the natural world to be.
>
> Then my girl, absolute manifestation of that goddess that she is. In such a split second she suddenly appeared underneath me. Suddenly she appears and [I experienced] this suddenly stilling the body and we just embraced. People started to clap and thought it was something out of the Strength [Tarot] card or something like that. That was

actually a really powerful, powerful, powerful experience for me. It was beyond words.

What was happening for Lewis in this moment? It is, as he says 'beyond words'. What we can say is that it was a moment of profound somatic liminal alterity. The experience of being with Lewis while it was happening had a significant impact on a number of participants.

Sauvage was close to Lewis during his dance with dirt and earth. Sauvage chose to remain there, among the chaos and dirt. Sauvage describes Lewis as engaging in testosterone-fuelled 'buffalo behaviour'. During an earlier ritual Sauvage wrestled with Lewis and found a sense of self-confidence and rejuvenation through the experience.

> **Sauvage:** I remember Lewis just being a complete Earth being. Throwing dust in the air and stuff like that. I have had various experiences with him in that circle over the years, all involving dirt and dust. I remember seeing him and just feeling privileged that I was watching somebody just fall into the Earth like that. I could really appreciate how connected he was and the strength that he was pulling from the Earth. I was next to him when he was doing that and [I was] getting covered in crap everywhere. I thought this is just part of the stuff that happens when you are near him. But I was learning from that. Every time I am somewhere near him in circle I gain something form it.
>
> [At an earlier ritual Lewis and I] wrestled in the dirt, and it was great. But it was really hard doing that because I did not want to connect initially. Here was this big, loud force [saying] 'I want to wrestle with you. Let's do it'. And I am going, 'No, I just want to quietly just be in my space, just go away'. I was really fortunate that there was something of him that I sensed I could trust in that instance, and that it was not just loud buffalo behaviour, it was something deeper and more honest than that. Because of that, I said, 'Ok, let's just have a go at being in the moment and see where this goes'. We just wrestled. In some strange way we bonded from that moment. [I discovered] I could face that energy and I could find a bit of it in myself, and I could engage with that and not come out of it feeling defeated or damaged, that I could actually come out of it feeling a bit rejuvenated, and that it is part of me, it is part of other people.

The next chapter takes up the themes of sensual intimacy and engagement with 'buffalo'-type aggression. The experiences are hedonistic. They are also profoundly transformative moments of liminal alterity through somatic consciousness. Engaging with these experiences includes dancing naked around a bonfire under a starry sky, kissing someone of the same gender, two men wrestling in the dirt and sexual play as part of a threesome. They are framed by a ritual that evokes and invokes a deity who represents the shadow selves of Western Christian culture, the repressed sexual and animalistic aspects of being human. The participants at Faunalia seek to develop new and healthier relationships with these aspects of themselves. Through ritual performance they find something that gives their lives a deeper sense of soul.

Endings

Participants drift off to bed at various stages throughout the night. Some participants stay until close to dawn. Sinead, for example said: 'I spent a long time there. I was probably one of the last eight there.' Some participants alluded to a closing of the circle at the end of the Baphomet rite that takes place close to dawn, although no one provided any detail of what this involved. For most other people the Baphomet rite finishes at some time in the early hours of the morning. Calvin, for example, said: 'I had drummed for a bit, talked to a few people, danced a bit more. I just wandered off. I think I ended up just going to bed at about three o'clock. Feeling sated, content, full.' The next day begins very slowly. Therion said: '[The next day] it was just the usual. Everyone is struggling to consciousness, walking around like zombies [laughs] for most of the day.'

CHAPTER SIX

Ethics

Baphomet is reinvented at Faunalia as a contemporary Pagan deity. During the Baphomet rite participants move from fear and terror of Baphomet to a more complex form of relationship. As a Pagan deity Baphomet represents the unpredictability of nature. Baphomet embodies paradox and contradiction as both male and female, human and beast. Baphomet also embodies many of the fears and anxieties associated with desire, bodies, unpredictability and ambivalence. In the Baphomet rite participants discover new ways of relating to these aspects of themselves and the world around them.

The pursuit of authenticity is at the heart of the Baphomet rite. Authenticity is found through release from fear, shame and guilt. Authenticity is found through developing a new form of relationship with erotic desire, and other confronting and unsettling aspects of the self. Erotic desire becomes a foundation for a new ethical way of relating both to others and to oneself. Authenticity, self-worth and confidence are found in relationships that respectfully explore the erotic possibilities of being human.

Baphomet: A Pagan deity

Baphomet originally emerged in the Middle Ages when the Catholic Inquisition accused the Knights Templar of blasphemously worshipping an idol called Baphomet (McIntosh 2011). Baphomet appears again in the work of the Golden Dawn, an occult magical order active in the late 1800s and early 1900s (McIntosh 2011), most notably in the image drawn by Eliphas Lévi. Among the influences that shaped the practice of Eliphas Lévi and the Golden Dawn were Christian mysticism, hermeticism,

Freemasonry and alchemy. For the Golden Dawn, Baphomet represented the balance that was required to work magically:

> The goat represents dense, Earth-bound nature, but has angel's wings representing heavenly nature. It has female breasts but a male phallus. The four elements are shown by the hooves resting on the globe (Earth), the fish scales on the belly (Water), the wings (Air) and the torch rising from the head (Fire). Darkness and light are present in the black and white crescent moons and in the black and white serpents curled around the caduceus-like phallus. (McIntosh 2011: 8)

The paradoxical and contradictory nature of Baphomet is emphasized in Baphomet's evolution to a Pagan deity at Faunalia. Similar to other Pagan deities, such as Hekate or Dionysos in Greek mythology (Lefkowitz 2003), Baphomet is neither despised, nor entirely embraced. Pagan deities are not entirely trustworthy, but they are nonetheless honoured.

Respecting or honouring a Pagan deity, such as Baphomet, does not mean obedience to that deity. Karen, a 42-year-old married Witch noted emphatically: 'We do not worship Baphomet. We simply honour the energy. It is a very different concept.' In many religious traditions worship is associated with obedience to a set of moral precepts and behavioural norms. In contrast, honouring suggests respect, but not necessarily obedience. Classical Greek accounts of rituals in honour of Dionysos (also referred to as Bacchus in Roman mythology) contain a similar understanding (Dalby 2003, Otto 1965). The deity was honoured, but the aim of the rite was for participants to develop a respectful relationship with the deity. The relationship between participants and the deity honoured is complex and ambivalent because Pagan deities do not necessarily act in the interests of humans (Lefkowitz 2003). In some ways this is similar to understandings of deities in other polytheistic religions such as Shinto (Kasulis 2004) and Hinduism (Flood 1996), and the structure of relationships with other-than-human persons in animist Indigenous societies (Harvey 2005). While a deity may be honoured and respected, ritualists are not necessarily required to love everything this deity might represent nor obey everything the deity might suggest they do. McGuire (2008: 35) suggests that some medieval Christians understood the activities of saints in similar ambivalent ways. Pagan ethics are typically relational, negotiated and not prescriptively dogmatic.[1] Participants' understandings of Baphomet illustrate this relational and ambivalent Pagan approach to deity.

Therion says he does not trust Baphomet, but, at the same time, he trusts that the ritual work he is doing with Baphomet is important and appropriate:

> **Therion:** Baphomet is not a comfortable deity. Baphomet is not a deity that you would say to: 'Here I place my trust in you and everything

would be OK.' Baphomet can hurt you, certainly not out of malice, I don't think. But there is always that sense that he, she may take people out of that comfort zone and that creates certain trust issues. I do not completely trust Baphomet. [But I still think that what happens in the Baphomet rite] is happening for a reason. I have got to trust that it is appropriate. I think in a way that is harkening back to a much more Pagan view of the world where deities were not something that you trusted.

Several other people made similar points about their ambivalent relationship to Baphomet. Heath, for example, noted that: 'I don't think Baphomet is safe. It is a very confrontational archetype to evoke.' Although Heath also said that: 'In some ways Baphomet was healing for me.' Similarly, Leonie said: 'I approach the Baphomet rite not with fear, but with respect.' Lewis says of Baphomet: 'To me a demon is of the natural world, in its natural place, undisturbed. In its quintessence it is primordial . . . A demon is wild.' Therion also compares Baphomet to something that is wild:

> **Therion:** [Baphomet scares me] because the energy is intense. When you are looking eye to eye with the priestess who has evoked Baphomet into herself, you are seeing Baphomet. You are seeing that energy and that energy is threatening on a very fundamental level because it is well outside your comfort zone. [I love Baphomet] as you might love a wild animal like a tiger.

Ambiguity, tension and paradox are central to all participants' understandings and experiences of Baphomet. The experience of intensely felt ambivalence towards a deity is one of the central outcomes of the Baphomet rite. In some ways the wildness of Baphomet is similar to the 'monsters' described by Kearney (2003). Kearney argues that monsters are symbols of the terrifying otherness of aspects of ourselves and the world around us. Rather than avoiding and ostracizing monsters, Kearney argues it is healthier to accommodate them and negotiate with them. Participants similarly describe a negotiated accommodation with Baphomet. Through engaging with Baphomet participants discover something about themselves:

> But monsters terrify and intrigue for another reason too: they defy borders. Monsters are liminal creatures who can go where we can't go . . . Transgressing the conventional frontiers separating good from evil, human from inhuman, natural from cultural, monsters scare the hell out of us and remind us that we don't know who we are. They bring us to no man's land and fill us with fear and trembling. In that sense we may say that monsters are our *Others* par excellence. Without them we know not what we are. With them we are not what we know. (Kearney 2003: 117; original emphasis)

Baphomet is not only a monster. Baphomet is also the subject of love and desire. Benjamin (1998) argues we need experiences that combine love and hate, desire and fear. Through them we learn to tolerate ambivalence within the context of relationships:

> Tolerating ambivalence, being able to feel both love and hate toward the same object, does not mean that love and hate are synthesized so that love triumphs over hate. Rather, it means that hate can be borne. Difference, hate, failure of love can be surmounted not because the self is unified, but because it can tolerate being divided. Inclusion of split off feelings or blocked aspirations is motivated not by a compulsion to restore unity but out of the wish to be less resentful and afraid of projected anger, less terrified of loss, less punitive toward what one desires. (Benjamin 1998: 105)

Pagan deities are often feared because they represent aggressive desires and destructive aspects of the world. Rituals that involve such deities are feared because it is incorrectly assumed participants will become subservient to, and obey, the injunctions of such deities. This is not the case at Faunalia, or with other Pagan rituals. The challenge of the ritual is to learn how to live with the bestial erotic desire that Baphomet represents. One reason participants seek to 'live with' the desire represented by Baphomet is that the opposite strategy of repressing and repudiating erotic desire has not worked well for them. The aim of the ritual is to allow erotic desire to exist, but not be controlled by it. Once these cut off and rejected feelings are reclaimed in the ritual, participants feel more in control of their erotic desire and more alive as a consequence.

There are some other religious groups that have created rituals involving the deity Baphomet. Baphomet appears in the rituals of the *Cultus Sabbati* (Chumbley 2010), Thelema (Duquette 1993) and Satanists (Lewis 2001, Flowers 1997). One or two interviewees reported they had read literature from these groups. In Thelema, as described by Duquette (1993), Baphomet appears in a number of formal rituals. Academic studies are rare, but the published ritual texts of Thelemites give the impression that they meet in small groups in urban locations, and have a formalized initiation process and liturgy. The *Cultus Sabbati,* Thelema and Satanism are quite different to Faunalia. Faunalia is an occasional ritual with no ongoing formal structure, and no initiatory membership. Further, in Satanism, Baphomet is interpreted as a representation of Satan. Whereas at Faunalia, Baphomet is re-interpreted as a Pagan deity, and the participants aim to escape or leave behind the association of Baphomet with Satan.

Paganisms are religions oriented towards nature. Pagan deities represent aspects of nature. The Greek God Apollo is a sun God, Hades is a God of the dead, Demeter a Goddess of fertility (Lefkowitz 2003). Pagan deities also represent aspects of being human: Aphrodite is a Goddess of love and erotic desire, for example (Cyrino 2010). Learning to relate to these deities is also a way of learning to relate to the world and to ourselves. These Gods, and the aspects of the world and being human that they represent, do not always act in the best interests of individual people. This requires people to develop complex ways of relating to these deities, and as a consequence complex ways of relating to the world and to their own fears and desires. At Faunalia, Baphomet is reinvented as a Pagan deity.

Baphomet, shadow and authenticity

Baphomet is a symbol of the shadow self. In particular, Baphomet is a symbol of sexual desire, pleasure and the body. Coming to terms with Baphomet as a shadow, or reflection, of internal psychological processes allows participants to feel less threatened by those parts of themselves they have split off or dislike. Further, once Baphomet is no longer a screen on which individuals project their own fears and shadows, this allows them to experience and relate to Baphomet as an 'other', in his/her own right. Participants begin to relate to Baphomet as he/she represents aspects of the other-than-human world such as 'totality' (Therion), 'wildness' (Lewis), 'life force energy' (Marie) and 'something else besides that's beyond our comprehension' (Harrison). Participants also begin to relate to their sexual desire, pleasure and their bodies as a valued aspect of themselves, rather than something to be feared.

Harrison provides one of the longer descriptions of Baphomet as deity. He explicitly makes the point that Baphomet is both an external being and a symbolic representation of his own psychological processes. He does not want to reduce Baphomet to one or the other of these, recognizing that both operate in his experience of her/him:

Harrison: My relationship with deity is complex and simple. At the simplest level, it is pretty much an emotional response. But the way I conceptualize that is fairly complex. Deity, for me, can be external and internal, subjective and objective. It is personal and personalized, but it is also abstract. What I mean is I can relate to Baphomet as a discrete entity, and objectively [as something] that exists somewhere, somehow. I can see that manifest in Phoebe when she takes on that part. That is Baphomet manifesting. I can relate to that entity when I do rituals on my own and invoke Baphomet. Baphomet is just there, and I can relate to him. But I also recognize a part of myself in it. Baphomet is part of me and I am part of Baphomet. The way I relate to Baphomet is [as] an archetype. It is a psychological process. When I relate to Baphomet and work with Baphomet, I am working with my own inner processes. But, Baphomet is also a lover. Our relationship is always ambivalent.

In the Baphomet rite, Baphomet is experienced as both external and internal to the participant – the beast within and the beast without. The participant enters into a relationship with those parts of themselves that Baphomet represents. However, Baphomet also represents something, or someone, which is other and separate. Baphomet is not simply a reflection of the self. As Harrison observes: 'I am conscious of the fact that when we do Faunalia, in a sense we are serving Baphomet. Providing a vehicle for Baphomet's expression and recognition.' Baphomet, as a being for its own sake, can only be known once participants understand, or come to terms with, their own fears and shadows that are projected onto Baphomet. This is an extension of the point made by Kearney (2003) and Benjamin (1998) about how the process of splitting projects fears and anxieties onto the other (see Chapter Four).

One of the most commonly experienced confronting aspects of Baphomet is his/her associations with, and resemblance to, the Christian Devil or Satan. In this sense Christianity is one of the 'symbolic resources' utilized in the Baphomet rite, although the aim is to escape the oppressive relational etiquettes that Christianity has embedded in people's lives. Leanan noted that her Christian upbringing made Baphomet confronting because it seemed blasphemous: 'But once I was in there and joining in the ritual, I just did it. Nothing very dreadful happened. I enjoyed the ritual very much.' Ruth also noted that she was dubious about using what seemed to her to be Christian imagery in a Pagan ritual, with its overtones of blasphemy. However, once she was in the ritual: 'I remember the sense of [being] just wild, free, an energetic shape-shifting around the fire, coming into the really primal idea of the medieval Witches' sabbat. It was an experience that I felt was very much akin to, it was extraordinary.' The accounts of René, Leanan and Ruth, all suggest that their fears of Baphomet were more a product of projected anxieties rather than any real experience of threat or danger associated with Baphomet.

Phoebe was at first scared of the 'energy of Baphomet'. She was brought up a Catholic, and felt that a lot of the parts of her that were important, such as her sexuality, smoking, dancing and enjoying herself, were seen as Satanic and evil by the Catholic Church. In the Baphomet rite she was able to embrace them as positive parts of herself, rather than as negative: 'I had to get rid of the Catholic fear of just being me. Me as the rebellious one, the one that destroyed the family's image' (Phoebe). Flora made a similar point about feeling good about herself and allowing herself to feel good about enjoying herself:

> Flora: It was just nice to feel good about myself and not feel guilty about it. I was raised a Catholic. You have got to be guilty for every pleasure you feel. It was so tantalizing. It was so different to any emotions or feeling I had ever had before. It was really a

self-indulgence, and that feeling OK. It is OK to do something for the sheer pleasure of it.

For many participants, childhood experiences of Christianity and contemporary consumerist culture had left them with a deep sense of fear and guilt about various aspects of their lives. They feared pleasure and their bodies, and felt guilty about choices to reject paths set down for them by tradition and family expectation. The Baphomet rite transforms these somatic, emotional understandings. 'Nothing dreadful happened' in the presence of Baphomet. Their fears are experienced as empty shadows. Baphomet, as a symbol of choice, pleasure and desire, is no longer feared as Satan. Participants begin to enjoy themselves in his/her presence, and in so doing begin to relate to pleasure and their bodies for their own sake, and not as projections of their own fears and shadows. Although Jessica Benjamin is not talking about Baphomet, she describes exactly this process: 'Owning the other within diminishes the threat of the other without so that the stranger outside is no longer identical with the stranger within us – not our shadow, not a shadow over us, but a separate other whose own shadow is distinguishable in the light' (Benjamin 1998: 108). Participants own their shadows: their bodies, sensual pleasures and rebellious choices. In so doing Baphomet appears as a separate other, who is no longer feared as a profoundly disturbing threat, although that does not mean Baphomet is totally embraced either. The new relationship is a mixture of ambivalence, pleasure and fear.

The celebration of pleasure and bodies for their own sake is a somatic and aesthetic experience. Such transformations are difficult to achieve simply by reading, thinking and understanding. Myth, ritual and aesthetic experiences are important because they engage with unconscious and semi-conscious self-understandings. It is not surprising that many people who read or hear about Baphomet feel afraid and remain deeply suspicious of the deity. It would be surprising if they were not afraid – because that is precisely the point of working with Baphomet. Baphomet represents that which many people fear. I suspect that Harrison's observation below relates to people who hear about Baphomet, but have not experienced the Baphomet rite, or something similar, themselves:

Harrison: Some people are afraid of the archetypal energy [of Baphomet]. They just cannot shake loose from that Christian devil association that the image provokes. I think most of the people coming to Faunalia are probably a fair way along that track, but, there are still some people who find that they cannot shake that off.

Experienced participants often reported that subsequent Baphomet rituals were less confronting, because some of their fears have been resolved. Their concerns turn to whether there is any actual inappropriate behaviour occurring. In the ritual they enter a state of trance and in that state they are able to engage with Baphomet in ways that are constructively transformative:

> **Sinead:** It was an interesting experience being in a ritual that encouraged the beast to come out. At no stage did I feel that inappropriate behaviour was acceptable within that ritual. People were releasing and really letting go, and there were quite a lot of people that were quite heavily into various trance states, and at a certain stage I was too. I sort of went in and out a bit. That beast aspect was quite powerful for me. And now I think it has actually, well, I have to say, it has changed my life.

The ritual changed Sinead's life, in part at least, because it enabled her to relate more confidently to some important people around her. She recounts a long story of an unhealthy relationship with an ex-husband. In the weeks following Faunalia she changed her interactions with her ex-husband and his new partner. She felt that Faunalia gave her a new courage and confidence to 'finally let this person go, and finally do it within myself'. The transformations that people experience in the Baphomet rite are often internal psychological transformations of emotional self-understandings with significant relational and interactional consequences.

Participants report they are less afraid, more confident, more prepared to take risks and pursue a path that is truer to their 'authentic' self. The movement from 'all that is wrong with life to all that is right' (Heelas 1996: 16) is a movement towards an 'authentic self' (Taylor 1991). In this sense, participants understand the shadows that Baphomet represents are the oppressive influences of other people and social processes that have prevented the expression of this authentic self. Celeste decides that she can no longer be married. Therion finds that he has shut his true self down emotionally. Phoebe and Flora are able to embrace pleasure as a part of their authentic selves. Harrison learns to relate to his inner feminine self as well as his masculine self.

This understanding is consistent with Charles Taylor's (1991) account of the moral ideal of authenticity. Authenticity is developed through reflexive self-awareness, which becomes an end in itself. According to Taylor, those who pursue authenticity as a moral ideal understand that each person has something unique that can only be discovered by being in touch with one's self. This authentic self is lost either through the pressures of conformity or through taking an instrumental stance to oneself. Authenticity is different to selfish individualism. Authenticity has relational implications because the self is developed dialogically. Authenticity requires 'recognition' (Taylor 1991: 50). That is to say, being authentic is not something that a person does on their own. Rather, authenticity is about being true to yourself in the context of relationships.

For Turner (1969), ritual transgression and liminal inversion are ultimately functional for society, reinforcing social norms. The norm that is reinforced at Faunalia is the ethic of authenticity. The aim of the Baphomet rite is to escape the binding influence of projected fears and misperceived threats so that participants can enjoy the pleasures of living an authentic life. Authenticity draws participants into new forms of relationship, or new ways of relating in existing relationships.

Participants argue that it is dangerous to ignore the 'energy' of Baphomet. Many participants made a link between self-discovery and nature, pointing to the primal energy of the Baphomet rite. Heelas (1996) notes the pursuit of inner spirituality is often linked to a sense of finding what is right within nature. Marie re-iterates Sauvage's observation in Chapter Four. The danger, she says, is not in working with Baphomet, but in failing to engage the 'archetype' that Baphomet represents:

> **Marie:** People criticize the working of the Baphomet because they say it is dangerous. But what we say is that it is more dangerous not to work with this. I think this is an archetype or a symbol, like Abraxus, the alchemical god, that is going to keep coming back to us. It is beyond good and evil. It is purely a primal, raw, life force energy.

The Pagan God Baphomet, as a symbol of nature, of 'primal, raw, life force energy', is respected, but not obeyed. In a ritual moment of mutual recognition the primal energy of Baphomet becomes an other who is honoured and respected but not obeyed, because she/he is 'beyond good and evil'. The aim is to 'dance' or 'play' with the energy of Baphomet. If Baphomet should lead them towards something they feel contradicts their own truth, participants feel confident to choose a path true to their own inner self.

The shadow work that occurs in the Baphomet rite is aesthetic and somatic, a form of 'iconic consciousness'. Phoebe, René and Flora emphasize the fear associated with the 'energy' of Baphomet. The lessening of this fear leads to new emotions of joy, pleasure and confidence. It also transforms their fears from vague and deeply disturbing shadows to more concrete concerns about actual behaviours and practices. This transformation happens in the context of the ritual performance, in dance, communion with Baphomet and erotic play with other participants. Changes to cognitive self-understandings do occur, but these are secondary to the primary transformation that occurs at a somatic, emotional and aesthetic level during the ritual. Pursuing an ethic of authenticity changes the way that people relate to each other, because the self is ultimately dialogical and relational. The relationship between self and Baphomet is complex, paradoxical and ambivalent, and, in the view of participants at Faunalia, this is the way it should be.

While the experiences at Faunalia are powerful, they require regular renewal. Participants feel they need to continue to work with their 'shadow selves' in order to continue to find ways of living authentically. I interviewed most participants in the month prior and/or the period two to six weeks after Faunalia. Their experiences were still fresh in their minds. Their discussion of participation in earlier festivals does provide some evidence of the longer-term impacts of attending Faunalia. Those who had been present at the 2000 Faunalia still remembered some of what they had experienced five years prior, sometimes vividly. However, the impact of the rituals seems to fade with time. The maintenance of ongoing self-understandings requires regular renewal, as is the case with seasonal rites (Turner 1983).

Desire and ethics

Richard Kearney (2001, 2003) develops an ethics based on desire drawing on the work of Emmanuel Levinas' (1979, 1985) and Luce Irigaray (1993). Mari Ruti (2006) develops a similar ethics, although her approach is informed by Lacan (1977). Kearney argues that religiously contextualized desire can lead to moments of self-transcendence and ethical concern for others. Irigaray describes a form of ethical erotic relationship that escapes, or transcends, oppression. Ruti examines how the surrender of self in erotic desire can lead to self-transformation. This section considers how these ideas might help explain the experiences of participants in the Baphomet rite.

Richard Kearney's (2001) book *The God who may be*, begins: 'God neither is, nor is not, but may be' (Kearney 2001: 1). He extends the analysis of erotic intimacy in Levinas' (1979) reading of the Biblical book the *Song of Songs*. Kearney develops the idea of 'fecundity' as a radical openness to what is possible. This approach to deity, and knowledge, is informed by love, desire and anticipation. Kearney's and Levinas' discussions engage desire constructively. Desire and ethics are not opposed. Rather, desire leads into the ethical moment of relationship. This is very different to understandings of ethics found in those ethical frameworks that emphasize the restraint of bestial or animalistic desire through adherence to normative rules.

Christianity, particularly the childhood experiences of Christianity of participants at Faunalia, often constructs desire as evil, associated with the pleasures of the body and the pursuit of selfish desires in contrast to traditional norms and expectations. Both Kearney and Levinas draw on different Christian traditions, such as the medieval mystics, in which the erotic aspects of relationships are metaphors for the relationship with the Divine. For Kearney anticipation (of sexual intimacy, social justice or other forms of relationship) comes out of a flirting with the pleasure of the possible, and working towards creating it, rather than a frustration with absence. Desire, experienced as the pleasure of the possible, focuses on the welfare of the other, as well as the pleasure of self. 'It is desire as such which points us toward transcendence . . . If love stops short at couples and coupling, desire cuts through toward the other' (Kearney 2001: 65).

Kearney's argument is that religiously contextualized love and desire encourages us to engage with the 'other' in relationships. Religion encourages self-transcendence. Religious mythology engages with that part of the world which is 'not us' – it brings us into relationship with God, community, nature, church, ancestors, the lost and those in need of God's love. For Levinas, and Kearney, it is desire that draws us into these relationships of transcendence. 'The caress' is a term that Levinas uses to describe the power of such encounters. The caress is: 'an erotic surge into the invisible, a transcendence . . . This erotic epiphany is the portal to ethics itself, the carnal trace of goodness' (Kearney 2001: 66).

The Baphomet rite is concerned with the possibilities of sexual desire. While the pursuit of sexual pleasure is part of the ritual, the ritual is more than this. The first Baphomet rite did not involve sex during the ritual. In 2005, while most people were nude, only a small number of people actually had sex during the ritual. A number of people said that if you focus on the sex you have missed the point of the Baphomet rite. Rather, the nudity and erotic performance of the ritual sacralizes sexual desire, and then challenges each participant to decide how they will engage in relationship in the context of that sacralized sensuality. It is in this context that each individual develops an etiquette for relating to their own, and to others', sensuality and sexual desire. Baphomet sacralizes desire and transforms it into an act of self-transcendence, an ethical moment of engagement with the other. Several participants, for example, who were married or partnered and their partner was not attending Faunalia, reported that their experience of the Baphomet rite was significantly shaped by the respect of, and commitments to, their absent partner. They still allowed themselves to be challenged and transformed by the ritual within the constraints of their existing relationships.

The performance of desire in the moment of relationship to Baphomet is respectful. It is not concerned with escaping restraint (which narcissistically focuses on the self), but with the pleasure of the possible (which focuses on the welfare of the other, as well as the pleasure of self). Mainstream narcissistic culture is obsessed with what can be possessed for me, focusing on rights and independence (Morrison 1998). For the participants at Faunalia such mundane culture misses the pleasure of the relationship – of what is possible, or 'may be'.

The Baphomet rite changes the way participants feel about their bodies, their sexuality, their relationships and their ability to be agents. During the

Baphomet rite, Leonie feels: 'fabulous and gorgeous about my body.' She is drawn into a new way of relating to her body that celebrates the pleasure of the body and that allows her to find alternatives to her 'shocking body image'. Dale kissed Harrison, a moment of homoerotic relationship that 'was just mind-blowing'. Another female participant was in a double bind of being married and feeling she was gay. At Faunalia she kissed a woman and it 'just freed me'. Sauvage wrestled in the dirt with the 'buffalo aggression' of Lewis and came out of it 'feeling a bit rejuvenated, and that it is part of me, it is part of other people'.

Desire leads into ethical relationship through its performative reframing in ritual. Ritual transforms the self-in-relationship at the emotional, somatic and aesthetic level. Religious ritual engages with that part of the world which is not us – the other. The other that the Baphomet rite engages is the other of the shadow, desire and the sensual self. The beastly, erotic desire that Baphomet symbolizes leads participants into moments of ethical relationship with themselves and others.

Desire that leads into ethical relationship requires an openness to the other. Luce Irigaray (1993: 208) differentiates a male lover who 'penetrates into flesh' without attention to the other and is unaware of the 'rape' in which he engages, from 'the caress' that seeks out 'the not yet of the female lover's blossoming' and the woman's ethics 'which is an opening of and to another threshold' (Irigaray 1993: 211). For Irigaray, when a male lover reduces the other to 'that which is not yet human in himself' he ignores the 'irreducible strangeness' of the other. In contrast, relationships founded on 'the caress' develop in a very different way. Irigaray's concept of the caress draws on the work of Emmanuel Levinas:

> What is caressed is not properly speaking touched. It is not the softness or tepidity of this hand given in contact that the caress seeks. It is this seeking of the caress which constitutes its essence, through the fact that the caress does not know what it seeks. This 'not knowing,' this fundamental disordering, is the essential. . . . And the caress is the anticipation of this pure future without content. (Levinas 1985: 69)

Participant accounts of the Baphomet rite echo some of Levinas' and Irigaray's sentiments of the caress. Many participants describe experiences of seeking, desire and longing. This is accompanied by a sense of the ineffability of their experiences – they are 'beyond words'. The transformations draw participants into something new and desired, but often elusive.

Ethical desire in erotic relationships is not a moment of possession or domination.[2] Rather, Ruti follows Irigaray (1993), Lacan (1977) and, I would add, echoes Benjamin (1988) and Levinas (1985), to describe love as 'an opening within the self that invites the other to enter while simultaneously respecting its integrity and distinctiveness' (Ruti 2006: 185). The moment of surrender disrupts idealized images of love. This is a moment of living with imperfection and alienation, held in the moment of loving surrender:

> Giving the gift of love must entail the loving subject's willingness to take a step back in order to create the clearing (in Irigaray's sense) necessary for the unravelling of the other's ideality. It must allow the other's alterity to surface in all of its strange – and perhaps even threatening – intensity. Enabling the other to surrender tells this other that it is loved both in its attempt to approximate the ideal and in its absolute failure at the moment of surrender, to do so. (Ruti 2006: 193)

It is precisely this sort of complex relationship to the erotic other that the Baphomet ritual makes possible. Participants re-discover themselves through caring erotic relationships with other participants. Other participants engage with them, but also step back and make space for the challenging otherness of the other. These interactions are not always comfortable and sometimes confronting, although most often described as 'amazing', 'powerful' and 'beautiful'. The complex mixture of desire and fear that participants describe in their relationship to Baphomet is characteristic of these forms of relationship. Through engaging with desire, participants develop new ethical stances towards others and themselves, rediscovering an authentic self. As Silverman (2000: 47), also drawing on Lacanian theory, puts it: 'it is through the practice of desire rather than through its renunciation that humans approach what has traditionally been called virtue'.

Ethical erotic relationships that open to the strangeness of the other are made possible by coming to terms with the threat of domination represented by Baphomet. Baphomet symbolizes the oppressive threat of domination through his/her representation of the shadow of the 'not yet human' (Irigaray 1993: 211) in ourselves – of bestial desire. At least, this is part of what is symbolized by Baphomet. The Baphomet rite does not involve either oppression by, or domination of, this bestial desire. Rather, the symbolic representation of the shadow in Baphomet dissolves the shadow's power, and allows for a moment of encounter in the erotic caress of the touch. This is equally as profound for women as for men. In the liminal moment of the Baphomet rite, women and men escape from the oppressiveness of the projected bestial shadow and find their own authentic sense of self in relationship with Baphomet. In that moment they are able to relate to each other through the caress.

Put another way, the liminal inversion and alterity of the Baphomet rite involves the removal, or deconstruction, of the domination and fear characteristic of many erotic relationships. Turner (1969) noted erotic transgression is often associated with liminality. Faunalia, and the Baphomet rite in particular, combines intense liminality and erotic transgression in the context of a ritual that inverts the dominating power of the shadow of sexual oppression. Oppressive expectations led some participants to fear, for example, their homoerotic desire. These oppressive expectations are dismantled. Similarly, Baphomet undermines the fear of emotional and erotic engagement that had closed Therion's emotional self down. This allows participants to engage creatively with alternative selves and etiquettes of relating. It is perhaps unsurprising that such experiences are profoundly transformative for participants.

Baphomet is a Pagan deity, and as such not always trustworthy. Desire in this context is framed by paradox and tension that is missed by Kearney's (2001) analysis and not examined in Irigaray's discussion of the caress. Baphomet is both a shadow, a projection of fears and repressed aspects of self, and a radically 'other' being who is feared and loved.

Solvé Coagula

> **Ruth:** Baphomet is not just the wild beast. There is an aggressive, angry side to it. There is also in the *solvé* and *coagula* a place for immense transformation and wisdom that can be learned.

The Baphomet rite is a moment of liminal transformation of self-understandings. In the liminal moment everyday rules and expectations are dissolved, so that they can be reformulated in new and creative ways. As Andy Letcher (2004) puts it: 'in the liminal phase, normal social relations are softened, melted, inverted, and broken down, only to be reformed again in the transition back to societas (van Gennep's aggregation)' (Letcher 2004: 20). The softening and inversion is not only of external norms but also of internally maintained self-understandings.

Solvé coagula is an alchemical Latin dictum which means to separate or dissolve and then to join or reassemble. It refers both to the chemical processes that some alchemists practised, and to a psychological transformation that occurs within the self (Gilchrist 1991). It clearly parallels the ritual process of separation, transition and re-integration. In the drawing of Baphomet by Elphis Levi, the word '*solvé*' is on the right forearm, pointing upwards, and '*coagula*' is on the left forearm, pointing downwards. Most participants are familiar with this drawing and are also familiar with the words *solvé coagula*. Towards the end of the interviews I asked if there was anything else participants wanted to add about Faunalia. Both Marie and Celeste raised the *solvé coagula* formulae. Marie argues, following Carl Jung, that scientists misunderstand alchemy, failing to see the psychological transformation to which it refers. Celeste also relates the formula to her own transformation in relationship status.

> **Marie:** *Solvé coagula.* The alchemy was very much misunderstood as the scientific age developed. I think probably where Jung had it right

was this notion that alchemy was about philosophy. This notion of *solvé coagula* is the notion that by dissolving psychic opposites and then reforming, we can create experiences or change consciousness. It is something unique about the Western mystery traditions. To me, Faunalia and the Baphomet rite is exactly that. It is a living tradition starting to develop an exploration of alchemy in its truer sense of how we can transform our lives.

Celeste: I think that *solvé coagula* is really important. This idea of people getting married for 60 years and that it will last forever . . . so clearly does not work. [We] should just accept that there is an expiry date, that we all change. The entire universe is about dynamic flux. If we don't grow, we die. People do not always grow in the same direction. They might happen to grow together for a while and then go their separate ways. That should not be regarded as a failure or as something to lament. I think people need to realize that we do not play by conventional rules at Faunalia but it does not meant that we are Satanist sluts either [laughs]. There is a deeper work going on.

The rituals at Faunalia facilitate the acceptance of life transitions that might otherwise be considered difficult or problematic. The destabilized, liquid, disembedded and transitional nature of contemporary life is well documented in sociological literature (Bauman 2000, Giddens 1991). The liminal rites of Faunalia assist participants to make sense of life transitions in this liquid and destabilizing social context. For Celeste the *solvé coagula* formula articulates an acceptance of the ending of her marriage as a normal life transition. Tradition expects that a marriage will last a life time. Celeste dissolves this expectation as an oppressive shadow and instead embraces transition as consistent with an ethics of authenticity.

The transformation of lives in the liminal rites of Faunalia follows a process of dissolution and re-aggregation, of separation, liminality and re-integration, of *solvé coagula*. Like the calendrical and seasonal rites of which festivals are a descendent (Turner 1983), this process returns participants to their mundane lives with a renewed understanding of their place in the world, a renewed confidence to face the challenges that life gives them, and a commitment to pursue an ethic of authenticity. Put another way, the rituals at Faunalia help participants pursue a life with soul. Through the somatic and aesthetic practices of the rituals, participants find a clearer sense of their authentic self and 'its place and purpose in the world' Ruti (2006: 20).

The liminal space of Faunalia, and the Baphomet rite in particular, dissolves expectations and allows participants to actively and creatively experiment with a range of alternative self-understandings. Psychoanalysis similarly engages with the creative reinterpretation of self-understandings so that individuals can engage with the world in creative and active ways.

Ruti (2006: 198) argues that analysis triggers a 'polyvalent discourse' that helps people 'speak and write themselves' in new ways as they engage with the destabilizing and open space of analysis. While speaking and writing are important to participants at Faunalia, the openness and destabilization at Faunalia occurs at the level of emotional and somatic knowing, and the reformulations of self also occur at this level. Transformations of self are somatic, performed and felt, as much as spoken, written and cognitively articulated. To paraphrase Ruti (2006: 218), the Baphomet rite aims to transform participants from people who are passively driven to act out and perform their desires to people who actively create, embrace and engage their desires. Part of what makes this active exploration possible is precisely the liminal dissolution of expectations.

> Psychotherapy is one way of coming to terms with the daimonic. By bravely voicing our inner 'demons' – symbolizing those tendencies in us that we most fear, flee from, and hence are obsessed or haunted by – we transmute them into helpful allies, in the form of newly liberated, life-giving psychic energy, for use in constructive activity. During this process, we come to discover the paradox that many artists perceive: That which we had previously run from and rejected turns out to be the redemptive source of vitality, creativity, and authentic spirituality. (Diamond 1991: 185)

Experiences in the Baphomet rite can be destabilizing of established identities. Successfully engaging with the transformative potential of Faunalia requires a willingness to change. René reported that some of her Pagan friendships had ended as a consequence of participation in previous Faunalia festivals. She saw this as a product of her being stuck in a particular way that meant that she, and some of her friends, resisted the *solvé* aspects of Faunalia. 'The Baphomet ritual tries to help you move through that stuff' (René). According to René, external circumstances meant that she was stuck and could not move forward. This created considerable tension because the Baphomet rite was encouraging her to experiment and change. However, in 2005 her experience was different: 'This year, I am not in that place where I am stuck anymore, I have been observing that *solvé* has been [acting] in a progressive way, helping me to release stuff and to move through old issues, and to get closure on things.'

For those that do embrace the liminal moment of inversion, of *solvé*, it is not completely destabilizing because participants know that the ritual will end and be followed by a stage of re-integration, of *coagula*. The ritual process contains, or restricts, the destabilizing and decomposing potential of the liminal moment. Nudity, for example, only typically happens around and during the Baphomet rite. Altered states of consciousness, such as states of trance, are also typically only experienced during the rituals. Participants feel confident to take their clothes off and to go into trance because they know the ritual will end, and they will be returned to 'normal'. Discussing Evelyn Underhill's mysticism and its links to creativity, Ruti makes a similar point:

> The same way as Bataille maintains that losing one's footing within erotic experiences calls for some sort of guarantee that one will not fall irrevocably, self surrender within artistic or other types of creative endeavors may only be feasible within securely established limits. This may also explain why mystical experiences tend to take place within the strict regime of monastic life. (Ruti 2006: 179)

In the moment of surrender of self to eros, mysticism or liminality, some guarantee is required that the self will not completely dissolve. I suspect that mystical experience in contemporary societies is more common on dance floors than in monasteries, at least in 'the West'. Nonetheless, Ruti's point is a good one. The experience of surrender, of dissolution of self, is difficult to endure if there is not a guarantee of closure and limits. The ritual process provides precisely this assurance at Faunalia: *Solvé* is always followed by *coagula*.

Andrew

Andrew provides a particularly candid account of why some people engage in inappropriate behaviour. I interviewed Andrew both before and after Faunalia. These excerpts are from the second interview. He is a single male in his forties who has been a Pagan for more than ten years.

> Andrew: This gathering has left a mark on me. It has been a big slap in the face to me. It has made me realize that I have been working too much with my ego. Some of my dearest friends have acknowledged that I have come to a point that I need to change things. I have come to the realization that socially and Pagan-wise, magically, I have [been] playing the fool at any cost [to my] friends. Even though I have not meant to hurt people, or have not meant to be a selfish, egotistical persona, that is what is coming across. It is coming across with some of my closest friends, and it has been building over several years. I am not willing to continue down that path. I don't like that side of me either. I am a very sensitive person. I am so fucking cynical about the world. [I am] always trying to prove myself. I have become a big whinger, and not showing much care and consideration for my close friends and others. I have just got to try and care more about my closest friends. This is an epiphany. This is a profound moment in my life.

[I did something that annoyed a few people at Faunalia] that afterwards, on reflection, I can see that I was being provocative. Then someone yelled at me and it made me realize this behaviour is not good. It is not just me. Faunalia leaves you raw and vulnerable. Your guard is down. I know that Baphomet has played a part in this realization that I am pushing some of my closest friends away. Not all of them. But quite a few. Enough. Enough pushing them away. This path, it is not working. It is broken. It starts with me. It starts with just trying to be more considerate, not being so lazy.

On the last night we were having a party. I was all dressed up, and no one would play with me. I felt so lonely. It was just a feeling of emptiness. It did not go away. I was almost crying at several stages. By the end the most beautiful thing happened that night. I was lying down after having several dances, and just thinking, I have got to surrender. I woke up in the morning, still feeling empty and feeling mad. I thought this is a sign. You can't continue down this track. You can't, you can't, you can't. I need to open up my heart basically. I have had this obsession with liberating myself and liberating others through wild, primal ritual, or eroticism, by basically being a misfit . . . I just need to surrender. I need to open up my heart to these people I love and care about.

Andrew's experiences at Faunalia led him to a realization about the problematic nature of his behaviour. In many ways the structure of Andrew's discussion reflects the central theme of this chapter – the movement away from self-centred behaviours that are disrespectful of others, and towards structures of relationship involving care and respect. However, Andrew's account is different to other accounts of epiphanies at Faunalia for a few reasons.

Andrew focuses on his sense of emptiness. This experience of emptiness remains overwhelming for the duration of Faunalia. Andrew has not engaged in a performance of new ways of relating to emptiness, or to other people. Andrew's experience is one of 'lack', to use Ruti (2006) and Lacan's term. Lacanian psychoanalysis sees humans as creatures defined by an experience of alienation or 'lack'. The aim of therapy is to find healthy ways of living with such experiences of alienation and emptiness. Healing is not found through removing the wound of the experience of lack. Rather, healing involves finding healthy ways to manage the experiences of alienation, isolation and suffering. Andrew seeks to escape from his sense of emptiness and isolation, rather than attempting to creatively engage with it. 'Reluctant to accept lack as a precondition of its existence, the subject flees from this lack by recourse to reassuring fantasies of plenitude and belonging' (Ruti 2006: 127).

Andrew's performances at Faunalia were primarily ones that performed disrespectful relationships. At Faunalia, in his own words, he engaged in performances that were annoying, egotistical and hurtful to others. The central change for Andrew is in his cognitive self-understandings. He describes a realization that his behaviour is inappropriate, but Andrew does not describe actually changing his behaviour. At Faunalia, changes to cognitive self-understandings are not the primary source of lasting changes to habitual relational practices. Rather, when changes are dramatized in performance, particularly liminal ritual performance, this tends to have lasting consequences. Dale kissed Harrison, and it transformed his experience of homoerotic desire. Sauvage wrestled with the buffalo energy of Lewis, and he found some of this energy within himself. Leonie danced naked and it helped her find constructive ways of living with her 'shocking body image'. Andrew found himself isolated and empty at Faunalia, and fantasizes about better ways of relating to people. The new ways of relating are fantasies and dreams, not yet performed or practiced.

It would be interesting to interview Andrew again, and perhaps his close friends, to discover if his subsequent behaviour has actually changed. It is quite possible that the realization he describes was just that, a momentary realization, with minimal lasting consequences for the way he interacts with other people. It is also possible that his realization has lead into further performances of respect and mutual recognition that have transformed Andrew's emotional and somatic awareness. Andrew, however, does not describe such experiences at Faunalia.

The selection from Andrew's account reproduced here is particularly candid and lends itself to deconstruction. Other parts of his interview are more in line with the positive transformations that other participants report. Other interviewees also provide hints of similar fantasies and possibly unrealistic hopes for transformation. Overall, it is probable that for a minority of participants, and a minority of experiences, the transformations associated with Faunalia will be only a passing fantasy. However, the evidence from longer-term participants suggests that a significant number of the transformations described by participants have substantive and ongoing consequences.

Mistakes

While participants celebrate Faunalia, they are also painfully aware of mistakes that have been made, and the all too human characteristics of those who participate in the event. At a basic level this is reflected in inconsiderate behaviour:

> **Harrison:** There was a guy who started off being a bit of a problem, and I had to have words with him about behaving himself on two or three

occasions. He brought a pushbike and a boom box, a ghetto blaster. He was rolling the pushbike around the central fire when everyone was sitting there, with his boom box on his shoulder. Being close, people got quite intimidated by him. So I asked him to stop, and he did.

The ritualists and organizers also make mistakes that undermine the ritual experience at Faunalia. Harrison described one ritual performed in an enclosed space at a previous Faunalia. They laid straw on the ground: 'it was really poor quality. It was damp and dusty. So it was really hard to breathe in the ritual. The next day, the energy was really low, everyone was really depressed and seedy and quiet and ritually hung over.' Another year there was a ritual 'which took a very long time to do, and was very cold' (Harrison). Ruth described this ritual as: 'Altered states of consciousness through hypothermia.' I suspect this was the same year that René mentions as being 'not the best organized'.

Technological and organizational failure can have significant emotional and interpersonal consequences. Harrison described how at one Faunalia they 'fucked up the party night'.

> **Harrison:** We had someone lined up to do the party, but then they couldn't make it. . . . So come the party night, nothing had been organized. [Some music was finally arranged, but] there was an argument about the music that had been on, and then people started mucking with the sound system and changing the CDs. So the guy that brought most of the CDs took all his CDs away. [Then someone] got a hold of a record player and put on this industrial/gothic noise that was really aggravating. The people that had complained that rock and roll was just too out of character [for] the magical space, instead of getting what they want, they get something even worse.

Phoebe reports that the year she did the cooking for Faunalia she began the festival by giving all the participants 'a big talk about community and contributing in a very positive manner'. Her roles as a ritualist and chief cook were exhausting. In the middle of the festival she overheard someone refusing to assist in the kitchen. They said: 'This is my holiday, I'm not here to work.' Phoebe suppressed her anger for a little while until it boiled over:

> **Phoebe:** I said 'I need you all to please sit down.' Well I think that was the politest thing I said. Thereafter I lost it. All I remember that came out of my mouth was a combination of a lot of fucks and community. It was our holiday too. Some people just thought I was kitchen staff. I was not short of help after that.

Various forms of interpersonal conflict, the sources of which are complex, have also disrupted Faunalia. Harrison described a year that 'was a pretty prickly year too. There was a lot of bickering between people and people upsetting each other over trivial things. Which didn't surprise me'. There was also considerable tension between some of the ritualists that 'had not been one hundred per cent resolved'. Several other participants mentioned similar problems and issues. Harrison and Phoebe were perhaps the most aware of these issues, and reflective about them, because of their organizational roles.

The decentred nature of authority, and the emphasis on an ethics of authenticity, makes it difficult for exploitative or manipulative leaders to succeed in Paganism. People would simply stop attending Faunalia if the leaders developed a reputation for being manipulative or engaging in inappropriate behaviour. However, particularly in small-group contexts, nefarious manipulation is possible. This is demonstrated by the Tim Ryan case, a Witch who used various manipulative techniques in association with ritual to abuse two young women (Ezzy 2013).

Perhaps the more significant threat to the ongoing existence of the festival is that it depends on a few particular individuals. It does not have a formal structure that will survive if one or more key individuals choose to withdraw from the festival. Faunalia, and Paganism in Australia more generally, does not have developed formal structures and tends to follow an organizational pattern in which individual groups and events develop, flourish and then die, subsequently to be followed by the emergence of new events and groups.

As noted in Chapter Two, various forms of inappropriate behaviour have occurred at Faunalia. However, such behaviour that was discussed with me during the interviews seems to be no more common than in any other community. A male who was pushy was more insistent than he should have been in asking women to hug him, and another participant received an unwanted kiss. These issues were resolved through people making complaints to the organizers who mediated a resolution. Constructive ways of responding to inappropriate behaviour have developed over time, as the organizers have been confronted by various events and developed procedures for dealing with them. Put another way, the participants at Faunalia do not always act in the interests of other participants. Such behaviour is not tolerated when it crosses clearly demarcated lines. Respect and consent are key criteria by which activities are judged. These have some normative characteristics – participants are required to sign a form outlining the expected standards of behaviour. However, the more important influence on behaviour at Faunalia is the etiquette of mutual respect that the rituals create. The rituals challenge participants to be respectful of both themselves and the others around them while also evoking powerful emotions of desire and fear. Respect is found within desire and fear, rather than by repressing these emotions.

Relational ethics

Judith Butler (2004) argues that when we engage in relationship with the other, the inter-subjective moment of encounter is inherently violent, often resulting in suffering. The communication of the other is not something we invite but comes to us without our choosing. The encounter with the other both constitutes us and transforms us. Commenting on the response of the United States to the September 11 destruction of the twin towers Butler makes the point that we should not rush to resolve the discomfort that suffering generates.

> Suffering can yield an experience of humility, of vulnerability, of impressionability and dependence, and these can become resources, if we do not 'resolve' them too quickly; they can move us beyond and against the vocation of the paranoid victim who regenerates infinitely the justifications of war. It is as much a matter of wrestling ethically with one's own murderous impulses, impulses that seek to quell an overwhelming fear, as it is a matter of apprehending the suffering of others and taking stock of the suffering one has inflicted. (Butler 2004: 149)

For Levinas and Butler it is these twin moments that are at the heart of ethics. The first moment recognizes and wrestles with one's own fear, and the desire to destroy the other, whose mere presence threatens me. The second moment recognizes the vulnerability and suffering of both self and other. It is the context of the interaction, the structure of the communication, the nature of the symbols and the framing narrative mythology, that makes this form of understanding possible, or not.

In the moment of recognition, of relational encounter, we are made vulnerable because the other with whom we are relating is a part of us that we cannot control. The ethical life is the one that actively engages with this precariousness, this vulnerability. The awareness of this vulnerability, our own and the other's, generates fear and anxiety. Fear that the other might overwhelm me or attempt to destroy me, and anxiety that I might need to fight the other in order to defend myself. For Emmanuel Levinas (1979) ethics is found in the active engagement with these emotions. 'For the nonviolence that Levinas seems to promote does not come from a peaceful place, but rather from a constant tension between the fear of undergoing violence and the fear of inflicting violence' (Butler 2004: 137). For most Pagans at Faunalia, the relationship to the other is a complex and ambivalent relationship. This ambivalence remains whether that other is Baphomet, a lover, an emotion, a self-evaluation or a male acting with 'buffalo' energy.

Butler suggests that language is inadequate to communicate the precariousness at the heart of relational encounters. 'One would need to hear the face as it speaks in something other than language to know the precariousness of life that is at stake' (Butler 2004: 151). She goes on to argue that literature and 'the humanities' has the potential to communicate this form of understanding at the limits of that which can be represented. Such forms of cultural criticism can help us to find the 'human where we do not expect to find it, in its frailty and at the limits of its capacity to make sense' (Butler 2004: 151).

Religious ritual can also provide an experience of the frailty of humanity at the limits of our ability to understand and communicate. In moments and experiences that are 'beyond words' participants at Faunalia engage with a threatening other that is also desired and loved. In a moment of mutual recognition they both pursue their own authenticity and an ethical concern for the other. Not all religious mythologies and rituals, or forms of cultural criticism in the humanities, communicate this frailty, this uncertainty. At Faunalia many participants discover and engage in a form of ethical relationality that embraces this frailty and vulnerability. The rituals at Faunalia draw participants into new ways of relating to desire, self and other.

The relational ethics nurtured at Faunalia embraces both desire and vulnerability. While embracing the pleasure of the possible, of the 'God who may be' (Kearney 2001), participants celebrate the joy of sensuality and of erotic relationships. Participants also experience fear and vulnerability during the rituals. They do not seek to escape these emotions, but rather seek new ways of relating to them, wrestling with their fears and vulnerabilities lest they lead them into unhealthy relationships and inappropriate actions. Both desire and vulnerability draw participants at Faunalia into respectful relationships, however human and flawed their performance may be.

Vignette: Phoebe

Phoebe played the role of Baphomet at Faunalia from 2000, when it began, until 2005, when I interviewed her. Phoebe's experience has already been discussed extensively throughout the book. This vignette focuses on her experience of Baphomet.

I was raised a strict Roman Catholic. I have to admit, until I [put on] the [Baphomet] mask myself six years ago, there was still a lot of fragments of Catholicism there . . . Looking at the mask, in my head and in my feelings, my emotions, the next step for me is to cut the ties of Catholicism. Baphomet is the god form, or Baphomet/Dionysus is the god form, that the Catholics chose to represent as Satan in the Bible and in their teachings.

I could not have sex with my [first] husband [laughs] until I got rid of a bloody family photo that I had on a dresser in my room. My father would come home and if we were watching telly and some of the soapies [and] a kiss was exchanged, he would turn it off, we all had to go to bed [laughs].

There were no hang-ups with the [Baphomet] ritual. But for myself to personally [put on] the mask as I did six years ago, that was the crucial point for me.

Baphomet was about accepting everything about myself. The Pagan Mardi Gras was the first time I experienced a passionate kiss with another woman. That blew me away. For months I was ringing up friends of mine that were gay, saying: 'What the fuck is going on here?' I remember coming home and telling [my husband]. It blew me away. [The challenge for me was] can you accept yourself? If I had a different upbringing, I definitely would have embraced bisexuality. I find women very, very appealing energetically, as I do men. So Baphomet was about accepting the sexual me. Accepting the balanced me, the male and female. I am a good person, and it is OK, everything is OK. There is no burning fire [of hell].

I know I am a good person. [Becoming a Witch] was about accepting. I wanted others to accept me. I struggled with that for a long time.

I learned a long time ago [that in ritual] the words mean nothing. I used to put such pressure on myself to memorize the entire ceremony. I [think it is important to memorize the words] because it [makes the ritual] flow. The energy has got to keep going. But when [a ritual is] just all words, to me, you lose it. If you are reading, having somebody there holding the Book of Shadows, people will start fidgeting and there is no energy. It is just, to me, empty words. If I am going to invoke a particular energy, element or a deity, I need to tune into that. So I do whatever I need to do to get into that headspace. Not the headspace, the heartspace.

I think the intensity of the energy [of Baphomet] scared me. The first maybe three years I would work with the energy for almost three months before the event. I would meditate. I would find myself doing housework and talking to Baphomet. I would say: 'You have seventy-five per cent' [laughs] 'but I want this much'. It is not even Phoebe, it is the mother, the wife. The monogamous one [laughs]. I was fearful of the fact that – what if? A lot of that fear, not only did it come from me, but also [from other people who were] really scared, what if? What if? . . . It would have been – oh, not quite seventy-five per cent, but I think it was eighty or eighty-five, and I had the fifteen per cent the first time.

I don't know all the history on Baphomet and that is OK. I understand the energy. That to me is important. I would meditate. I would go to bed during the day. I would lie down. I would say things like, 'You are old. I know that you are primitive, I know that you are primal'. I would go through some of the chants in [the] Baphomet [rite]. But I continuously have had that energy with me for almost three months. This year [was different], it was a matter of reading a poem and the picture. That was it. It was only a couple of weeks. All I found myself doing this time was just reciting [the poem]. The more I recited it, the more I could feel the energy building up. This year I think I gave myself one hundred per cent. Even last year there was still just five per cent [of me kept back from Baphomet]. Over the years I have gotten more comfortable with the energy. I was the empty glass that was going to carry the energy.

Phoebe has also channelled other deities such as Hekate. I asked how Hekate is different to Baphomet.

Hekate is in the context of a [small] ritual. It does not come in its full force. It is there but it is on a nice level. Baphomet is for a group. It has got to come in to [a much greater] degree for everyone to get a taste, for everyone to touch. When I invoke Hekate, I zone out, but nowhere near like Baphomet.

With reference to the 2005 Baphomet ritual, I asked: Do you remember anyone's face or a conversation you had with somebody afterwards? Is there something somebody said that gave you a sense of what Baphomet did for them?

Other than wow, I guess. I think a lot of people struggled with words after it. The words came after their experience. Not even on the Sunday morning. I think people found words after. That is why I say, it was a world between. We were taken back in time to our ancestors. We had energies there that were old, and had danced the dance thousands of times before. We were honouring ourselves as this generation, but we were also honouring way back when.

Jenny, in particular, I just wanted to take her pain. I, Baphomet, was saying: you do not need it any more, let it go. I could have put my hand in her, and taken out all the shit . . . She hurts so much. There was pain from everyone, but she hurt so much. I felt pain. I felt people's pain this year. I felt the heaviness. She stood out the most. It was internal, the chaos was internal, it was not external like previous years. I think Baphomet, the energy, I wanted to take it [the pain]. It was about taking it, saying that you do not need it anymore, let it go.

Baphomet is the healer. He is the confronter and confronts you. But this year it was more healing. Look at the shit we bury. Look at our feelings. Bring them up, vomit them out. Do not hang on to it anymore. It has taken from you more than it needed, now it is time for you to take back.

I remember Baphomet was there and I was there, and there were parts of me that were interacting. There were aspects of Baphomet that were stronger than me, and participants were aware when it was Baphomet and when it was me. [After I had taken the mask off] a lot of them actually saw that I still had my mask on, they were not even aware that the mask was no longer there. So he was there, I was there. He was attentive. Since then I have felt the healthiest I have been in ten years. There is a sense of clarity.

The world needs to know not to fear Baphomet. It is an energy that is primal that is in all of us. To embrace it. Not to fear it. To embrace it. Because the aspects or qualities of Baphomet are the energy [of life]. I am energy. It is what makes us alive today. Only we have ignored it, we have been scared of it through society, through religion . . . There is the fine line between doing what is acceptable and what is not acceptable. Baphomet is in all of us. To me, Baphomet is all gods, or goddesses, he is everything. He has the qualities of all the gods and goddesses. But it is just the one name.

I do not fear Baphomet anymore. I fear losing myself totally to that. [The consequences would be] everything. Nothing. Too much. Not enough. I don't know [laughs].

Ego inflation. [I have seen it before with Kim]. Kim's whole attitude was basically kiss my arse, wipe my feet. She demanded absolute respect. People had to kneel before her. Not literally. She wanted all the power, I think. She wanted control. She was not nice. She was using people.

I do not want to lose myself in ego. All of this experience over eight years [of being a leader of the Pagan community] is still humbling. I want it that way. I have my moments of ego. [But] I do not want to be a handful of people that I have come across over eight years that have lost themselves and are now empty souls. I do not want to be the guru. To me, we are all gurus. We are all followers and we are all leaders. We are all teachers and we are all students. The fear that I have with the Baphomet is losing that side of me.

I asked how Phoebe thought Faunalia, and in particular the sense of community, had changed over the six years it had been running.

It has changed because it has had to. You have got to allow things to grow. You nurture that growth. We have kept an open mind, hence we have always encouraged both the positive feedback and the negative feedback to help this develop and grow . . . [It is about] not putting it into a container and saying this is exactly how it has to be. It is about letting it evolve and letting it grow. Every year is a different year.

I think because community starts right from the start. It is as the participants start to arrive. It is instigated right from the onset. They are shown their cabin, then once you have settled in they all ask is there something they can do, because they see a lot of others busy doing things. I think that that really helps. I think it is the way we approach them as well. There are no orders, we do not give orders. With people that I am very familiar and comfortable with, I do tend to say, 'Oh, look, can you help us in the kitchen? We just need five minutes'. A lot of the times they will actually come. The majority of participants have been year after year after year. That has actually helped. As the first-timers come in, they see this group that is contributing, whether it be with the firewood or setting up something. Even something like sweeping the dining hall and setting the tables up, arranging tables. So they automatically get in there. Harrison and I blend.

There is no authority, we do not walk around with that authority. I think that because we are on their level, and they are on our level. We are all walking side by side. I believe that actually contributes a lot. Other than the initial welcoming ritual, welcoming talk, and going through the guidelines and what we expect of people. It is an openness. It is very much an openness. It is an openness of heart. Every year that has improved. So every year people are already walking in there with open hearts. There are a couple of people that choose to remain closed. That is OK too, because they are still accepted and they are still treated in the same manner. It is definitely a spiritual [growth]. The rituals that have taken place over the years open people. I am a firm believer that when you are working magic or ritual with individuals, you see them skyclad. I am not saying the outer skyclad, you see them raw inside. Baphomet broke down a lot of personal boundaries. There is that acceptance and there is the openness. I do not know how it happens. It happens. I do not know what the key is, I do not know whether it is my relationship with Harrison. Harrison and I contribute a lot to that [openness] because we, ourselves, also get down and get our hands dirty.

CHAPTER SEVEN

Religion

The religious rituals at Faunalia help participants make sense of some of the most troubling aspects of their lives. Specifically, they work with the inevitability of death, and deep ambivalences associated with sexual desire. The rituals change the way participants relate to death, suffering, sexual desire and their bodies. The rituals primarily change participants' feelings and somatic understandings. The rituals also change what participants think about these things, but these changes are secondary. There is little possibility of thinking clearly when your mind is 'blown' and your heart takes control. As Phoebe notes, the words come later.

Contradiction, tension, performance and half-conscious understandings play a central role in ritual. The rituals move participants out of the everyday world where meaning and order are paramount, through a liminal space of trance and inversion, and safely return participants to the mundane world. The absence of rational thought in the liminal moment does not lead to anything 'terrible' happening. Rather, in that moment in which control is relinquished to their hearts participants discover something that changes their lives and restores their souls. This 'something' is beyond words. How could it be anything else? These aspects of the ritual experiences at Faunalia are interpreted in this chapter drawing on the philosophy of Friedrich Nietzsche, the art historian Carl Einstein and the psychoanalytic theory of Mari Ruti and Jessica Benjamin.

The religious rituals at Faunalia change the way participants relate to themselves and to the world around them. They discover that death is indeed something to be feared, but that fear is bearable. They discover that naked bodies are indeed erotic and sensual, imbuing interactions with lust and desire, but that these desires can be negotiated with respect and loving care. Aesthetic experiences and somatic knowing transform relational etiquettes. In the ritual moment of 'flow' their sense of self dissolves and they experience deep and intimate relationships with other ritual participants, the deity and the world beyond. When your heart is open it is much easier to care deeply for the person who stands before you in all their naked vulnerability. These experiences draw participants out of narcissistic self-absorption into relational commitments to the others around them, even if, for many people, these relationships do not extend beyond the end of the festival.

Religion is non-rational, at least partly. This is because rationality is inadequate to encompass the religious experience of being human. Words point towards religious experiences, as if through a glass darkly. Accounts of gods, spirits and energies *point towards* religious experiences. In this context asking if the beings represented by these words are 'real' or 'true' in a scientific sense makes no more sense than trying to measure the amount of someone's love. The gods, like love, have their own arithmetic which is more real than any scientific experiment. If academic studies of religion are to adequately grasp the significance of religious ritual and experience, then religion must be valued on its own terms.

Aesthetics

Nietzsche, developing a theme from classical Greek Paganism, provides a strong argument for the importance of aesthetics in representing the conflictual aspects of life and the inevitability of suffering and death. At the heart of Nietzsche's vision is an 'insistence on contradiction as an attribute of nature [which] implies that it must be understood as a conflict of forces rather than as a set of laws or as a chaotic formlessness' (Pan 2001: 44). The contradictory and tension-ridden nature of the world is best understood as an aesthetic phenomenon, Nietzsche argues, rather than conceptually described through logical laws. According to Pan (2001), this does not mean that understanding is impossible. Rather, it means that aesthetic forms of understanding are preferable because they represent this conflictual and unpredictable nature of the world. In *The Birth of Tragedy*, Nietzsche (1993) builds on Schopenhauer's argument for the value of aesthetic forms of understanding:

> [Nietzsche] believes it is impossible to approach the totality of nature through scientific means based on critique that seeks to grasp nature as a set of laws. Rather, nature's totality can only be approached through aesthetic means grounded in the intuition of the artist, whose visions depend on the ability to identify 'with the primal unity, its pain and contradiction'. (Pan 2001: 45)

Nietzsche distinguishes between Apollonian gods representing 'reason, proportion and control' and Dionysian gods representing 'emotional intoxication and orgiastic ritual practices' (Collins 2007: 22). Dionysian practices embrace an aesthetic appreciation of contradiction and paradox. While Nietzsche's association of these two forms of religion with historical periods has been criticized (Rampley 2000), the distinction, shorn of its historical associations, is nonetheless useful. Nietzsche argued that 'Christianity was a development of the Apollonian religion of self-control, which resolutely repressed Dionysian practices' (Collins 2007: 22). Weber (1963) made a similar point, identifying the rationalizing and disenchanting tendencies of Protestantism that shaped the modern spirit of capitalism. The modernist project 'had at its centre an attempt to subject the world to human control, and this required the obliteration of all that could not be controlled' (Mellor and Shilling 1997: 10). In this context the 'Dionysian sense of abandon and sensuality . . . continued to constitute a "fearful Other" in Renaissance and Enlightenment visions of an ordered, controllable world' (Mellor and Shilling 1997: 10).

Contemporary Christianity in the West is predominantly Apollonian, although the Christian tradition is much more complex than this. Christianity is often represented as intransigently monotheist with an overriding tendency to unify and rationalize, integrating or destroying the threatening other. While there is some truth to this characterization, this principle is transgressed in 'a thousand and one ways' (Maffesoli 1996: 111). The cult of saints, the mystics and a range of other practices demonstrate that 'the foreign or the stranger have had many havens enabling a resistance to the simplification of unitary reduction' (Maffesoli 1996: 111). Maffesoli discerns a similar Dionysian ambivalence in contemporary 'tribes': 'The tribes he [Dionysus] inspires demonstrate a troublesome ambiguity: although not disdaining the most sophisticated technology, they remain nonetheless somewhat barbaric' (Maffesoli 1996: 28). The tribes, or 'neo-tribes' identified by Maffesoli are formed around subcultures and new forms of consumption, and include Goths, music and fan subcultures, and Pagans (Letcher 2001).

The Dionysian and Apollonian co-exist in most epochs. 'It is possible to trace both Apollonian dimensions of control and Dionysian tendencies toward transcendence throughout those epochs and events which have caught the attention of such thinkers as Schopenhauer, Nietzsche, Weber, Freud and Elias' (Mellor and Shilling 1997: 13). Charles Taylor (1989) similarly argues that romanticism is the often-ignored counterpart of modernist enlightenment rationalism. From this perspective, the Dionysian aspects of neo-tribes are not the return of something lost, but the manifestation of the Dionysian in this particular epoch. The Apollonian and Dionysian appear in all epochs in various guises.

While the 'notion of art as the sensuous embodiment of truth' (Rampley 2000: 191) is undoubtedly central to Nietzsche's thought, Rampley (2000) argues that aesthetic modes of engagement for Nietzsche are not an alternative way of approaching an external 'reality'. Rather, aesthetic moments of engagement represent the impossibility of ever conveying the one truth about an external reality 'because it does not exist' (Rampley 2000: 192). Aesthetic modes of engagement represent both the multiple possibilities for interpreting experience, and the necessity of choosing an interpretation.

There is an implicit morality to the Apollonian rationality of enlightenment thought. It assumes that rationality can plumb all depths and correct all errors, thus avoiding pain. 'The good' is unified, and can be understood rationally. In contrast, and following the classical Greek Pagan understanding of tragedy, Nietzsche argues for 'the incommensurability of nature and the consequent inevitability of human suffering' (Pan 2001: 47). The Apollonian and Dionysian ways of engaging with nature, self and others, have very different moral consequences, they construct different etiquettes of relationship.

To put this in Levinasian terms, Dionysian aesthetics represent the incommensurability and conflictual nature of relationships. In contrast, Apollonian aesthetics attempts to eliminate the conflictual and unpredictable nature of relationships. In some ways this is inconsistent with Levinas's thought, because he does not see the world as basically conflictual, as Nietzsche does. However, it can also be seen as an extension of Levinas's account of the inaccessibility of the other, and the tensions and self-disruptions that arise through engagement with such an other. Levinas argued that both the desire to control or destroy the other and the desire to respect the other exist simultaneously. Ethics lies in the way we respond to these desires. The enlightenment modernist project attempts to escape the contradictions of myth, providing solutions. Carl Einstein, similar to Nietzsche, and Ruti (2006), grapple with the idea that there are no solutions and argue that myth and ritual are 'a return to those contradictions and their irresolvability' (Pan 2001: 188).

The Baphomet rite at Faunalia combines liminal ritual and Dionysian intoxication with eroticism and deliberate engagement with the shadow aspects of self and the world. The paradoxical and aesthetic aspects are central to the rite.

> **Heath:** Baphomet is the archetype of man, woman, beast. It is a cocktail of primal lust and primal magic. In Baphomet I am not in my head. My unconscious comes through, it is a feeling rite. If you questioned it, then I do not think you could get into it. You just have to get out of your mind in the Baphomet rite otherwise you are nothing. You are just going to run out of the space. No matter how much you think you are used to it, I can't speak for others, but I am never used to it.

The Baphomet rite does not make sense when you are in 'your mind', and when it is viewed from the perspective of Apollonian cognitive categories.

Baphomet confronts participants with the necessity of aesthetic and performative engagement with the fundamentally contradictory nature of the world and the paradoxical nature of their own fears and desires. This Dionysian experience is contained within a liminal rite that removes people from, and then returns participants safely to, the Apollonian world of mundane reality. Participants value the ritual for precisely these characteristics.

Religion and ritual conceived and practised within the Dionysian frame is very different to religion and ritual conceived and practised within an Apollonian frame. This application of Nietzsche's observations to religion extends Harvey (2013) and McGuire's (2008) arguments that religion is primarily about practices. Religions that focus on practise embrace a different ontology and epistemology. They understand, or experience, the world as primarily conflictual and tension-ridden, and apprehend it aesthetically and performatively.

Dionysian ritual

Dionysian ritual is ritual that transforms participants' mode of engagement with the world such that they value and understand aesthetic modes of communication. Aesthetic modes of engagement are typically somatic and performed. In the rituals at Faunalia, participants also describe an experience of loss of the self. As a consequence of this dissolution of the self, participants develop a greater appreciation of the relational and communal sources of their self-understandings. They find what they consider to be healthier selves through relationships of mutual recognition.

This is Phoebe's point in the final paragraphs of her vignette. Over time people at Faunalia have increasingly engaged in actions that contribute to the collective and create community. This generosity is a product of the leadership provided by Phoebe and Harrison, the actions of others at Faunalia and the rituals, particularly the Baphomet rite.

The rituals at Faunalia transform participants' mode of engagement with the world. Specifically, they draw people into an appreciation and understanding of aesthetic and symbolic ways of relating:

> **Marie:** I have a friend who is an artist. She was a member of our coven. We started working together [doing ritual]. She would have long conversations with me which, quite frankly, I could make no sense of because she seemed to always talk round and round in circles. Whereas I had been trained very much to think in a very linear way. I always got annoyed by her conversations. The strange thing was that when I came back from Faunalia the first time, I spoke a different language. Suddenly what she was saying actually made perfect sense

IMAGE 7.1 *Seline and Tania.*
Photo by Philippe.

to me. I felt like it opened up an aspect of my psyche which had been lost.

Such aesthetic modes of communication are central to people's understandings of their experience of Faunalia. This is what Carl Einstein means when he argues that: 'Mythic reality is not a backward or pathological fantasy world but the foundation of human perception, functioning to determine the structures through which humans experience the world' (Pan 2001: 134). When asked how he responded to the early festivals, Lewis replied:

> Lewis: Well, one day I was caught in a whirlpool in a river, and many people die. You know what I did? I jumped into the whirlpool and I went under the actual river and I followed it all the way out into the other end. That is what you have got to do. It's a lot of fun.

In cognitive linear terms, this answer does not seem to address the question about Lewis's experience of a particular Pagan festival. However, Lewis uses parables and metaphors much of the time to explain himself. He is explaining something that is beyond a linear conceptual narrative. His experiences of the festival are characterized by embracing natural forces and processes that are beyond his control and swimming with them.

> Lewis: Working in disorienting the senses is very important to transcend the mind, getting beyond the mind, and actually take it to that God, Goddess, to that place in the soul, in the being, to get to that nakedness and transcend from beyond there.

An experience of a life with soul is associated, for Lewis, with disorienting experiences, with getting beyond the rational conceptual mind. This is central to his experience of Faunalia. The point for Lewis is not to abandon rational thought. Rather, it is that self, nature, God and Goddess, cannot be completely understood from within the bounds of rational linear thinking. This is similar to Carl Einstein's understanding: 'Rather, nature's totality can only be approached through aesthetic means grounded in the intuition of the artist, whose visions depend on the ability to identify "with the primal unity, its pain and contradiction"' (Pan 2001: 45). Einstein here parallels Nietzsche's thought and reflects the influence of the late nineteenth-century romantic movement that emphasized aesthetic approaches to nature (Taylor 1989). Einstein's discussion is important because he extends these ideas to analyse the significance of religious experience.

> Rather than basing religion on the presupposition of faith in a dogma, Einstein constructs a model of religion in which faith is the result of an aesthetic experience of the parable, and the eternal is not a pure form but is always linked to bodily experience. (Pan 2001: 158)

The relationship of bodily experience to aesthetic engagement is clearly articulated in Sauvage's experience at the dance party. On the last night of Faunalia there was a relaxed dance party with different kinds of music in four different venues. The gymnasium played old time 'rock and roll' music, which attracted Sauvage, and had a flat concrete floor with a central cauldron fire and little else in the room. This made it very easy for Sauvage to manoeuvre in his wheelchair. His account illustrates how aesthetic modes of understanding emerge out of, or are bound up with, somatic, performed and relational experiences.

> Sauvage: The disco [on the last night], in a strange sort of way, for me was probably the most powerful, even though the other two rites were extraordinary. I think it was set up really well, but for some strange reason I felt safe enough to just be who I was at that point in time, and just explored that. I found myself spending a lot of time dancing. I felt that I could be there without my armour and feel safe. And not just feel safe, but feel really vibrant and big. And be able to dance with

beings, with yourself, with your shadow, with your past, with others that you felt a bond to or an attraction, or were trying to resolve something. Yeah, yeah.

At the disco Sauvage dances with his shadow. He also dances in his wheelchair. He feels safe to 'be without my armour', by which I think Sauvage is referring to something like the Dionysian openness to experience and the dissolution of self. The self does not completely dissolve, rather people experience themselves as more porous and open for the duration of the festival. In that time and that place it is safe to be without one's armour, but the armour will be put back in place once Faunalia is over. This somatic, aesthetic, ritually contextualized practice changes the way Sauvage feels about himself, and helps him to resolve some things that were troubling him.

> **Sauvage:** It is funny because [the disco in the gym is] the one part of the event that I have probably not talked about to anybody else because I do not really know how to explain it, that sense of being able to dance. It is something that I do not do. The last time I have done anything like that is probably twenty or thirty years ago. I thought, well, what made me do that? Where did that come from? I think it is the safety [that I feel] and it is [a context that enables] that physicality of your being to work in unison with your spirituality, and not have a disjointed relationship there.

The rituals at Faunalia bring people's physicality, their somatic experience, into relationship with their spirituality. Sauvage is attuned to this dimension of experience because he uses a wheelchair. Many other participants also pointed to the somatic nature of their experiences at Faunalia. Whether it was circling round the fire waiting to be taken in the Underworld rite, lying in the mock grave, dancing naked in the Baphomet rite or being confronted by Baphomet, participant descriptions emphasize how they felt, their somatic awareness, and often explicitly note the absence of thought or the difficulty of formulating their experience in words. Dionysian ritual engages somatic experience to transform aesthetic orientations to both self and the world.

Sauvage's reference to being 'without my armour' can also be understood as a reference to engaging with his shadow. Conger (1991) draws on the psychoanalytic theory of Wilhelm Reich to identify a parallel between the body as shadow and the body as armoured. According to Reich, the armoured body is divided: the body, the mind, emotions and spirit are all kept separate. The armoured body contains the 'energy' of the repressed shadow by defensively armouring itself through rigidity and muscle contractions. The aim of therapy is not to remove one's armour completely, as 'everyone needs some armour as protection' (Conger 1991: 88). Rather, the aim is to engage in creative relationship with the somatic 'armoured' expressions of one's shadow: 'Therapy seeks not only to dissolve armour but to introduce flexibility and conscious choice to what had been a rigid, unconscious, defence structure' (Conger 1991: 88).

Most participants at Faunalia describe an experience, similar to that of Sauvage, of feeling open, of dropping their barriers or shields, which points towards a sense of dissolution of the boundaries of self. This dissolution is temporary. For the duration of the festival, and particularly during the rituals, the sense of radical openness and vulnerability, of having one's 'armour' down, is a powerful experience. The experience of the dissolution of the boundaries of the self is welcomed, desired and celebrated. It reflects a deep emotional intimacy, an experience of communitas in Turner's (1969) sense. This experience of openness, or having a porous self, is central to the transformative processes that occur at Faunalia.

Many participants develop a stronger appreciation of the social and communal foundations of the self as a consequence of the ritual experience of the loss of self. This outcome has many similarities to the consequences of near death experiences – which also lead some people to value relationships and social goals and reject selfish individualistic life-goals (Kellehear 1996). Several people made comments similar to those of Phoebe in Chapter One that pointed to the importance of 'heart friendships' that they had developed during the rituals at Faunalia. I understand 'heart friendships' to refer to relationships of 'mutual recognition' (Benjamin 1988). The rituals at Faunalia enable participants to disentangle themselves from relationships that involve projected shadows and rediscover a self in relationships of mutual recognition. For example, Leonie's poor body image is partially a product of her assumption that other people view her as ugly. She projects onto other people her shadow, assuming incorrectly that they view her body as ugly. In the Baphomet rite she realizes that this assumption is wrong and begins to feel and see herself as beautiful because this is the way she perceives that other participants see her. Such transformations are made possible through embodied participation in ritual that engages aesthetically apprehended etiquettes of relating.

The point that Dionysian ritual transforms people's self-understandings is one Durkheim (1976) made some time ago. Shilling and Mellor (2011) clearly describe Durkheim's argument:

To be intoxicated, for Durkheim, is to be open to transcendence of the individual, egoistic characteristics of one's physical self. Stimulated by the collective experience of congregating amidst the sacred, participants are 'pulled away from . . . ordinary occupations and preoccupations', and moved to the point of delirium akin to 'the religious state' (Durkheim, 1995: 386). It is through this intoxicating feeling of hyper-excitement that individuals become attached or cathected to the collective dimensions of their bodies, and motivated to pursue impersonal ends and collective 'rules of conduct' (Durkheim, 1973). (Shilling and Mellor 2011: 22)

At Faunalia ritual intoxication does not create commitment to transcendent normative rules. Rather, ritual intoxication allows for the transformation of relationships with shadow aspects of the self and with others. Further, Dionysian ritual leads to a greater appreciation of aesthetic ways of relating to the world and of relationships and shared experiences. While the process is different, the effect is similar, in that it transforms the individual's moral stance in the world – the way they relate to others. The religious ritual at Faunalia transforms the participants' etiquette of relationships.

Baphomet is 'all'

The Baphomet rite is an aesthetic moment of apprehension of the totality of nature and its inherently contradictory character. In the interviews, participants consistently describe Baphomet as both a symbol of 'all', 'everything', 'totality' and as having many conflictual and contradictory characteristics. Both Phoebe and Flora make this point:

> Phoebe: Baphomet is everything. Baphomet is all the fears, Baphomet is all the OKs. Baphomet is everything. Baphomet is the chaos. Baphomet is the light in the chaos. Baphomet is the darkness in the chaos. Baphomet is the all, and yet he is the nothing. I do not have words. He is the confronter and confronts you. But this year it was more healing.

> Flora: Baphomet is the most incredible concept, archetype. It was perfect. Baphomet is everything. He is not androgynous, she is hermaphrodite. She is not no sex, she is both sexes, all sexes. All creatures. Everything. She is the centre where everything meets. To have the opportunity to meet him, and to bow down before him . . . There is no other archetype or deity who has such power to release us from oppression as him. He is everything. Everything and nothing. All at the same time. So I was very taken by it, of course. I loved the goat head, the goat being the symbol of not following the herd, doing exactly what he wants to do. If the goat wants to go and eat your clothes off the line, it will [short laugh]. They won't just follow blindly.

Engaging with Baphomet, as a representation of the ambivalence and contradiction at the heart of 'the all' leads participants to develop an ethic of self-responsibility and authenticity. This is Flora's point. While she chooses to 'bow down before him', this does not mean that she will 'just follow along blindly'. Flora echoes the ambivalence towards Pagan deities discussed in Chapters Four and Six. Flora also echoes Marie's points in Chapter Six, that at Faunalia they honour rather than worship Baphomet. Further, when participants engage with Baphomet as a complete and inherently contradictory representation of the universe, this does not lead to despair, to selfishness or to violence. Rather, it challenges participants to find their own ethical way of relating to the radical otherness of Baphomet, and the world he/ she represents.

In the Baphomet rite participants experience release from oppression. The healing and transformative power of the Baphomet and Underworld rites comes precisely from the apprehension and participatory acceptance of the inherent ambivalence of life. This is Nietzsche's point, and, following Nietzsche, Einstein, Lacan and Ruti's. Ruti, drawing on Lacan, describes the sense of alienation that humans experience as 'lack' (Ruti 2006: 15). The participants at Faunalia do not conceptualize their experience in terms of 'lack'. Rather, Baphomet represents a broad range of tensions, desires, fears and frustrations. Nonetheless, the point is similar. The aim is not to suture over these tensions, desires, and fears, but to learn to live with them. In the Baphomet rite participants see Baphomet as a symbol of the tensions, contradictions and paradoxes of nature, and of these tensions, contradictions and paradoxes within themselves.

Participants talk about experiencing Baphomet 'within' themselves. Natasha, for example, reported: 'I felt Baphomet was within, in a way.' Baphomet is both the 'beast within' and the 'beast without'. Baphomet reflects inner psychological tensions, and is the focus of their projections. The experience of Baphomet is also created through ritual and social processes, embodied in the priestess. However, Baphomet cannot be reduced to projections and social processes:

> **Harrison:** When Baphomet manifests in the circle, she is not just in the priestess. To some degree she has got to be in everyone. Or they have got to be aware that she is in everyone. I see her as a part of all of us, and we are all a part of her. I see it anthropomorphically, as an entity, but also as an energy, as a force that is basically all life, well, all everything. Everything that I can conceive of in existence. That is the underlying reality of Baphomet for me. It is huge. Primal. It is awesome. So we only manifest a very small part of that, and can only see a very small part of that.

Phoebe describes Baphomet as a healer and destroyer. Baphomet represents the murderous impulses within ourselves, and the capacity for generosity and compassion. When participants describe Baphomet as 'primal', they are pointing to the all-encompassing nature of Baphomet. Yet, in some ways Baphomet is a lover for both Phoebe and Harrison.

Harrison thinks of Baphomet as also 'something else besides that is beyond our comprehension.' Engaging with Baphomet involved an acceptance, for many participants, that life, the universe, is beyond comprehension. Participants still engage with 'a very small part of that', but accept that it is impossible to apprehend everything. This acceptance for Harrison is part of the mystery and pleasure of the ritual experience: 'The heart of the relationship with magic and deity is mystery. We just engage with it as best we can' (Harrison).

Baphomet represents something more, beyond human projection, that is in and of itself revelatory. This can be interpreted sociologically in various ways, but with Edith Turner, I argue that such experiences should be valued for their own sake: 'It's true that I once had an experience of religion, after which I didn't see the point of disbelieving other people's experiences' (Edith Turner 1992: xiii). The participants at Faunalia point to an aesthetic apprehension of something that is difficult to put into words, and which is central to finding a life with soul. I am not arguing for the truth of any particular religious experience, whether of Baphomet, Christ or an Ndembu Ihamba (Turner 1992). Rather, I argue that these experiences should be understood on their own terms, as somatic, aesthetic, religious experiences that have value in and of themselves.

Sociologically, the important point is that in the Baphomet rite participants engage aesthetically with a representation of 'the all' that is inherently paradoxical and conflictual. This engagement transforms the etiquette of relating to both self and others. Specifically, it provides a way of learning to live with, rather than suturing over, a broad range of tensions, desires, fears and frustrations. This transformation in the way that participants relate to themselves and others is made possible by the liminal experience of the Baphomet rite.

Liminal flow

Csikszentmihalyi (1974) originally used the term 'flow' to describe the internal mental states of artists who became immersed in their work:

Flow refers to the holistic sensation present when we act with total involvement. It is a kind of feeling after which one nostalgically says 'that was fun', or 'that was enjoyable'. It is the state in which action follows upon action according to an internal logic which seems to need no conscious intervention on our part. We experience it as a unified flowing from one moment to the next in which we are in control of our actions, and in which there is little distinction between self and environment; between stimulus and response; or between past, present, and future. (Csikszentmihalyi 1974: 58)

Csikszentmihalyi's account of flow is very similar to the liminal experience of participants at Faunalia. The rituals create an experience of unified action and awareness in which the focus of participants is wholly and completely on the ritual. There is a participatory acceptance of the ritual accompanied by a sense of confidence in one's self to do what is required. However, this is counterbalanced with the sense of ambivalence characteristic of engagement with Pagan deities. Participants willingly suspend disbelief and accept the rules and presumptions of the rituals while maintaining confidence in their own ability to make choices consistent with their own sense of authenticity and their commitments to ongoing relationships.

Phoebe notes that, for her, ritual is about flow and energy, and not about the words. Experiences of flow at Faunalia are documented in earlier chapters. For example, as noted in Chapter Three, René reports that during the Underworld rite she was wholly focused on the ritual: 'At no point did any mundane thought or thoughts of the outside world, or my kids, or my life out there ever intruded for a minute.' Similarly, during the Baphomet rite Calvin noted that: 'part way through the ritual I found that my clothes were somewhere in a corner and was not quite sure when or why they had come off but that was that. I was just really, really enjoying the sense of it.' René and Calvin, similar to most other participants, experience ritual as a moment of 'flow'.

Turner (1979) uses Csikszentmihalyi's concept of flow to differentiate the experience of liminality from the liminoid. He suggests that liminality is found in societies where ritual is compulsory. In these ritual contexts experiences of flow are shared, culturally endorsed experiences, and generate commitment to the established social order. In contrast, the liminoid is found in industrialized societies where rituals are optional, experiences of flow are individualized and established social structures are therefore experienced as oppressive: 'we might say that liminal genres put much stress on social frames, plural reflexivity, and mass flow, shared flow, while liminoid genres emphasize idiosyncratic framing, individual reflexivity, subjective flow, and see the social as problem not datum' (Turner 1979: 494).

The experience of flow at Faunalia is somewhere between the liminal and the liminoid. Established social structures are experienced as restrictive or oppressive (liminoid), but participants return to commitments in mainstream society with a renewed sense of purpose and fulfilment (liminal). A number of participants make comments similar to Calvin. They describe a sense of craving for something more, that Faunalia fulfils, followed by a renewed acceptance of mainstream commitments:

> Calvin: I would get to the end of the week and think, 'is that it?' What is this other depth? Sometimes in really passionate sex it had a similar sort of touch. [It is a] third cousin of this feeling that you are looking for . . . My first Faunalia allowed me to put aside that craving, that

call. Being able to say that I can operate in the world with this craving and fulfil it whilst still being sane, participating in the world.

It is not quite accurate to say that participants at Faunalia return to mundane life with a sense of commitment to the values of mainstream society. The absence of routine experiences of flow and liminal communitas are understood to point towards something that is deeply disconcerting about mainstream society. Participants at Faunalia report that their experiences allow them to participate and cope with mainstream society, but with a sense that there is something outside of it, or beyond it, which the culturally endorsed routines of mainstream life do not provide. Once he returns to mundane life, Sauvage expresses a sense of surprise at what had happened at Faunalia. The memories of these experiences are difficult to believe. He could almost say that he needs to pinch himself to remind himself that he was not dreaming. Interviewees commonly express a sense that the experiences of liminal flow and communitas are 'extraordinarily rare'.

> **Sauvage:** I felt a sense of belonging there in the place and with those people that is extraordinarily rare, and I just want to hold on to that. I had to keep telling myself in the week after that it happened. Because I kept thinking, no, it can't happen, no, that sort of shit does not happen. Then I thought, hmm, no, must do, I think it did. I better remember it did. I think there is proof of it somewhere. Other people tell me I did these sort of things, so I must have.

The rarity of experiences of flow and communitas in contemporary Western societies makes it difficult for people to construct a life with soul. This absence is one of the causes of the soul-destroying character of contemporary Western culture. Weber (1930), and many others, link the decline of religion, the disenchantment of contemporary life, to the experience of life as an 'iron cage'. Participants at Faunalia do not seek to escape the cage of calculative rationality and replace it with a new sacred canopy (Berger 1967). Rather, they seek ways of being able to live in the world as it is. Ritual experiences of flow and communitas transform the frustrations and numbing quality of the iron cage back into a 'light cloak' again. Marie makes this point in an extended discussion of ritual, ecstasy and joy:

> **Marie:** Faunalia was magical and beautiful. Experiences like being in a rite, like a Baphomet rite, and dancing all night with people who you don't know, and feeling the energy so strongly that you lose your sense of self. Suddenly you become a part of the dance, you become part of a mesmerized pull of energy that transforms you into another world, another dimension, not physically, but, psychically.

You experience a completely different sense of what we are, and who we are, and where we are, and what reality is about.

The closest I can get to it is the readings from the Greeks, when they talk about the Dionysian rites . . . there is this joy of connecting, being one with the Gods. That loss of self is that sense of just being one with all of that, and not being something separate. That enables or allows or precipitates a sense of joy in the moment that is indescribable. It is ecstasy. That is what it is.

But it is true ecstasy, it is not drug induced ecstasy. I think the shocking thing about the [ecstatic experiences at Faunalia] is that they are real, that you know it is something that is experienced that is a part of reality. It is not just something going on in your head that is affected by a chemical change. I mean, obviously chemical changes occur when you are in a natural trance state anyway. But the fact that it does not require anything to induce it means that it is natural, which means that it is actually just a part of life that we are missing out on in our culture. Day to day. That is shocking because what it is saying to us is, what are we doing? We are constructing a reality which is omitting this incredibly important part of life, joy. If we are doing that, why are we doing that? What is this about? That is a terrible price to pay, if we have abandoned joy. Because joy feeds us with hope. It feeds us with meaning in our lives. It is like the spiritual acorns to get us through the winter of our lives.

If we don't have that [joy that comes from ecstasy], what are we going to rely upon? Taking anti-depressants? Or trying to fill our lives with consumer items. We promote [how important it is to] succeed professionally, but we know that when our careers are over, who are we going to be? We will be a retired x or y or z, we are no longer part of that machine, that professional machine that is achieving x, y and z. So what does sustain us? What will sustain us through all these things? I think when you have these experiences, it tells us that there is something that we can do and be part of, that will give us that nourishment.

Turner (1979) suggests that people seek out experiences of flow if existing social practices do not routinely provide them. The experience of 'flow' is 'autolectic'; it is its own reward. This means, suggests Turner, that if experiences of flow are restricted or repressed, that people will seek them outside socially approved practices: 'people will deliberately manufacture cultural situations and frames which will release flow, or, as individuals, seek it outside their ascribed statuses or stations in life, if these are, for one reason or another, "flow resistant," that is, conducive to boredom or anxiety' (Turner 1979: 488). When experiences of flow are not part of existing social practices, society is experienced as oppressive and restrictive.

In many ways the liminal experience of flow at Faunalia is one of the main aspects of the festival that is attractive to participants.

Liminal flow is an experience of the dissolution of self in 'the all', a moment of joy and celebration of life. These experiences allow participants to return to, and live more comfortably within, the mundane everyday world of families, friendships and work. The religious experience of flow in ritual makes the inevitably painful and challenging character of human lives more bearable and meaningful. Similar to the earlier calendrical and seasonal rites (Turner 1983), these ritual experiences require regular renewal to maintain the sense that life is worthwhile and emotionally satisfying.

Transcendence and religion

Central to the liminal experience of flow and communitas at Faunalia is the sense of being part of something bigger, of an experience of engagement with 'the all'. This is a form of transcendence, although not typically in the sense of contact with something that is in a higher realm. Rather, it is a form of self-transcendence in the sense of an understanding and experience of the self in a relationship with others, nature, spirit, life or deity, that transcends the individual. That is to say, in Pagan ontology deities and the spiritual realm are typically understood to exist alongside humans, as part of this world, rather than to exist in some separate transcendent plane. The experience of transcendence has two main consequences. First, it provides a greater sense of self-confidence and self-worth. Second, it leads into an ethical moment of offering of self for the other. It is an act of 'mutual recognition' in Jessica Benjamin's (1988) sense and a Levinasian (1979) moment of ethical engagement. However, the other is not always a human person but often an other-than-human person, 'the all', spirit, nature or deity.

I define religion as a set of ritual practices that engage symbolic resources to provide an etiquette for relationships and an emotional and cognitive sense of self-worth and purpose. The religious rituals at Faunalia engage the symbolic resources of contemporary and classical Paganisms, Christianity and Jungian psychoanalysis to transform etiquettes of relating to deity, to self and to others. The ritual practices provide a somatic, emotional and cognitive sense of self-worth and purpose; they provide a life with soul.

Most concepts of religious and spiritual transcendence emphasize transcendence through awareness of greater meaning. Kellehear's (2000) tripartite conception of situational, moral and religious transcendence experienced by those undergoing palliative care is an excellent example.

The basic concept of spirituality upon which the current model is based is the idea that human beings have a desire to transcend hardship and suffering. In other words, people need to seek and find a meaning beyond their current suffering that allows them to make sense of that situation. (Kellehear 2000: 150)

'Meaning' in the ritual context is not simply cognitively articulated. It is also emotional, relational and performed. Both suffering and desire are important themes at Faunalia, and the meanings of both suffering and desire are found through locating the self in a relational frame that transcends the isolated individual. Ritually experienced religious transcendence is an act of mutual recognition, locating the individual in a broader frame of relationships with deity, nature and social networks. This simultaneously gives the individual a sense of self-worth and enables them to live more easily with both suffering and desire.

As described in the vignette, René developed a stronger sense of self-respect after rediscovering spirituality through joining a Witchcraft coven. Her account echoes that of Phoebe in Chapter One. She says that 'reconnecting to spirit' gave her confidence and a sense of self-worth that resulted in her leaving her marriage: 'Basically I realized that I was worth more than what I was putting up with.' Religious transcendence through opening her heart and mind to spirit and a greater meaning results in a greater sense of self-worth and self-confidence. This awareness transforms her etiquette of relating to her husband. René was no longer willing to accept the way she was treated in her marriage, and as a consequence chose to end the marriage.

Experiences of transcendence are also moments of the dissolution of self. Harrison describes his preparedness to 'give everything to love' resulting from his merging with deity, in this case Baphomet. He moves between describing his love for deity and his love for other people. The loss of self becomes an ethical moment of self-sacrifice.

> Harrison: [Talking about love for Baphomet:] when I love, I'll give everything to love. Do anything for the person except negate myself. When you interact with someone that you love, or when I do, when it is really close, and when you are making love, or doing magic, or invoking and embodying there is a point in that where you lose all sense of yourself. You just dissolve into the partnership. Then there is no sense of separation, there is no sense of self. It is not a negation, but an immersion beyond limits.

The self-confidence and self-worth associated with religious transcendence is not a form of selfish individualism. Rather, as Harrison highlights, religious transcendence locates the self in relationships of ethical responsibility. This is similar to Taylor's (1991) conception of the ethics of authenticity and Levinas's (1979) relational ethics in which we are responsible for the 'other'. The conception developed here places greater emphasis on the somatic, performed and aesthetic dimensions of ethical relations.

The ritual experiences of flow, liminality and communitas shape the way people interact in mundane life. The everyday ethical and relational practices of love, relationships and self-evaluations are significantly shaped by ritual experience. This is what Carl Einstein means when he argues that: 'Aesthetic experience thereby transcends normal experience by creating the forms that govern the creation of normal experience' (Pan 2001: 134). Religion derives its power to shape moral orientations from the aesthetic experiences of rituals that shape relational etiquettes. Belief may be important, but for participants at Faunalia it is the emotional, somatic and performed relationships that are primary in shaping their ethical practices.

Participants' love for Baphomet has an erotic character that underlines the somatic and emotional aspects of meaning generated by the rituals at Faunalia. Desire and love motivate the ritual encounter with Baphomet. Leanan captures the interwoven qualities of desire, transcendence, contradiction and self-transformation in the Baphomet rite:

> **Leanan:** Baphomet is a very strong, solid, symbol. I know it is a person dressed up, but in another way, she isn't, he isn't [pause of three seconds]. It is a very difficult symbolism to come to terms with because it is hermaphroditic, it is masculine, it is feminine, it is the everything. This year I was sexually aroused by it. I know others who have had the same experience. But even knowing who it is, and it is another woman in there, yes, it can be arousing, or it is arousing. That never happens to me with other women outside of that circle, so definitely there are other energies, other powers, other things, swirling around in that circle. I think it is the God energy, the Goddess energy, the Baphomet energy, in the whole sacred space, rather than the person I know that is behind it. This year, at one point I saw Mórrígan for about a second, and then it was Hekate for about a second, and then the Goddess went into Kali. So there was three Goddesses I saw, one after the other, and they were all crone-type, transformational [Goddesses].

Leanan, a 59-year-old retired woman, sees three Goddesses that represent her stage of life. In this quote she does not explain how she understood the significance of this vision. Rather, after the experience: 'I just did some drumming.' The significance of the experience exists at the level of 'acting', half conscious, not fully articulated, but engaged with somatically and emotionally through performance. The experience is a moment of transcendence through engagement with deity that provides Leanan with a somatic sense of meaning.

In the rituals at Faunalia participants engage with a deity in mutual recognition that is also an experience of transcendence. The ritually

IMAGE 7.2 *Hawthorn.*
Photo by Philippe.

produced experience of flow facilitates this engagement. The boundaries of the self become porous and dissolve into the all. This is a moment of transcendence in which there is a sense of becoming part of something bigger. It definitely does not, however, involve a sense of escaping from physical fleshly existence. The recognition of deity is also a moment in which the physical nature of the self is recognized by deity. For Leanan this recognition by deity is erotic, and embraces 'crone-type' deities associated with the physical transitions of old age, death and dying.

Religious experience

The anthropology and sociology of religion is deeply ambivalent about the authenticity of religious experience: 'ever swaying between rationalization and deep understanding' (Turner 1992: 29). At times academic studies of religion seem to assume that religious practitioners are delusional, that atheism is the only objective viewpoint and that religion can be reduced to a symbolic reflection of social processes and realities. At other times, ethnographies of religious practices are respectful, sympathetic and ethnographically rich in description. Victor Turner's defining work on the religious ritual of the Ndembu in Central Africa is an excellent example of precisely these tensions (Ezzy 2008). When Turner analyses religious rituals in terms that solely emphasize the social structural functions of religion, the underlying assumption is that ritual is rational from the point of view of the Ndembu, but that they are epistemologically mistaken and ethically inferior. Rituals are 'symbolic compensations' in the absence of secular processes to deal with social conflict and adversity (Turner 1957: 197). Social structure is described as 'actually existing', whereas Ndembu Paganism is 'epistemologically' subordinate or 'naive' in comparison to Western understanding (Turner 1957: 192).

In his later work, notably his account of the Chihamba ritual in *Revelation and Divination in Ndembu Ritual*, Turner (1975) argues that religion has 'ontological value', it tells us something important about the nature of the world.

> After many years as an agnostic and monistic materialist I learned from the Ndembu that ritual and its symbolism are not merely epiphenomena or disguises of deeper social and psychological processes, but have ontological value, in some way related to man's condition as an evolving species, whose evolution takes place principally through its cultural innovations. (Turner 1975: 31)

This approach echoes Carl Einstein's argument that religion is not 'fantasy', but central to what it is to be human (Pan 2001: 134). Turner (1975: 31) goes on to argue: 'I became convinced that religion is not merely a toy of the race's childhood, to be discarded at a nodal point of scientific and technological development, but is really at the heart of the human matter.'

Turner's appreciation of the value of religion is linked to an appreciation of the inability of language to encompass the complexities of human experiences. Myth, ritual and other forms of cultural expression, Turner argues, engage with the aspects of human experience rational explanation fails to grasp. The Ndembu Chihamba ritual in particular, Turner felt, 'proved intractable' to explanation solely in terms of 'social processes and symbolic action'. Instead, Turner draws on Kierkegaard to argue that paradox is the 'inevitable result' of human reflection (Turner 1975: 20), and that the paradoxical message of the Chihamba ritual must be respected. In the performance of the Chihamba ritual Turner (1975: 20) discovers an attempt to 'say the unsayable'. The experiences of the ritualists 'exceed the . . . possible limits of thought'. Turner urges his readers not to dismiss these insights as mystical simply because it is difficult to frame them in the language of atheist and materialist anthropology. The experiences point to something important about human social life that is impossible to describe in other ways.

Turner draws parallels between the experience of communitas during the Chihamba ritual and the Christian mystic Meister Eckhart's encounter with the 'Godhead'. He suggests that both may reflect a 'primal ground' that underlies all social experience, and sits behind Durkheim's analysis of collective effervescence in ritual (Turner 1975: 23). Turner's discussion privileges Christianity. He argues that Ndembu Paganism is legitimate because it parallels the religion of Christianity. It is not necessary to make Christianity the reference point, or to agree that there is a 'primal ground' or 'Godhead', to accept Turner's point that both Christian and Ndembu religion have 'ontological value'. In contrast, and more inclusively, I argue that the ontological value of religious ritual and myth is that it indicates something about social life and human experience that can only be experienced and understood through aesthetic, somatic, performed ways of knowing, or 'iconic consciousness' (Alexander 2008).

Turner goes on to argue that if anthropologists, and I would add sociologists and religious studies scholars, are to understand ritual, they must themselves engage in performative and experiential learning. 'The religious ideas and processes I have just mentioned belong to the domain of performance, their power derived from the participation of the living people who use them' (Turner 1975: 29). Edith Turner's (1992) work is an example of precisely this form of anthropological research that engages through participation.

> Religion, like Watergate, is a scandal that will not go away. We have to live it through; it cannot be dispelled by magical incantation or reduced to a non-sense by positivist or linguistic philosophy, for it is concerned with negative or midliminal experience of the sort which perhaps provoked Ludwig Wittgenstein's ultimate aphorism 'whereof one cannot speak, thereof one must be silent'. (Turner 1975: 32)

I argue that religion and ritual are important to many people because they provide a life with soul. A life with soul is one lived with 'heart', passion and sense of being authentic. This is an extension of Turner's point. Religion does not always provide a life with soul, and religion is not the only way of discovering a life with soul – it is clear that artistic and musical endeavours, and various other practices, can also engage with the 'soulful' side of life. However, I think Turner is correct to argue that there is something central to religion of which one cannot speak, or at least not speak in reductionist and scientific terms. Religious rituals are a 'midliminal' experience, a form of 'acting' (Benjamin 1998). Understanding how these processes influence human lives is vitally important: 'Deciphering ritual forms and discovering what generates symbolic actions may be more germane to our cultural growth than we have supposed' (Turner 1975: 31).

Religious experiences and symbols are ways of engaging with somatic knowledge that embraces tension and contradiction, and then draws on aesthetics and ritual to shape the way people live in the world. As I understand it, to say that Baphomet acts and is present at Faunalia is a way of indicating that the semi-conscious, somatic knowing people experience at Faunalia is equally, if not more, important than other scientific and cognitive ways of understanding and knowing the world. Further, the participants at Faunalia argue, and I suspect they are right, that the disenchanted world of late modernity empties their lives of soul. Religious ritual does not universally create lives with soul. Ritual, like science, can be used to enhance *and* to destroy life. Rather, religious ritual is a morally neutral 'technology' that transforms somatic knowledge that is central to the human experience of purpose and self-worth.

Religious experiences and ritual transformations are a product of social processes and can be rationally analysed. However, religion cannot be reduced to these aspects. Social processes and rational analysis do not explain away religion any more than they explain away love, gender or social inequalities. What is important sociologically and anthropologically is how particular religious cultures and ritual practices create particular forms and etiquettes of relationship. How does religion contribute to, or detract from, a life with soul?

Religion redefined

Participation in the religious rites of Baphomet and the Eleusinian-inspired Underworld transform most participants in deep, long-lasting and profound ways. Participants come to terms with difficult issues associated with body image, sexual desire, death, transition and suffering. The participants at Faunalia are not concerned with belief, and neither is their practise institutionalized. These life-affirming transformations are made possible because the rituals at Faunalia draw participants in new etiquettes of relationship.

The power of the rituals at Faunalia derives from a Dionysian engagement with intoxicating emotions that transform somatic self-understandings. Rituals that are theatrically elaborate and experientially immersive generate liminal experiences of flow and transcendence. They engage aesthetically and somatically with the paradoxical and inherently conflicting nature of self, other and the relationships within which we are embedded. These practices are the religion of Faunalia.

Participation in Faunalia's religious rituals transforms relational etiquettes. Sexual desire and the fear of death are represented in ritual as relational others, as Gods with a reality that goes beyond mere representation, and who must be respected in their own right, although not necessarily obeyed. Ethics, new forms of relational etiquettes, are created in these ritual moments of respectful engagement with divine others. Participants journey with Hades and Persephone into the Underworld, and death loses its sting as a feared other. They dance naked with Baphomet, a goat-headed deity with an erect phallus and breasts, and sexual desire becomes something to be celebrated. These ritual experiences lead participants into a moment of self-transcendence and relational practices of deep intimacy and genuine care for others.

Religion is a set of ritual practices that engage symbolic resources to provide an etiquette for relationships and an emotional and cognitive sense of self-worth and purpose. Faunalia combines ritual practices that are extraordinarily powerful and immersive with a relational ethics, or etiquette, that allows participants to open their hearts to their deepest fears and desires. In those moments of extreme vulnerability they find new hope, courage, purpose and self-worth.

Conclusion

It is impossible to write about the events at the centre of Faunalia. Words fail me. 'You have to be there to experience it, to appreciate it' (Dingo). Put another way, when I asked Harrison why he invested so much effort into organizing Faunalia, he said: 'Fucked if I know.' I understand this to indicate that it is difficult to articulate the reasons for his efforts. It is not just that words are inadequate; it is that the reasons and motivations cannot be consciously articulated. The reasons and motivations are emotional and somatic. People do it because it feels right. This is not some deficiency in participant self-understandings. Rather, it is an insight into what it is to be human: *Humans create lives with meaning and purpose through somatic performances often driven by unconscious or half-consciously articulated purposes and reasons.*

The ineffable nature of the rituals at Faunalia is bound up with a desire to keep it secret. Marie began her interview with a quote that she says is credited to Julian the Apostate, the last Pagan Emperor of Rome and participant in the Eleusinian Mysteries that inspired the Underworld rite:

> **Marie:** Shall we divulge what has been hidden? Shall we open what is to remain closed? Shall we speak words that are not to be spoken? For this is a hymn to the mother of the Gods.

The theme of hidden knowledge is central to many magical traditions and religious practices. We will never know the details of the rites of Eleusis in ancient Greece, because it was forbidden to write them down (Burkett 1985). Perhaps part of the reason for the prohibition is because to attempt to articulate the secrets of the rituals in writing or speech would inevitably result in misunderstanding. Mystery rites can only be understood in the experience. In that sense, the error is the belief that the meaning of ritual can be captured in words. Words can only point to the aesthetic ritual practice that inspires them. It is the practice that is primary. Cognitive interpretations are secondary, inevitably partial and often misleading.

Many participants feel deeply ambivalent about revealing their participation in Faunalia, and the existence of Faunalia itself. Harrison said: 'We have resisted [the temptation] to publicize Faunalia beyond the Pagan community. We do not really think [the broader community will] understand what we are doing. A lot of Pagans do not understand what we are doing.' Towards the end of the interviews I asked participants what they thought the world needed to know about Faunalia. Several people made comments similar to Leonie:

> Leonie: I don't think that the world needs to know about Faunalia. I don't think it needs to be common knowledge. Faunalia needs to be kept private.

Leonie made this statement despite having agreed to be interviewed twice, and having read and signed a document explicitly stating that I intended to use the interviews as the basis for publications about Faunalia. I think Harrison and Leonie's statements indicate that Faunalia is understood by participants as for a time and place, and a particular group of participants. There is no desire for Faunalia to become an organization like a church, or to seek to expand the influence of the movement. Rather, they wish to keep Faunalia private. In response to reading this, Harrison commented:

> Harrison: We didn't want to keep Faunalia private. Anyone who heard about it could book and attend, if they got in quickly enough. But, we didn't want it to be a mass media sound bite. We didn't want it to provide a few moments entertainment for a passive audience. Faunalia was for the people that went and engaged with it.

What participants at Faunalia do want to share is the discovery that rituals can facilitate a soulful life, a life of 'joy' as Marie articulates in her long quote in Chapter Seven. They want the world to know that rituals like those at Faunalia provide experiences that are enriching and soulful. Similar moments can be found in the samba dance of the rituals of the *candomblé* (Browning 1995), ecstatic praise during a Pentecostal service (Anderson 2004) and a multitude of other practices. In the lives of participants these extraordinary ritual practices are balanced with mundane everyday lives dominated by scientific rationality, cognitively articulated myth and planned work schedules. Engaging with both aesthetic and rational, Dionysian and Apollonian, has significantly enhanced the lives of participants of Faunalia.

> Soulfulness is a matter of learning to live with the volatility and unknowability of existence without falling into states of psychic

rigidity . . . while our impulse might be to demand clarity from the world as well as from ourselves, *soulfulness implies knowing how to experience states of non-mastery as enabling rather than threatening.* (Ruti 2006: 223; emphasis added)

The rituals of Faunalia are states of 'non-mastery'. They invoke, and evoke, the inevitability of death and the immutability of desire. The rituals work with these experiences such that they become enriching as well as threatening. I say 'as well as threatening' because participants at Faunalia do not seek to overcome their fears or master their desire. Rather, as personified in their understandings of Baphomet, they work towards, and such work is never finished, a détente between enriching and threatening responses to sex and death. Rituals make possible respectful relationships.

The Dionysian rituals of Faunalia are a liminal experience. It lasts for a time, and then is gone. Making the transition back into the mundane world of everyday life can be traumatic.

> Calvin: When I came home after Faunalia, I felt as though someone had taken a cheese grater and rubbed it all over my body. Not that I had that experience of [physical] pain, but [I had] the rawness that would give you. [I felt] open and exposed to anything, everyone. I had this feeling that everything had been stripped away. I remember going down to the supermarket, just down the road, on that first day back for general groceries with my partner. It was painful when we were out, just looking at the people, feeling their moods, feeling completely exposed to whatever was going through them emotionally. It is as though any defence, any barrier, whatever, had just gone. That took me quite a while to assimilate. I can remember coming home and crying saying: 'It is so beautiful, I do not want to let this feeling go.' But I can't live with it either. There is no way I could function in society feeling like that.

> Leonie: I had the rest of the week off from work and I hid. I did not go out at all except to the supermarket, to a friend's farewell and to Pagans in the pub. I felt, not fragile, but open and too raw. The supermarket felt harsh and hard and too bright. Other years I have gone back to work straight away, that was very unpleasant. I had more time off this year, and that was good, but perhaps I had too much time off. Catching the train on Monday and going back to work was very hard. I didn't want to lose what I had. I didn't want the mundane world to take it away.

> Phoebe: [At the end of Faunalia I feel] sad. There is always this sadness, there is a sense of loss. Coming back into the mundane world, the responsibilities, the rules, the obligations, all of that. It is a big shift.

Some participants suggested that the emotional openness people felt after Faunalia was a product of the failure to properly 'ground'. 'Grounding' refers to a ritual practice in which intense emotions and magical 'energies' are understood to be drained away back into the Earth (Starhawk 2005). I wonder whether these sorts of post-Faunalia experiences also suggest that we could do more to make our everyday lives more soulful.

At the end of a three-hour interview, I asked Sauvage what he thought the world needed to know about Faunalia. He points beyond the sexualized content of the rituals to the structure of the relationships at Faunalia. He articulates the irresolvable tension between self and community that is at the heart of Taylor's (1989) ethics of authenticity and Benjamin's (1988) mutual recognition. The rituals of Faunalia, if only partially, temporarily and flawed in their performance, allow participants to both discover themselves more authentically, and to care for the unsettling 'other'.

In the first paragraph Sauvage describes an ethic of authenticity, privileging the self and self-discovery. He moves seamlessly from this into a discussion of community, in which the ego is subsumed by group purposes and the task of caring. An unsettling confrontation with sex and death provides the energy that fuels the rituals of Faunalia. The outcome is a moment of self-discovery made possible by respectful relationships.

> **Sauvage:** [short laugh] I don't know that the world is ready [to know about Faunalia]. I think we need to re-visit what we consider to be dark and a bit self-indulgent. I think people focus on the high sexual content of Faunalia, and the fact that it can be liberating. That is there, but that is not really the big ticket items to me. It is about giving you the confidence to feel safe to be yourself, and to go about unarmoured. In so doing you become more of who you are or can be. I think that is what it can offer people. It is one passage, and there are probably many others [that provide a similar journey].
>
> I was totally knocked out by the capacity for that group of people to form a community, and to work together without ego. To really honour each other's essence to find ways to include people that are difficult in any number of ways . . . I think that is a pretty impressive model for other people to look at and see where they can learn from that. It can work. People can honour one another and work together and form a cohesive community. If nothing else, that is huge.

METHODOLOGICAL APPENDIX

'Faunalia' is a pseudonym for an annual Pagan festival that took place between 2000 and 2009 in a rural location in south-eastern Australia. About 80 people attended the 2005 festival, many being good friends who had attended previous festivals together, although there was a good representation of participants attending for the first time. Phoebe reports that 80 per cent of the participants at the first Faunalia were strangers, but that in 2005 more than half the participants knew each other well. In 2005 I interviewed 23 participants, including 12 that I interviewed both before and after the festival. I also interviewed two non-attending partners of participants. The interviews took place in various locations, including people's homes, at cafés and restaurants, and at a University where I was a visiting scholar. Twelve of the participant interviewees were women and 11 were men. Their average age was 37, ranging from 21 to 59 years old. On average they had attended four Faunalia festivals, including the 2005 festival, with six interviewees attending Faunalia for the first time in 2005. They had been Pagans for an average of nine years, ranging from one year to 25 years. Thirteen were married or partnered, and ten were single. Of those who were married, five people were attending the festival without their partner and eight were attending with their partner. I received ethics approval for the research from the University of Tasmania Human Research Ethics Committee.

As part of the pre-festival information distributed by the organizers, participants were sent information about the research and an invitation to contact me if they were willing to be interviewed. Most interviews lasted approximately one hour, with one interview lasting six hours. Most interviews were recorded and transcribed in their entirety. A few interviews were not recorded and I took extensive notes. Quotations from the interview transcripts have been 'cleaned'. Repeated words are deleted, as are repetitive phrases such as 'sort of' and 'you know'. Words and short phrases such as these that have been deleted from quotations are not indicated in the quotations. Where extended sections have been deleted, this is indicated by '. . .' Words that I have added for clarity and that go beyond the words from the interview are included in [square brackets]. Potentially identifying information has been deleted, or changed. All names used are pseudonyms. In some cases I have given one participant two different pseudonyms and split the interview into two different 'participants' in order to further protect anonymity.

It would be very difficult to conduct participant observation at Faunalia, if not impossible. I attended Faunalia as a participant in 2005, but not as an observer. At the first opportunity during a collective briefing I explained that I was interviewing participants before and after the festival, but that I was not doing fieldwork or observing participants while at the festival. I did not take fieldwork notes during my participation, and I did not record fieldwork observations afterwards. I have not recounted my own memories of Faunalia. I have subsequently made it clear to various participants of Faunalia in various forums that the only information I am using for the current book is information people have given me during the interviews. This is the only information for which I have explicit and informed consent. The addition of my own

IMAGE A.1 *The author at Faunalia, writing poetry the morning after a Baphomet rite.*
Photo by B. Dalton.

memories about the festival would not significantly change or add to what I have written here. I could add some interesting details, stories and some poetry, but these would not be anything more than elaboration of the main themes already present in the book. I sent an early draft of the entire book to the organizers of Faunalia and selected chapters to some other participants. This was an extremely useful exercise allowing me to rewrite the book in a way that represents what occurred at Faunalia more accurately. Some of their comments have been reproduced in the text.

When people ask me what I believe, my usual response is to say that I believe that religious practices are important because they tell us something about ourselves and the world. My own religious practice is complex and difficult to articulate in a simple categorical label. Pagan rituals are an important part of what I do, and in many senses I am a Pagan. My practice is inclusive, eclectic and often includes practices derived from mystical Christianity, Hinduism and Shinto. I feel comfortable participating in a variety of religious practices and symbolic universes. Kasulis (2004) reports that most Japanese people move comfortably between religious traditions, preferring Shinto rituals for birth and marriage and Buddhist rituals for funerals. He also notes that most Japanese people do not identify as being religious on surveys because the word 'religion' in Japanese is associated with belief and creeds. However, if asked whether they had worshipped a fox in the last month, Kasulis speculates that 90 per cent of Japanese people would say 'yes'. The fox is a common *kami* (deity/spirit) found at Shinto shrines. I am not Japanese, and the traditions of religious practice I draw on are more eclectic, but my practice and self-understanding are similar.

Faunalia certainly has its share of selfish individuals who engage in unhelpful behaviour. The consequences of these actions can be hurtful and exploitative. None of the people I interviewed suggested that these behaviours were of the order that Greenwood (2000) describes in her account of manipulative leaders of a British Witchcraft coven. If there had been major ethical transgressions I would have expected some of my interviewees to raise such issues. None raised any such issues.

I actively sought to distribute invitations to participate in the research to people who had unpleasant experiences at Faunalia. The organizers of Faunalia suggested this approach and assisted with forwarding invitations to these people. Unfortunately, none of these people volunteered to be interviewed. Perhaps if I had interviewed these people the book could have provided a more detailed account of some of the failures of Faunalia, such as the ritual that Ruth describes as: 'Altered states of consciousness through hypothermia.'

I am aware that the book focuses on the positive aspects of Faunalia. This is a bias inherent in any qualitative study – interviewees tend to avoid describing actions that might portray them in an unfavourable light. Nonetheless, it is my judgement, and the interview selections reproduced here support this claim, that Faunalia has had a profoundly positive effect on most of those who attended the festival.

Participants provided some interesting reflections on the effect of participating in the interviews. It is appropriate to leave the last words to them:

> **Leonie:** Faunalia has made me more tolerant of my husband. I think it has affected us because I am happier with myself and therefore happier with him. We have been really good since Faunalia. Hmm, I had not put that together until you asked me. I will have to think about that.

> **Calvin:** After the first interview I did a lot more thinking and reflecting. So the interview itself was part of the Faunalia experience for me. Tidying up previous years. Making me wonder, will I approach this time differently. [The interview] was a great thing. [As I was talking to you I realized] each of the two Faunalias I have been to were expressed in terms of a theme. The first year was dealing with psychological, sexual and fitting into group type things. The second year had lot less of that. It was far more of a magical type emphasis. As a result of expressing them in those one sentence summaries on my way into this year's Faunalia, I was starting to wonder what I would like to take out of it.

NOTES

Introduction

1 All names are pseudonyms, including 'Faunalia'. For more detail on the ethics, protocols of transcription and other methodological aspects of the research, see the Methodological Appendix. The two quotes that open the Introduction have been more heavily edited than the other quotes in the remainder of the book. I have changed the tense in some parts, slightly rearranged the word order and deleted some words without indicating the deletions.

2 At Faunalia, Baphomet is pronounced Baff-oh-may.

3 Most of the photos are from the 2005 Faunalia. The first and last photos in the book are from the 2007 festival. All photos are used with the permission of the photographers and the people in them.

4 This is different to the Northern Hemisphere where widdershins is usually understood to mean casting a circle anti-clockwise. This is because in places such as the United Kingdom and North America the sun appears to travel through the southern sky, hence travelling clockwise.

Vignette: Therion

1 In the three Vignettes, my words are in italics and the participants words are in plain text.

2 'Pagans in the Pub' is a monthly gathering of Pagans that occurs in most cities in Australia where Pagans meet to discuss topics of interest. It is typically a social and networking opportunity where Pagans meet and chat over a meal or a pint of beer.

3 Confest is an annual Australian alternative lifestyle festival (see St John 2000).

4 At the second Faunalia in 2001, the 'Dark Night' ritual was performed on the second night, followed by the Baphomet rite on the third night. The 'Dark Night' ritual was not performed in 2005. Instead the Underworld rite was performed on the second night.

Chapter Two

1 Some Pagans spell the word 'magick' with a 'k' to differentiate it from sleight of hand magic.

Chapter Three

1 The Australian dollar coin is a small, round, gold coloured coin similar in size to a one Euro coin or a US one dollar coin.

2 There were about 12 ritualists performing key roles, about 65 participants going through the journey and a few people who did not participate in the ritual.

Chapter Four

1 'Non-rational' or 'arational' are probably better terms than 'irrational'. To say that ritual is irrational suggests that it fails to meet the criteria of rationality, whereas to describe ritual as non-rational suggests that the criteria of rationality do not apply. I use 'irrational' here for consistency with Benjamin.

Chapter Six

1 Some Pagan groups, such as the racially based forms of contemporary Heathenism, are very dogmatic with fundamentalist characteristics (Gardell 2003).

2 Benjamin's approach does not seem to encompass the possibility that bondage and domination can be consensual and liberating. See Zussman and Pierce 1998 for a discussion.

REFERENCES

Ahmed, Sara. 2004. *The Cultural Politics of Emotion*. New York, NY: Routledge.

—. 2010. *The Promise of Happiness*. Durham, NC: Duke University Press.

Alexander, Jeffrey C. 2008. 'Iconic Experience in Art and Life'. *Theory Culture Society*, 25, 5: 1–19.

—. 2010. 'Iconic Consciousness: The Material Feeling of Meaning'. *Thesis Eleven*, 103, 1: 10–25.

—. 2012. *Trauma: A Social Theory*. Cambridge UK: Polity.

Alford, C. Fred. 1997. *What Evil Means to Us*. New York, NY: Cornell University Press.

Allen, William. 1984. *The Nazi Seizure of Power* (rev. edn). New York, NY: Franklin Watts.

Anderson, Allan. 2004. *An Introduction to Pentecostalism*. Cambridge, UK: Cambridge University Press.

Armstrong, Karen. 2005. *A Short History of Myth*. Edinburgh, Scotland: Cannongate.

Arnal, William and McCutcheon, Russell. 2013. *The Sacred Is the Profane: The Political Nature of Religion*. Oxford, UK: Oxford University Press.

Asad, Talal. 1993. *Genealogies of Religion: Discipline and Reasons of Power in Christianity and Islam*. Baltimore, MD: Johns Hopkins University Press.

—. 2003. *Formations of the Secular: Christianity, Islam, Modernity*. Stanford, CA: Stanford University Press.

Bado-Fralick, Nikki. 2005. *Coming to the Edge of the Circle: A Wiccan Initiation Ritual*. New York, NY: Oxford University Press.

Bauman, Zygmunt. 1993. *Postmodern Ethics*. Oxford, UK and Cambridge, MA: Blackwell.

—. 2000. *Liquid Modernity*. Oxford, UK: Blackwell.

Bell, Catherine. 1992. *Ritual Theory, Ritual Practice*. Oxford, UK: Oxford University Press.

—. 1997. *Ritual: Perspectives and Dimensions*. New York, NY: Oxford University Press.

Benjamin, Jessica. 1988. *The Bonds of Love: Psychoanalysis, Feminism, and the Problem of Domination*. New York, NY: Pantheon.

—. 1998. *Shadow of the Other: Intersubjectivity and Gender in Psychoanalysis*. New York, NY: Routledge.

Berger, Helen and Ezzy, Douglas. 2007. *Teenage Witches*. New Brunswick, NJ: Rutgers University Press.

Berger, Peter. 1967. *The Sacred Canopy: Elements of Sociological Theory of Religion*. New York, NY: Doubleday.

Bernasconi, Robert. 1997. 'The Violence of the Face: Peace and Language in the Thought of Levinas'. *Philosophy and Social Criticism*, 23, 6: 81–93.

Blain, Jenny. 2002. *Nine Worlds of Seid-Magic: Ecstasy, Neo-Shamanism in North European Paganism*. London, UK: Routledge.

Blazer, Dan. 2005, *The Age of Melancholy: 'Major Depression' and its Social Origins*. New York, NY: Routledge.

Bordo, Susan. 1995. *Unbearable Weight: Feminism, Western Culture, and the Body*. Los Angeles, CA: University of California Press.

Bourdieu, Pierre. 1977. *Outline of a Theory of Practice*. Cambridge, UK: Cambridge University Press.

Bowden, Hugh. 2010. *Mystery Cults of the Ancient World*. Princeton, NJ: Princeton University Press.

Browning, Barbara. 1995. *Samba: Resistance in Motion*. Bloomington, IN: Indiana University Press.

Buber, Martin. 1958. *I and Thou*. Trans. Ronald Smith. New York, NY: Collier Books.

Burkert, William. 1985. *Greek Religion*. Oxford, UK: Blackwell.

Butler, Judith. 2004. *Precarious Life*. London, UK: Verso.

Chumbley, Andrew. 2010. *Opuscula Magica, Volume 1, Essays: Witchcraft and the Sabbatic Tradition*. Richmond Vista, CA: Three Hands.

Collins, Randal. 2007. 'The Classical Tradition in the Sociology of Religion'. In James Beckford and N. Jay Demerath (eds), *The Sage Handbook of the Sociology of Religion*. Los Angeles, CA: Sage, pp. 19–38.

Conger, John. 1991. 'The Body as Shadow'. In Connie Zweig and Jeremiah Abrams (eds), *Meeting the Shadow: The Hidden Power of the Dark Side of Human Nature*. New York, NY: Penguin, pp. 84–88.

Cotterill, Pamela and Letherby, Gayle. 1993. 'Weaving Stories: Personal Auto/ biographies in Feminist Research'. *Sociology*, 27, 1: 67–80.

Crites, Stephen. 1971. 'The Narrative Quality of Experience'. *Journal of the American Academy of Religion*, 39, 3: 291–311.

Csikszentmihalyi, Mihaly. 1974. *Flow: The Psychology of Optimal Experience*. New York, NY: Harper and Row.

Csordas, Thomas. 1994. *The Sacred Self: A Cultural Phenomenology of Charismatic Healing*. Berkeley, CA: University of California Press.

Cyrino, Monica. 2010. *Aphrodite*. New York, NY: Routledge.

Dalby, Andrew. 2003. *Bacchus*. London, UK: British Museum Press.

Daniels, Michael. 2005. *Shadow, Self, Spirit: Essays in Transpersonal Psychology*. New York, NY: Imprint Academic.

Dante, Alighieri. 1949. *The Comedy of Dante Alighieri the Florentine: Cantica I: HELL*. Trans. Dorothy L. Sayers. London, UK: Penguin Books.

Davis, Colin. 1996. *Levinas*. Cambridge, UK: Polity.

de Certeau, Michel. 1992. *The Mystic Fable*. Trans. Michael Smith. Chicago, IL: University of Chicago Press.

Diamond, Stephen A. 1991. 'Redeeming our Devils and Demons'. In Connie Zweig and Jeremiah Abrams (eds), *Meeting the Shadow: The Hidden Power of the Dark Side of Human Nature*. New York, NY: Penguin, pp. 180–186.

Douglas, Mary. 1966. *Purity and Danger*. London, UK: Penguin.

Driver, Tom. 1991. *The Magic of Ritual: Our Need for Liberating Rites that Transform our Lives and our Communities*. San Francisco, CA: HarperCollins.

Duquette, Lon Milo. 1993. *The Magick of Thelema*. Boston, MA: Weiser.

Durkheim, Emile. 1973. 'The Dualism of Human Nature and its Social Conditions'. In Robert Bellah (ed.), *Emile Durkheim on Morality and Society*. Chicago, IL: Chicago University Press, pp. 149–163.

—. 1976. *The Elementary Forms of the Religious Life*. Trans. Joseph Swain. London, UK: Allen and Unwin [first published in Paris: F. Alcan, 1912].

—. 1995. *The Elementary Forms of Religious Life*. Trans. Karen Fields. New York, NY: Free Press.

Earl, Mary. 2001. 'Shadow and Spirituality'. *International Journal of Children's Spirituality*, 6, 3: 277–288.

Ezzy, Douglas. 2002. *Qualitative Analysis: Practice and Innovation*. London, UK: Routledge.

—. 2008. 'Faith and Social Science: Victor and Edith Turner's Analyses of Spiritual Realities'. In Graham St John (ed.), *Victor Turner and Contemporary Cultural Performance*. New York, NY: Berghahn, pp. 260–275.

—. 2013. 'Minimising Religious Conflict and the Racial and Religious Tolerance Act in Victoria, Australia'. *Journal for the Academic Study of Religion*, 26, 2: 54–72.

Ezzy, Douglas, Gary Easthope and Victor Morgan. 2009. 'Ritual Dynamics: Mayor Making in Early Modern Norwich'. *Journal of Historical Sociology*, 22, 3: 396–419.

Farrar, Janet and Farrar, Stewart. 1981. *The Witches Bible Compleat*. New York, NY: Magical Childe.

Featherstone, Mike. 1982. 'The Body in Consumer Culture'. *Theory, Culture & Society*, 1, 2: 18–33.

Fish, Jonathan. 2005. *Defending the Durkheimian Tradition*. Aldershot, UK: Ashgate.

Flood, Gavin. 1996. *An Introduction to Hinduism*. Cambridge, UK: Cambridge University Press.

Flowers, Stephen. 1997. *Lords of the Left Hand Path*. Smithville, TX: Runa-Raven.

Gardell, Mattias. 2003. *Gods of the Blood: The Pagan Revival and White Separatism*. Durham, NC: Duke University Press.

Gennep, Van. 2004 [1909]. *Rites of Passage*. Trans. Monika B. Vizedom and Gabrielle L. Caffee. New York, NY: Routledge.

Giddens, Anthony. 1991. *Modernity and Self-Identity*. Stanford, CA: Stanford University Press.

Gilchrist, Cherry. 1991. *Alchemy*. London, UK: Element Books.

Gilmore, Lee and Proyen, Mark Van. 2005. *AfterBurn: Reflections on Burning Man*. Alberquerque, NM: University of New Mexico Press.

Ginsburg, Carlo. 1992. *Ecstasies: Deciphering the Witches' Sabbath*. Trans. Raymond Rosenthal. London, UK: Penguin.

Greenwood, Susan. 2000. *Magic, Witchcraft and the Otherworld*. Oxford, UK: Berg.

Grimes, Ronald. 2000. *Deeply into the Bone: Re-inventing Rites of Passage*. Berkeley, CA: University of California Press.

Haar, Michel and Gillis, Marin. 1997. 'The Obsession of the Other'. *Philosophy and Social Criticism*, 23, 6: 95–107.

Harvey, Graham. 1997. *Listening People, Speaking Earth: Contemporary Paganism*. London, UK: Hurst.

—. 2005. *Animism: Respecting the Living World*. New York, NY: Columbia University Press.

—. 2013. *Food, Sex and Strangers: Redefining Religion*. London, UK: Equinox.

Heelas, Paul. 1996. *The New Age Movement: The Celebration of the Self and the Sacralization of Modernity*. Oxford, UK: Blackwell.

—. 2006. 'The Infirmity Debate: On the Viability of New Age Spiritualties of Life'. *Journal of Contemporary Religion*, 21, 2: 223–240.

Heelas, Paul, Woodhead, Linda, Benjamin Seel, Bronislaw Szerszynski and Karin Tusting. 2005. *The Spiritual Revolution: Why Religion Is Giving Way to Spiritualty*. Oxford, UK: Blackwell.

Herbert, Frank. 1965. *Dune*. New York, NY: Chilton.

Hodkinson, Paul. 2002. *Goth: Identity, Style and Subculture*. Oxford, UK: Berg.

Horowitz, Allan and Wakefield, Jerome. 2007. *The Loss of Sadness*. Oxford, UK: Oxford University Press.

Howell, Julia. 1997. 'ASC Induction Techniques, Spiritual Experiences, and Commitment to New Religious Movements'. *Sociology of Religion*, 58, 2: 141–164.

Hume, Lynne. 1997. *Witchcraft and Paganism in Australia*. Melbourne, AU: Melbourne University Press.

Huskinson, Lucy. 2004. *Nietzsche and Jung: The Whole Self in the Union of Opposites*. New York, NY: Brunner-Routledge.

Hutton, Ronald. 1999. *The Triumph of the Moon: A History of Modern Pagan Witchcraft*. Oxford, UK: Oxford University Press.

Ingold, Tim. 2011. *Being Alive: Essays on Movement, Knowledge and Description*. London, UK: Routledge.

Irigaray, Luce. 1993. *An Ethics of Sexual Difference*. Trans. Carolyn Burke and Gillian C. Gill. London, UK: Athlone.

—. 2001. *Two Be Two*. Trans. Monique Rhodes and Marco Cocito-Monoc. New York, NY: Routledge.

Ivakhiv, Adrian. 2003. 'Nature and Self in New Age Pilgrimage'. *Culture and Religion*, 4, 1: 93–118.

Jantzen, Grace, 1998. *Becoming Divine: Towards a Feminist Philosophy of Religion*. Manchester, UK: Manchester University Press.

Johnson, Robert. 1991. *Owning Your Own Shadow: Understanding the Dark Side of the Psyche*. San Francisco, CA: Harper Collins.

Karp, David. 1996. *Speaking of Sadness: Depression, Disconnection, and the Meanings of Illness*. New York, NY: Oxford University Press.

Kasulis, Thomas. 2004. *Shinto: The Way Home*. Honolulu, HI: University of Hawai'i Press.

Kearney, Richard. 2001. *The God who may Be: A Hermeneutics of Religion*. Bloomington, IN: Indian University Press.

—. 2003. *Strangers, Gods and Monsters: Interpreting Otherness*. London, UK: Routledge.

Kellehear, Allan. 1996. *Experiences near Death*. New York, NY: Oxford University Press.

—. 2000. 'Spirituality and Palliative Care: A Model of Needs'. *Palliative Medicine*, 14, 2: 149–55.

—. 2007. *A Social History of Dying*. New York, NY: Oxford University Press.

Kemp, Peter. 1997. 'Introduction to Special Edition on Emmanuel Levinas'. *Philosophy and Social Criticism*, 23, 6: 1–3.

King, Richard. 1999. *Orientalism and Religion*. London, UK: Routledge.

Kristeva, Julia. 1991. *Strangers to Ourselves*. Trans. Leon Roudiez. New York, NY: Columbia University Press.

Lacan, Jacques. 1977. *Ecrits: A Selection*. London, UK: Tavistock.

Latour, Bruno. 2010. *On the Modern Cult of the Factish Gods*. Durham, NC: Duke University Press.

Lefkowitz, Mary. 2003. *Greek Gods, Human Lives*. New Haven, CT and London, UK: Yale University Press.

Letcher, Andy. 2000. '"Virtual Paganism" or Direct Action?' *Diskus*, 6. www.basr.ac.uk/diskus/diskus1–6/letcher6.txt, accessed December 2011.

—. 2001. 'The Scouring of the Shire: Fairies, Trolls and Pixies in Eco-Protest Culture'. *Folklore*, 112: 147–161.

—. 2004. 'Bardism and the Performance of Paganism'. In Jenny Blain, Douglas Ezzy and Graham Harvey (eds), *Researching Paganisms*. Walnut Creek, CA: Alta Mira, pp. 15–42.

Levinas, Emmanuel. 1979. *Totality and Infinity*. Trans. Alphonso Lingis. The Hague, Amsterdam: Martinus Nijhoff.

—. 1985. *Ethics and Infinity: Conversations with Philippe Nemo*. Trans. Richard Cohen. Pittsburgh, PA: Duquensne University Press.

Lewis, James. 2001. *Satanism Today: An Encyclopedia of Religion, Folklore, and Popular Culture*. Santa Barbara, CA: ABC-CLIO.

Luhrmann, Tanya. 1989. *Persuasions of the Witch's Craft*. Oxford, UK: Blackwell.

MacIntyre, Alasdair. 1981. *After Virtue*. London, UK: Duckworth.

Maffesoli, Michel. 1996. *The Time of the Tribes. The Decline of Individualism in Mass Society*. Trans. D. Smith. London, UK: Sage.

McCloud, Sean. 2011. 'Toward a Materialist Theory of Metanoia'. American Academy of Religion Annual Meeting, San Francisco, CA, November, pp. 19–22.

McGuire, Meredith. 2008. *Lived Religion: Faith and Practice in Everyday Life*. Oxford, UK: Oxford University Press.

McIntosh, Christopher. 2011. *Eliphas Levi and the French Occult Revival*. New York, NY: State University of New York Press.

McNamara, Beverley. 2001. *Fragile Lives: Death, Dying and Care*. Sydney, AU: Allen and Unwin.

Mellor, Philip. 2006. 'Religion as an Elementary Aspect of Society: Durkheim's Legacy for Social Theory'. In James Beckford and John Walliss (eds), *Theorising Religion: Classical and Contemporary Debates*. Aldershot, UK: Ashgate, pp. 3–18.

Mellor, Philip and Shilling, Chris. 1997. *Re-forming the Body: Religion, Community and Modernity*. London, UK: Sage.

Morgan, David and Wilkinson, Iain. 2001. 'The Problem of Suffering and the Sociological Task of Theodicy'. *European Journal of Social Theory*, 4, 2: 199–214.

Morrison, Andrew. 1998. *The Culture of Shame*. London, UK: Jason Aronson.

Murray, Margaret. 1921. *The Witch Cult in Western Europe*. Oxford, UK: Oxford University Press.

Nietzsche, Friedrich. 1993. *The Birth of Tragedy*. Trans. Shaun Whiteside. Harmondsworth, UK: Penguin.

Nussbaum, Martha. 2004. *Hiding from Humanity*. Princeton, NJ: Princeton University Press.

Olaveson, Tim. 2001. 'Collective Effervescence and Communitas: Processual Models of Ritual and Society in Emile Durkheim and Victor Turner'. *Dialectical Anthropology*, 26, 2: 89–124.

—. 2004. '"Connectedness" and the Rave Experience'. In Graham St John (ed.), *Rave Culture and Religion*. London, UK: Routledge, pp. 85–106.

Orr, Emma, 2007. *Living with Honour: A Pagan Ethics*. Winchester, UK: O Books.

Orsi, Robert A, 2005. *Between Heaven and Earth: The Religious Worlds People Make and the Scholars who Study Them*. Princeton, NJ: Princeton University Press.

Otto, Walter 1965. *Dionysus: Myth and Cult*. Trans. Robert Palmer. Bloomington, IN: Indiana University Press.

Pan, David. 2000. 'The Struggle for Myth in the Nazi Period: Alfred Baeumler, Ernst Bloch, and Carl Einstein'. *South Atlantic Review*, 63, 1: 41–57.

—. 2001. *Primitive Renaissance: Rethinking German Expressionism*. Lincoln, NE: University of Nebraska Press.

Pike, Sarah. 2001. *Earthly Bodies, Magical Selves: Contemporary Pagans and the Search for Community*. Berkeley, CA: University of California Press.

Rampley, Matthew. 2000. *Nietzsche, Aesthetics and Modernity*. Cambridge, UK: Cambridge University Press.

Rappaport, Roy. 1999. *Ritual and Religion in the Making of Humanity*. Cambridge, UK: Cambridge University Press.

Ricoeur, Paul. 1985. *Time and Narrative*, vol. 2. Trans. Kathleen McLaughlin and David Pellauer. Chicago, IL: University of Chicago Press.

—. 1992. *Oneself as Another*. Trans. Kathleen. Blarney. Chicago, IL: University of Chicago Press.

Riis, Ole and Woodhead, Linda. 2010. *A Sociology of Religious Emotion*. Oxford, UK: Oxford University Press.

Rose, Herbert. 1959. *The Handbook of Greek Mythology*. New York, NY: Dutton.

Ruti, Mari. 2006. *Reinventing the Soul*. New York, NY: Other.

Sandford, John. 1991. 'What the Shadow Knows'. In Connie Zweig and Jeremiah Abrams (eds), *Meeting the Shadow: The Hidden Power of the Dark Side of Human Nature*. New York, NY: Penguin, pp. 19–26.

Shilling, Chris. 2005. 'Embodiment, Emotions, and the Foundations of Social Order: Durkheim's Enduring Contribution'. In Jeffrey Alexander and Philip Smith (eds), *The Cambridge Companion to Durkheim*. Cambridge, UK: Cambridge University Press, pp. 211–238.

Shilling, Chris and Mellor, Philip A. 1998. 'Durkheim, Morality and Modernity'. *The British Journal of Sociology*, 49, 2: 193–209.

—. 2011. 'Retheorising Emile Durkheim on Society and Religion: Embodiment, Intoxication and Collective Life'. *The Sociological Review*, 59, 1: 17–42.

Silverblatt, Irene. 1983. 'The Evolution of Witchcraft and the Meaning of Healing in Colonial Andean Society'. *Culture, Medicine and Psychiatry*, 7, 4: 413–427.

Silverman, Kaja. 2000. *World Spectators*. Stanford, CA: Stanford University Press.

St John, Graham. 2000. *Alternative Cultural Heterotopia: ConFest as Australia's Marginal Centre*. PhD thesis, La Trobe University, Melbourne, Australia. www.confest.com/thesis/, accessed 2 October 2012.

—. 2004. 'The Difference Engine: Liberation and the Rave Imaginary'. In Graham St John (ed.), *Rave Culture and Religion*. London, UK: Routledge, pp. 19–45.

—. 2006. 'Electronic Dance Music Culture and Religion: An Overview'. *Culture and Religion*, 7, 1: 1–25

—. 2010. 'Liminal Culture and Global Movement: The Transitional World of Psytrance'. In Graham St John (ed.), *The Local Scenes and Global Culture of Psytrance*. New York, NY: Routledge, pp. 203–219.

Starhawk. 1979. *The Spiral Dance*. San Francisco, CA: Harper and Row.

—. 2005. *The Earth Path: Grounding your Spirit in the Rhythms of Nature*. San Francisco, CA: HarperOne.

Stevens, Anthony. 1991. 'The Shadow in History and Literature'. In Connie Zweig and Jeremiah Abrams (eds), *Meeting the Shadow: The Hidden Power of the Dark Side of Human Nature*. New York, NY: Penguin, pp. 27–29.

Sutcliffe, Steve. 2003. *Children of the New Age: A History of Spiritual Practices*. London: Routledge.

Taylor, Charles. 1989. *Sources of the Self*. Cambridge, UK: Cambridge University Press.

—. 1991. *The Ethics of Authenticity*. Cambridge, MA: Harvard University Press.

—. 2007. *A Secular Age*. Cambridge, MA: Belknap Press of the Harvard University Press.

Tramacchi, Des. 2000. 'Field Tripping: Psychedelic Communitas and Ritual in the Australian Bush'. *Journal of Contemporary Religion*, 15, 1: 201–213.

Turner, Victor. 1957. *Schism and Continuity in an African Society*. Manchester, UK: Manchester University Press.

—. 1969. *The Ritual Process*. Ithaca, NY: Cornell University Press.

—. 1975. *Revelation and Divination in Ndembu Ritual*. Ithaca, NY: Cornell University Press.

—. 1979. 'Frame, Flow and Reflection: Ritual and Drama as Public Liminality'. *Japanese Journal of Religious Studies*, 6, 4: 465–499.

—. 1983. 'The Spirit of Celebration'. In F. Manning (ed.), *The Celebration of Society: Perspectives on Contemporary Cultural Performance*. Bowling Green, OH: Bowling Green University Press, pp. 187–91.

Turner, Edith, with W. Blodgett, S. Hakona and F. Benwa. 1992. *Experiencing Ritual: A New Interpretation of African Healing*. Philadelphia, PA: University of Pennsylvania Press.

Vásquez, Manuel A. 2011. *More than Belief: A Materialist Theory of Religion*. Oxford, UK: Oxford University Press.

Weber, Max. 1930. *The Protestant Ethic and the Spirit of Capitalism*. Trans. Talcott Parsons. London and Boston, MA: Unwin Hyman.

—. 1963. *The Sociology of Religion*. Trans. Ephraim Fischoff. Boston, MA: Beacon [first published in Germany in 1922 by J. C. B. Mohr as 'Religionssoziologie'].

White, Lynn, 1967. 'The Historical Roots of our Ecological Crisis'. *Science*, 155, 3767: 1203–1207.

Whitmont, Edward. 1991. 'The Evolution of the Shadow'. In Connie Zweig and Jeremiah Abrams (eds), *Meeting the Shadow: The Hidden Power of the Dark Side of Human Nature*. New York, NY: Penguin, pp. 12–18.

York, Michael. 1995. *The Emerging Network: A Sociology of the New Age and Neo-Pagan Movements*. London, UK: Rowman and Littlefield.

—. 2003. *Pagan Theology: Paganism as a World Religion*. New York, NY: New York University Press.

Zussman, Mira and Pierce, Anne. 1998. 'Shifts of Consciousness in Consensual S/M, Bondage, and Fetish Play'. *Anthropology of Consciousness*, 9, 4: 15–38.

Zweig, Connie and Abrams, Jeremiah. 1991. 'Introduction'. In Connie Zweig and Jeremiah Abrams (eds), *Meeting the Shadow: The Hidden Power of the Dark Side of Human Nature*. New York: Penguin, pp. 3–5.

INDEX